Soldiers a

Memoirs of Alexander Gardner Colonel of Artillery in the Service of Maharaja Ranjit Singh

Hugh Wodehouse Pearse

And

Alexander Haughton Campbell Gardner

(Editor: Major Hugh Pearse)

Alpha Editions

This edition published in 2019

ISBN : 9789353298937

Design and Setting By
Alpha Editions
email - alphaedis@gmail.com

COLONEL ALEXANDER GARDNER

"The untented Kosmos my abode
I pass, a wilful stranger:
My mistress still the open road
And the bright eyes of danger."

—R. L. S.

Swan Electric Engraving Co.

Colonel Alexander Gardner.

At the Age of 79

Soldier and Traveller

MEMOIRS OF ALEXANDER GARDNER

COLONEL OF ARTILLERY IN THE SERVICE OF
MAHARAJA RANJIT SINGH

EDITED BY

MAJOR HUGH PEARSE

2ND BATT. THE EAST SURREY REGIMENT

WITH AN INTRODUCTION BY

THE RIGHT HON.

SIR RICHARD TEMPLE, BART., G.C.S.I.

WITH PORTRAITS AND MAPS

WILLIAM BLACKWOOD AND SONS
EDINBURGH AND LONDON
MDCCCXCVIII

NOTE.

The Editor desires to express his grateful thanks to all who have assisted him in the preparation of this volume; and he would specially acknowledge the kind help and encouragement afforded him by Captain Claude Clerk, C.I.E., and Mr Herbert Compton.

CONTENTS.

CHAPTER I.

THE MAN AND HIS WRITINGS.

CHAPTER II.

EARLY LIFE AND TRAVELS, 1785-1819.

CHAPTER III.

ADVENTURES AMONG THE HAZARAS, 1819.

CHAPTER IV.

WANDERER AND FREEBOOTER IN CENTRAL ASIA.

CHAPTER V.

A SOLDIER OF FORTUNE AMONG THE AFGHANS.

CHAPTER VI.

A FUGITIVE.

CHAPTER VII.

THROUGH BADAKSHAN.

CHAPTER VIII.

AMONG THE KIRGHIZ.

CHAPTER IX.

A REMARKABLE JOURNEY.

CHAPTER X.

ADVENTURES IN THE PANJAB.

CHAPTER XI.

THE LION OF THE PANJAB."

CHAPTER XII.

INTRIGUE AND ANARCHY.

CHAPTER XIII.

THE DEFENCE OF LAHORE.

CHAPTER XIV.

"HORROR ON HORROR'S HEAD."

CHAPTER XV.

THE FIRST SIKH WAR.

CHAPTER XVI.

"PORT AFTER STORMY SEAS."

APPENDIX.

INTRODUCTION.

A goodly portion of Colonel Gardner's eventful life was spent in the Panjab kingdom or province during the palmy days of Ranjit Singh. His adventurous travels were in the regions adjacent to or beyond the Panjab frontier. The early years of my own active service were passed in the Panjab, and I was accustomed, indeed obliged, to study the affairs of the regions beyond its north-west frontier, even though I had no chance of travelling in them. Thus the names mentioned by Gardner in his Memoirs regarding countries beyond the Panjab have long been known to me from anxious study. The names of men and places mentioned by him in the Panjab are still better known to me — those of men either from personal acquaintance or very near tradition, those of places either from frequent visits or from actual residence. Major Pearse has now arranged these stirring and interesting Memoirs in a lucid and satisfactory manner; and I willingly comply with his request that I should write a brief Introduction. It is indeed hard for me to describe to an English reader the memories which a perusal of these Memoirs summons up in my imagination,—the potent figures whom I used to see moving on the historic stage, now described by one who knew them even more intimately than I did; the workings of human nature in the most mountainous regions of the earth, which I often heard narrated by many an Asiatic, now recorded in my own language by one who saw them in their very midst; the tremendous events, on which I constantly pondered while standing on the very spots or places where they occurred, now depicted by one who was a witness of, or participator in, them!

As is often the case in the men who live a daring, dashing life that sustains nervous tension and excites the imaginative faculties, Gardner evidently possessed a power of narration and description in a high degree—clear in facts, graphic in touches of detail, picturesque invariably—applicable equally to human motive, action, and habit—appreciative towards others, modest respecting himself—indicating that presence of mind, whether in distress or in peril, whereby his aptitude for accurate observation never for an instant failed him. In the middle and later part of his career he must have been a fairly diligent writer. Had he been able to preserve all his papers, and if, after the loss of some among them, he had been at the pains of bringing out all he had, under his own eye, with the requisite supplements, a capital record would have been handed down to us. The tale of his career would have been as good as that which Othello told to Desdemona. As it is, his life-story is something of that nature, and though not so complete as it might have been under the auspices of the narrator himself, has yet been made sufficiently so by Major Pearse's good care and skill. It well deserves the attention of our rising manhood in the British Isles. Though relating not to the British dominions nor to the British service, it shows what men of British race can do under the stress of trial and suffering. It illustrates that self-contained spirit of adventure in individuals which has done much towards founding the British Empire, and may yet help in extending that Empire in all quarters of the globe.

To the Memoirs also are appended some useful memoranda regarding the several European officers employed together with Gardner in the service of Ranjit Singh.

Alexander Gardner was born in 1785 in North America, on the shore of Lake Superior, and died at Srinagar, the capital of Kashmir, in 1877. His father was a Scottish emigrant to the then British colonies of North America, who took part in the War of Independence. His mother was an Englishwoman resident in South America, and had an admixture of Spanish blood. Her distinguished son wrote of her in terms of the highest admiration. He inherited an adventurous disposition from both sides, paternal and maternal. He sought first for a position in the Russian service, but accidentally lost it on the eve of attainment. Then he crossed the Caspian Sea, and entered on a career of adventure in Central Asia, from Kokan across the Hindu Caucasus to Herat, amidst ambuscades, fierce reprisals, hairbreadth escapes, alternations between brief plenty and long fasting —amidst episodes sometimes of brutality and cruelty wellnigh inconceivable, at other times of hearty charity and fidelity unto death. For some time he was prominent in the service of Habib-ulla Khan, the first Afghan opponent of the great Dost Muhammad Khan. During two years he actually enjoyed a term of domestic happiness, when he was peaceful indoors though generally at war out-of-doors. This was the one oasis in the wild desert of his whole life. To the last he could never refer to it without tears, case-hardened as he was, with his memory seared by many horrors, and his visage hardened by looking at terrors in the face. It met with a bloody and piteous termination; and then for some time he had to get through an existence fraught with extremity of hardship and of crisis, during which he was preserved by his own intrepidity and penetration. At length he succeeded in entering the Panjab, being engaged in the service of the Afghan chiefs who held Peshawar, and who were subdued by Maharaja Ranjit Singh. While there he received a command to enter Ranjit Singh's service, and proceeded to Lahore. He was employed in the Maharaja's service as commandant of artillery for several years. Then he was transferred to the service of Dhyan Singh, the Prime Minister, a

Rajput of the lower Himalayas, who with his brother, the famous Gulab Singh, became the chief feudatories of the Sikh sovereignty. He made the acquaintance of Henry Lawrence, then a rising political officer at Peshawar, at the time of the British disasters at Kabul in 1841. After Dhyan Singh's death he served Gulab Singh alone. He witnessed, or was in close contact with, the sanguinary revolutions that followed one after another upon the death of Ranjit. He was at Lahore during the first Panjab war in 1845-46. He then returned to the territories of Gulab Singh, who became sovereign of Jammu and Kashmir. He died a pensioner under Gulab Singh's successor in Kashmir at the advanced age of about ninety years. His constitution, originally magnificent, must have become somewhat worn out by the severe vicissitudes of a long career, and he dreamed the evening of his life away.

It is wonderful how he retained the power of writing English simply, gracefully, graphically, inasmuch as for several years consecutively he could never have heard it spoken nor had any opportunities of reading it. For long intervals he could have used no language but Mongolian or Pushtoo, and later on little but Panjabee. He must also have learnt at least something of Persian and Russian.

In this widely extended record, almost entirely autobiographical, beginning in the latter part of the last century and ending past the middle of the present century—stretching from the Caspian Sea across the Indus and on to the Sutlej—the diverse matters group themselves under certain heads as follows for a bird's-eye view:—

First. The geography of Central Asia, especially the country of the rivers Oxus and Jaxartes, the Turcoman desert, the western extremity of the Himalayan range, Badakshan, the Pamir with sources of the Oxus, and Chitral.

Second. The characteristics, mental and physical, of the men and women of these regions, the dispositions of individuals, the customs of tribes.

Third. The court and camp of Ranjit Singh, which formed the most potent organisation of this kind ever erected by the natives of India in modern times.

Fourth. The tragic and sometimes terrific events which ensued after the death of Ranjit Singh, and which led to the first war between the Sikhs and the British,—a war which broke the back of that community, religious, military, and political, saluted proudly by the Sikhs as the Khalsa.

Fifth. The scenes, strange, weird, pathetic, unlucky, lucky, in Gardner's life, relating to him in particular.

I proceed to offer a few observations on each of these groups.

In respect to the first group, the geographical details, though not quite all that they might have been, owing to the loss of papers in time of dire trouble, they are yet notably considerable, and are in themselves valuable. Gardner has been highly esteemed as a geographical authority upon the regions he had visited by such men as Sir Alexander Burnes, Sir Henry Rawlinson, Sir Henry Durand, and Mr Ney Elias. Much attention was paid to his work at the time by the Royal Asiatic Society in India. Fifty years ago, when he travelled or sojourned in those mountains and uplands, there was a sentiment, a prevision, in the British mind to the effect that our interest in these regions must one day grow and rise. By this time, indeed, it has grown and risen; for a large, perhaps the greater, part of them has come within the British sphere of influence after delimitation of boundaries by treaty with a European Power. We have therefore rendered ourselves nationally responsible for learning all that can be learnt about these regions. Much, indeed, has been done in this way since Gardner's time. Still, these Memoirs of his deserve study, for they will clear up some points that are obscure, confirm others that may have been doubtful, add others not previously verified, and render our general view more correct and better subservient to our comprehension of political relations. The more the geographical features are brought home to the minds of our politicians, the better will they know how to guard our own domains. Moreover, we are now concerned to understand the origin, the progress, the history of geographical discovery in this quarter. To all this the Gardner Memoirs greatly conduce. They do not consist merely of topographical description, but while conveying sound information, they are replete with varied interest.

Regarding the second group, that of the men and women, it is to be remarked that if, in the words of the poet, "the noblest study of mankind is man," then here is to be found some material for that end — material, too, specially useful to us Europeans, because since some centuries at least we find little or nothing of that sort on our own European continent. Gardner narrates the divers incidents—which happened under his own eyes, and wherewith he was closely concerned or had immediate contact—with artless naïveté, each point being limned by a master hand, like those touches in a sketch which, to artists' eyes, indicate that it has been taken from nature. The internal evidence convinces us that these characters are drawn from the life in Central Asia. Now and again the rapine, the revenge, the thirst for blood, the disregard of life, the throes of agony, the effacement of all sentiment, the destruction of all faith and honour, make us wonder whether these creatures are like human beings—whether they are not predatory animals, birds of prey, in human form. Yet there are simultaneously afforded proofs that into these poor souls there has been breathed something of the divine spirit which is not yet extinct—that through all the clouds and brooding darkness there sometimes break the rays of light from the conscience given by the Creator. The same narrative presents instances among the same men of fidelity, truthful, honourable, enduring, and disinterested—for danger or safety, for plenty or hunger, for heat or cold, for peace or crisis. Again, there are cases of hospitality with many of the best qualities of charity as we understand it—of protection accorded to one who seemed helpless, friendless, destitute, maintained proof against temptation and inviolable under trial. After terrific scenes there closely follow ceremonies, graceful, gallant, chivalric, almost recalling the legends of the Golden Age. The character of the women is often romantic and courageous in the extreme. In what we should call Baronial warfare, where one wild chief will be the conqueror and another the conquered, the women, generally numerous, of the vanquished are infamously seized as the spoil of the victor. But often the pride of the women will not brook this. When they see that warlike defence is over, they will die rather than fall into the hands of their foes: the wife will beg death from her husband's sword, the sister from her brother's dagger. Apart from all this, several episodes are briefly recounted which, as tragic plots, would be worthy of Shakespearean treatment, and as dramas would be as complete as anything that a dramatist could frame. In reference to the dreadful faults of these poor people in Central Asia, the charitably considerate reader may remember that some centuries ago the devastating inundation of Gengiz Khan and his Mongol hordes swept over these garden-like territories, which probably were among the original habitations of mankind. By this dread series of events there came about that which the historian eloquently and truly describes, "a shipwreck of nations." There was not only a dislocation but a disruption of society. Morally as well as materially every root was torn up, every foundation dug out, every landmark swept away, everything that pertained to civilisation was flung into a vortex of barbarism. The damage then done to countries at that time among the fairest on earth has proved irreparable during the succeeding centuries. Yet the plant of divine affection once sown in a race of mankind never quite dies—the light of other days is never put out—the spark is still in the embers ready to burst forth into white flame. No doubt, since Gardner's time the Russian supervision will have done much for social improvement, and British influence, advancing in the same direction, may do still more. Still, if we are to prepare for the better things that are to be, we ought to know the things that have been, and therefore weigh well such authentic narratives as those of Gardner.

Referring to the third group, that concerning Ranjit Singh, we may observe that it relates hardly at all to the condition of the Panjab at the time. Gardner had but scant notions — I might almost say no notion — of civil government. But after quitting the turbulent Peshawar and its cut-throat neighbours, and on crossing the Indus, he was evidently struck with the comparative peace, the rule and order, which reigned in the Panjab. In the absence of any account from the author, I may explain to our reader the character of Ranjit Singh's civil rule in a few words,—having myself had to study it while the memory of it was fresh among the people, and while evidence on every point was forthcoming. It was as bad as it dared to be with such a people as the Panjabi — just that and no worse. It took all that it could venture to take from the people—that much and no more. It took no thought for judgment and justice, — that was relegated to feudatories of degrees and sorts; but they were men of the country, locally respected or feared, and they would not carry things too far. The Sikh sovereignty—as a political and military institution only—was popular in the Panjab. It was the symbol of a national faith, founded on a sort of theocracy, but victorious by force of arms. The people were in no humour to quarrel with it needlessly. So long as they could go on paying their way, they did not want any revolution —they would bear a burden sooner than rebel, they would yield up a large percentage of their crops before they turned out to fight. They would so turn out, however, instantly if provoked beyond a certain point, and this too with grenadier-like force. The knowledge of this kept the conduct of the Government within bounds.

Still, Gardner gives us much material for the historical completion of the portraiture of Ranjit Singh, who — considering his comparatively humble birth, his mean bringing up with really no education, his want of personal gifts, the disadvantages arising from debased habits and the lowest life — was the most extraordinary native that ever rose to power in India within modern times,—power effectively great and long sustained over the manliest race on the Indian continent —personal, too, to himself alone, so that when it dropped from his dying hands no successor could be found to take it up. Thus the reader will doubtlessly note the various meetings which Gardner had with Ranjit Singh, the cautious inquiries about military affairs, the instinctive dread of the approach of the British Power, the employment of European officers in the field, the march with the army to the Afghan frontiers with the Sikh sovereign at its head, the strange affairs at the mouth of the Khyber Pass, and the several other operations on the Trans-Indus border. He gives some instructive notes regarding Ranjit Singh's management of the Sikh or Khalsa army. While presenting a high estimate of Ranjit's capacity for kingship, he abstains from noticing—perhaps he even throws a veil over—the king's vices, which were scandalously overt and destructive of respectability in the State. He must have seen these more or less, but he is loyal when leaving them unmentioned. This is the more noteworthy in that he deals quite differently with the character of Gulab Singh, who was equally his patron and ultimately his sole employer. His analysis of Gulab Singh's conduct and disposition amounts to ruthless vivisection, and must doubtless be true. On the other hand, he attributes many wise and able qualities to his master, to whom this particular praise—well deserved, no doubt—was most acceptable. Strangely enough, it appears that this character was published at the time, and gave no offence to Gulab Singh. This would be incredible had it not been authenticated. The fact must be, that Gulab Singh had been so inured to the commission of crime, and Gardner to the sight of it, that both had ceased to be horrified by it. Therefore the one did not hesitate to impute it, nor did the other mind the imputation, so long as a certain sort of praise was attributed which the one knew how to render with discrimination and the other appreciated highly.

The fourth group relates to the events ensuing on the death of Ranjit Singh. The events in the palaces of native princes in India have now been known to European authorities for a century and a half. I do not remember any so grave as those which occurred in quick succession at the capital of the Panjab, Lahore, at this epoch. Upon most of these a lurid light is thrown by Gardner's narrative, he being an eyewitness of some, or in immediate proximity to others. I must refer the reader to Gardner's word-pictures of these grim occasions —their effect would be marred by any attempt at reproduction. The story of how Dhyan Singh the Vizier receives a deadly threat from Cheyt Singh within the next twenty-four hours—how Dhyan

Singh (Gardner with him) follows up Cheyt Singh that very night into the recesses of the palace, and after a tiger-spring stabs him to the heart, saying that the twenty-four hours are not over—is dramatically tragic. Rarely do we have such a tale authenticated at first hand by an eyewitness. Of a similar character is the murder of Dhyan Singh, shot in the back, and the *sati*-burning of his young widow—she declaring that her funereal fire shall not be lighted till the heads of her husband's murderers are placed at her feet; and she, when they have been thus placed by Gardner himself, mounting the pyre and applying the torch with her own hand, her little maid in her lap sharing the same fate. Equally graphic is the account of the murder of the Maharaja Sher Singh. He has a stormy interview with a great feudatory. At the end he asks to look at the handsomely-worked barrel of a musket which the feudatory bears. Admiring it, he gets the muzzle close to his breast; the feudatory pulls the trigger and the king drops dead. The last scene at Lahore is remarkable, when the Sikh army, governed no longer by its sovereign but by its own military committees, is shortly to march and cross the Sutlej as an act of war against the British.

There is now an infant Maharaja as sovereign, with his mother as regent, assisted by a brother, who is especially unpopular with the army. All three are summoned to attend a great parade: they come in state, she and her boy on one elephant and he on another. They are received with an ominously resounding salute of artillery. Her elephant is first made to kneel down; she with her boy is dragged shrieking to a sumptuous tent; then the brother's elephant is made to kneel, and he is promptly despatched in the face of the army. Such was the discipline with which the Sikh army on the eve of contest prepared itself to cross swords with the British. Lastly, while the army is fighting a losing battle, a big deputation comes back from it to Lahore to see the Regent and complain to her against the commissariat. She receives them, the complaints grow louder, and the fate of the capital is trembling: suddenly (Gardner standing just behind her) she flings off her loose outer skirt and flings it at their heads, saying, "Wear that, you cowards, while I go to fight in man's equipment!" The men are abashed, and the crisis is for the moment averted. I have held out only a few signals, but to realise these romances of real life, the reader must peruse Gardner's narrative.

The last or fifth group contains the scenes affecting Gardner personally. These are so frequent throughout the Memoirs that to array them all would be like counting the beads in a long necklace. I shall only advert to a very few in order to give some idea of the whole. On the last day of his married life in Afghanistan, after an adverse fight he is told that his little fort (*castello*) has been captured, and that all is over within it. He rushes thither and ascends to his desolate chamber. There he sees his young wife lying dead with her boy, also dead, in her arms. From out her dress there just protrudes the left hand with which she has driven the dagger to her heart to avoid becoming the prey of the captor. Anon he and his few followers, afraid to light a fire in the Afghan cold at the mouth of their cave for fear of discovery, desperate from wounds and hunger, stop a party of traders, overhaul their effects, taking some of their provisions, such as fat sheep-tails preserved in snow, and a ball of salt well rounded off from constant licking, but leaving them to proceed with their more valuable things. Later on, when in Moslem service, he hangs round his neck a clasped Koran which none will dare to touch. Between the leaves of this he places his notes and memoranda; when the book shall thus become suspiciously thick he means to say that these are extra prayers. During the early days of his service with Ranjit Singh some guns presented by the British Governor-General have arrived. He is shown the shells and fuses in the tumbrils, and asked if he can fire them. Fortunately for him, he finds among the fuses a slip of paper which he can read while his employers cannot, and which gives the necessary instructions. Possessed of this knowledge, he is able to fire them with entire success; and so in Sikh estimation his reputation as an artillerist is made. On one dire occasion after Ranjit Singh's death he makes havoc with his guns. A fight at the closest quarters is going on between two rival parties for the possession of the palace fortress of Lahore. He has to defend the gate, which has been destroyed, and at the entrance he contrives to pack his ten guns with their muzzles all together: these he fires simultaneously as the fanatical Akalis with shouts and brandished swords are pressing in a mass up the narrow way—and lo! the assailants are literally blown into the air.

These Memoirs, published just half a century after the event, corroborate the conclusion formed by many, as I remember, after the first Sikh war in 1845-46. On the death of Ranjit Singh in 1839, Sikh rule in the Panjab became an impossibility. The members of a brave but unruly confederacy, extending over the Land of the Five Rivers, had been united and held together by the rough genius of Ranjit Singh, but never welded nor consolidated. He was not statesman enough for such consolidation, being merely a rude organiser, and a fighting commander without being a soldier in any higher sense. On his death it became, from Gardner's narrative, clearer than ever that there were four parties clutching with lethal violence at each other's throats—the Court party, the so-called blood princes, the Dogras (Dhyan Singh and Gulab Singh), and the Sindhanwala chiefs. Above all was an unmanageable army acknowledging no power but its own. The destruction of all these elements, the one by the other, was about happening when the first Sikh war broke out. On a retrospect we may almost regret that the British Government could not then annex the country, the native rule having become demonstrably impossible. That would have saved all the bloodshed in the second war. As it was, a further respite was allowed in the hope of better things. But the fire of disturbance burst forth worse than ever. The second war had to be undertaken, and after that the annexation of the Panjab became inevitable. If any one should doubt the ultimate necessity of that annexation, let him consult these Memoirs of Gardner.

RICHARD TEMPLE.

COLONEL ALEXANDER GARDNER.

CHAPTER I.

THE MAN AND HIS WRITINGS.

MR FREDERICK COOPER AND COLONEL GARDNER — SIR LEPEL GRIFFIN — MR EDGEWORTH'S ABSTRACT OF COLONEL GARDNER'S JOURNAL—SIR HENRY YULE AND SIR HENRY RAWLINSON—MR NEY ELIAS—SIR HENRY DURAND'S 'LIFE OF A SOLDIER OF THE OLDEN TIME.'

In the hot weather of the year 1864 the Government of India deputed, as was then the annual custom, an officer to the valley of Kashmir to act as referee between the large body of English visitors and the subjects of his Highness the reigning Maharaja.

The officer selected for duty on this occasion was Mr Frederick Cooper—a man well known in his day for a terrible act of severity performed by him in the execution of his duty during the suppression of the great mutiny of the Indian army.

Mr Cooper was a man of talent and imagination, and while making such inquiries concerning the affairs of Kashmir as seemed to him a desirable preliminary to the performance of his new duties, he heard for the first time of the existence at Srinagar of an old European commandant of the name of Gardner.

Feeling sure that the conversation of this veteran would supply information of great interest concerning the history, manners, and customs of Kashmir, Mr Cooper lost no time in requesting the old adventurer, who bore the rank of commandant or colonel of artillery, to favour him with a visit.

The desired visit was speedily paid, and Mr Cooper's description of his new acquaintance, written down at the time, presents to us the hero of the following narrative of travel and adventure.

"The old colonel," he writes, "while on the verge of his eightieth year, had a gait as sturdy and a stride as firm as a man of fifty. Some six feet in height, he usually wore a tartan-plaid suit, purchased apparently from the quartermaster's stores of one of the Highland regiments serving in India. In consequence of a severe wound in the neck, received in battle many years before, the old commandant had long been unable to eat solid food; he had, moreover, lost from age nearly all his teeth. The photograph"—a copy of which forms the frontispiece of this work—"while indicating the outline of the countenance, gives but a dim idea of the vivacity of expression, the play of feature, the humour of the mouth, and the energy of character portrayed by the whole aspect of the man as he described the arduous and terrible incidents of a long life of romance and vicissitude.

"The English he spoke was quaint, graphic, and wonderfully good considering his fifty years of residence among Asiatics.

"In the course of our first conversation I discovered the stores of experience, adventure, and observation which the old man could unfold; his memory, too, except as to precise dates, I found singularly tenacious. He complained of the loss and abstraction at various times of his manuscripts. A whole volume, which contained an account of his visit to Kafiristan, perished at

Kabul in the destruction of the house of Sir Alexander Burnes.

"Sir Alexander, whose interest in Kafiristan is well known, had borrowed the book in question from Gardner before starting with the army of the Indus on that march from which he was never to return."

The outcome of this interview was a series of conversations between Mr Cooper and Gardner, in the course of which the latter related those wanderings and adventures, an account of which I have pieced together to the best of my ability in the following pages.

Colonel Gardner had from time to time written down in his quaint, crabbed handwriting many anecdotes connected with his service under Maharaja Ranjit Singh; and these pictures of a bygone conqueror, and of the mighty army which he welded together, possess a unique interest and value.

Mr Cooper unfortunately did not live to complete his history of Gardner's travels, and for some years after his death the unfinished work and Gardner's own manuscripts entirely disappeared.

In a footnote to Sir Lepel Griffin's masterly Life

of Ranjit Singh occurs the following reference to these papers: "Colonel Gardner . . . allowed me to read his manuscript narrative of the later years of the Maharaja, and the events which succeeded his death. These most interesting and valuable papers, which were intrusted to the late Mr Frederick Cooper, C.B., have disappeared, and the loss, from a historical point of view, is considerable."

I will conclude this reference to Mr Cooper's share in preparing the narrative by mentioning the fact that his rough draft of Gardner's travels, as far as the point where Gardner left the Pamirs, was corrected throughout by Gardner himself; and therefore it may be assumed that the traveller accepted the draft as a faithful record of his adventures.

It is perhaps unnecessary to relate to the reader how it was that Gardner's papers came into my hands: suffice it to say that this occurred some four years ago, and that the vicissitudes of the papers by no means came to an end with Mr Cooper's death. Two very high authorities on Central Asian geography successively took the papers in hand with a view to investigating their value, and both unhappily died while the papers were in their possession.

I must now say something on the subject of the credibility of Colonel Gardner's narrative.

Those interested in the study of geography may be aware that an abstract of a portion of Gardner's travels appeared in the 'Journal of the Asiatic Society of Bengal' of February 1853. This abstract was furnished to the Journal by Mr Edgeworth, an officer of the Bengal Civil Service; but as Mr Edgeworth was unfortunately prevented "by want of leisure and other causes" from properly editing the abstract, its publication throws but little light on Gardner's exploits, and has no value for us save that it affords positive proof that Gardner had written at some period prior to 1853 an account of his travels, "thrown," as Mr Edgeworth writes in his introductory remarks, "into the shape they now have, occupying several volumes of country paper."

The abstract was, in fact, so carelessly put together, and so barbarously mangled by native printers, that its publication permanently injured Gardner's reputation, and even caused many persons to express their disbelief that he had ever visited the regions he professed to describe.

Such, however, was not the opinion of geographers so thoroughly qualified to give an authoritative opinion on the subject as the late Sir Henry Rawlinson and Sir Henry Yule. Thus the latter, in his preface to the second edition of Wood's 'Journey to the Sources of the River Oxus,' after making severe comments on the inaccuracy of Mr Edgeworth's abstract of Gardner's Journal, says: "Colonel Gardner is not only a real person, and one who has real personal acquaintance with the regions [Badakshan and the Pamirs] of which we are treating, to a degree, it is believed, far surpassing that of any European or native traveller whose narrative has been published, but he appears to have acquired the esteem of men like the late Sir Henry Durand, whose good opinion was of unusual worth."

Sir Henry Rawlinson repeatedly refers in his geographical writings to Gardner's travels, and in his well-known 'Monograph on the Oxus' says, "Colonel Gardner did certainly visit Badakshan in person"; and again, "Gardner actually traversed the Gilgit valley from the Indus to the Snowy Mountains, and finally crossed into Chitral, being, in fact, the only Englishman up to the present time (1872) who has ever performed the journey throughout.

These remarks of Sir Henry Rawlinson and Sir

Henry Yule were written, it must be remembered, before Mr Cooper had set about the task of writing a corrected version of Gardner's travels, and these two eminent geographers had nothing before them on which to settle Gardner's claim to be considered a great traveller but the mangled "abstract," the inaccuracies of which they so severely criticised. Nevertheless, barbarous spelling, unrecognisable names, and incorrect distances notwithstanding, they agreed in believing that Gardner had verily and indeed traversed Badakshan and the Pamirs, and had found his way from those regions to India by the way of Gilgit and Chitral.

About a year ago I placed the entire MS. of Gardner's geographical notes and Mr Cooper's rough draft of his travels in the hands of that "mute, inglorious Milton," the late Mr Ney Elias, a man whose invincible modesty alone prevented his being known as one of the greatest of English travellers, and one of the highest authorities on Eastern geography.

Mr Elias took the greatest interest in the MS., and at the time of his sudden and lamented death had, in part, written a note on Gardner's travels.

Having himself a personal knowledge of Badakshan and other portions of Gardner's route, possessed by no living European, Mr Elias's opinion may be accepted as final. The following extract should satisfy all but the most incredulous:—

"There appears to me to be good internal evidence that, as regards the main routes he professes to have travelled, Gardner's story is truthful. When he tells us that he visited the east coast of the Caspian, Northern Persia, Herat, the Hazara country, even Khiva; that he spent some time in and about the district of Inderab, and afterwards passed through part of Badakshan and Shighnan, thence crossing the Pamirs into Eastern Turkestan, I see no reason to doubt him. At the time he speaks of, such journeys were almost as practicable for Europeans as for Asiatics. Most of the countries in Central Asia were in a more or less disturbed and lawless condition—much more so than in later years—but that was a condition which affected Asiatic and European alike. . . . The times were, on the whole, sufficiently favourable to render belief in the main features of his narrative possible; and it is, in a sense, the truth of the general narrative that enables us to excuse the untruth of many of the details.

"In other words, had Gardner not travelled over a great part of the ground he professes to describe, it would not have been possible for him to interpolate the doubtful portions of his story. He could not have known enough of the surrounding conditions or even the names of places and tribes, nor have met with the people whose clumsy inventions he at times serves out to us. It is necessary, for instance, that a man who could never have read of the Pamir region should at least have visited that country or its neighbourhood before he could invent or repeat stories regarding Shakh Dara or the Yaman Yar, or be able to dictate the name of Shighnan."

I will conclude this brief introduction of Colonel Gardner and his writings with a summary of his career with which Sir Henry Durand completed a sketch entitled 'Life of a Soldier of the Olden Time: An unwritten Page of History':—

"Even in outline the story is of great interest, —a life drama indeed, as full of incident and adventure as drama can well be. The story of Dugald Dalgetty is nothing to this, as it will be seen by the light of times to come.

"To take the two ends of the long tangled line is something wonderful, — one end bright and sunny on the banks of Lake Superior in the Far West; the other end approaching, where the chapter will close, in lands watered by the Indus. And then the schooling in Ireland, and the teaching in Lahore; the parting from home for ever for a life from end to end of perils such as very few men have ever imagined, still less known.

"It is difficult perhaps to comprehend all the career, but much may be understood. There is no mistake about the high heart, the undaunted courage, the unflagging will. Colonel Gardner's personal influence, too, must have been great—what is called magnetic; for how else could he have bound to himself for nine months, and he all the time a prisoner, men who seemed to have an interest in separating from him as far as possible? And how else could he have drawn to himself those Sowars and others whom he led to Kabul and elsewhere?

"That such a man has been so little mentioned in the history of the times is a marvel. But we must remember that he was a man without a country, though England or any country might be proud to claim him.

"Faithful to his standard, whatever it was, obeying without questioning military orders, he presented and presents, perhaps, one of the finest specimens ever known of the soldier of fortune.

"He must have been a man, too, who did not care to force himself into notice so long as he could obtain employment; and the fact that he secured the respect and confidence of so many persons, of characters so widely different, is enough to show that besides being a bold soldier, he was possessed of rare tact and skill, of qualities indeed which, if the love of adventure had been urged on by anything like an equal share of ambition, would have gone far to gather together the turbulent elements among which he lived, and make of them a more devastating flame than even Gardner himself ever saw."

Such a tribute, coming from so honoured a source, surely entitles Gardner to "a fair field and no favour," and never in his life did he ask for more.

CHAPTER II.

EARLY LIFE AND TRAVELS, 1785–1819.

PARENTAGE AND BIRTH OF THE TRAVELLER—A WANDERER FROM CHILDHOOD—THE JESUIT SCHOOL IN MEXICO—FIVE YEARS IN IRELAND—GARDNER RETURNS TO AMERICA—VISITS LISBON, MADRID, CAIRO, TREBIZOND, AND ASTRAKHAN—GARDNER'S ELDER BROTHER; HIS SUDDEN DEATH—GARDNER'S FIRST VISIT TO HERAT—FIRST WANDERINGS IN ASIA.

About the middle of the last century a certain Scottish surgeon named Gardner accompanied his father to North America, and subsequently took an active part in the War of Independence. It appears that he was intimately associated with several of the leaders of the rebellious colonists, particularly with George Washington and the Marquis de Lafayette, and he long preserved their correspondence with him.

After the War of Independence had ceased Dr Gardner obtained employment under the Mexican Government, and while living in Mexico married the daughter of an Englishman named Haughton, who was the principal official of a town and district on the banks of the river Colorado. Haughton's wife was of Spanish descent and belonged to a good family, through whose influence Haughton had obtained preferment. Haughton himself was the son of a major in the English army, well known in his day as a traveller in Africa, in which mysterious continent he eventually lost his life.

Soon after the marriage Dr Gardner and his wife moved northwards and made their home on that portion of the shore of Lake Superior which is nearest to the source of the Mississippi, and here in the course of time they became the parents of three sons and as many daughters.

The youngest of these sons, the hero of these pages, who was born in the year 1785, received the names of Alexander Haughton Campbell, and, like his brothers, was brought up in the Unitarian religion, the creed of their father. The daughters, on the other hand, followed their mother and became Roman Catholics.

Although in his old age Alexander Gardner became devout in his language, and, perhaps from long association with Orientals, interlarded his letters with pious phrases, it does not appear that religion came much between him and worldly objects during his adventurous career. For many years he passed as a Mussulman, and apparently felt no scruple in the matter.

This may possibly have resulted from the contentions which took place in his childhood, as the strict views of Mrs Gardner impelled her to endeavour to draw her sons as well as her daughters into the fold of her Church.

Alexander Gardner's travels began early in life, for before his fifth birthday Dr Gardner returned to Mexico and made a new home there, near the mouth of the river Colorado and not far from the town of St Xavier. At the same time he permanently entered the Government medical service, and in course of time acquired considerable property in addition to some inherited by his wife.

Mrs Gardner was, to use her son's words, "in all respects a well-educated and accomplished woman, of a rare sweetness and strength of character." She educated her sons and daughters in their early years, and as a man may be in some measure judged by his appreciation of that priceless blessing, a good mother, it is worthy of note that Gardner attributed to that early training whatever of good there might be in his character.

She was, he adds, an accomplished linguist, speaking French and Italian well, in addition to English and Spanish, which she naturally knew in virtue of her mixed descent.

Dr Gardner was cast in a rougher mould, but he was a well-educated man, and taught his sons Greek and Latin, with the severity customary at that period, until they reached the age of twelve, when (no doubt at the desire of their mother) they went successively to the Jesuit school at St Xavier.

As was natural, Gardner, when recording his early recollections, had no very definite memories of this school, but remembered creating a sensation on his first arrival there by a sturdy refusal to attend the daily mass and the confessional. The contempt with which he was treated by the priestly masters galled him to the quick, and he was even more infuriated by the haughty disdain, such as Spaniards alone can exhibit, with which his schoolfellows received both friendly overtures and warlike challenges.

Isolation in youth is hard to bear, yet no doubt Gardner had to thank it in part for the stern and inflexible courage that enabled him to endure, and even to enjoy, the much greater isolation—

that of the European dweller among Orientals—that was his lot for the greater part of his life.

Alexander Gardner's chief consolation during his lonely school-life was derived from the incessant study of a book of travels among the American Indians, the property of the Principal of the school. Gardner discovered this book, he relates, in the Principal's library, while waiting there for chastisement. He begged for a loan of the book, but being refused, took an opportunity of possessing himself of it; and the successful lawlessness of the act, coupled with the romantic character of the book, no doubt permanently influenced him. In his own words, "From this early period of life the notion of being a traveller and adventurer, and of somehow and somewhere carving out a career for myself, was the maggot of my brain."

Gardner remained nearly nine years in the seminary, mainly at the intercession of his mother, for his father would have preferred his being educated in England.

Mrs Gardner died early in the year 1807, when Alexander was between twenty-one and twenty-two years old; and there is some mystery as to the manner in which he passed the following five years. He himself states that he was in Ireland during the greater part of the time, preparing partly for a maritime life, to which he was then inclined. It is probable that while in Ireland he acquired a certain knowledge of the science of gunnery, and also assimilated the tenacious accent of "the distressful country." In after-years his knowledge of artillery and his strong Irish brogue gave occasion to those unfriendly to him to accuse Gardner of being a deserter from the British artillery. This charge was, however, quite unsubstantiated, and there are no grounds for giving it the slightest credit. It should also be stated that Gardner came in contact, after the Sikh war, with very many English officers and soldiers, and that, had the statement been true, more would certainly have been heard of it, as every effort was being made at the time to remove the European and foreign officers who were in the service of the Sikh Government.

In 1812 Gardner returned to America, landing at New Orleans in the month of March. Here he received the news of his father's death, conveyed to him in a letter from his second brother, and immediately embarked on the career of adventure to which his inclination led him.

The spirit of unrest, inherited from both sides of their parentage, was no doubt strong in the Gardner family; and Alexander's eldest brother had for several years been employed by the Russian Government as an engineer at Astrakhan. By his advice Gardner left Philadelphia, where he had been staying with one of his uncles, and sailed for Lisbon, whence he proceeded to Madrid. There he realised his father's Spanish property (derived from his wife) on behalf of the family, it having been arranged that the portions of himself and his eldest brother should be provided from this source.

Having realised the property, Gardner transmitted the proceeds to his brother at Astrakhan, retaining only a sum sufficient for his own travelling expenses to that city.

While preparing for this journey, Gardner made the acquaintance of a man named Aylmer, whom he describes as very clever and an experienced traveller, and, moreover, a relation of the Principal of Gardner's old Jesuit school in Mexico. Aylmer was a Jesuit himself, and had no difficulty in persuading Gardner to join him in a journey which he was about to make to Alexandria and Cairo. His complete knowledge of Persian and

Turkish made him a desirable travelling companion for Gardner, and the latter seized the opportunity offered him of gaining an acquaintance with those languages.

Early in the year 1813 they accordingly set out from Madrid together, and arrived in due course at Cairo, where Gardner found (as Aylmer had promised him) a friendly and intelligent French society. A Monsieur Julien welcomed them to his house, and they found other visitors there in the persons of two German mineralogists. These men, one of whom was named Dallerwitz, having been dissatisfied with the salaries offered them by the Egyptian and Persian Governments, had determined to try their fortune in a military career, and to wend their way to the Russian frontier, as reports were current that European military officers, particularly those trained as engineers, were in request by that Government.

Having made the acquaintance of these Germans, Aylmer and Gardner determined to proceed to Trebizond with them. Another member of the party was a highly accomplished Frenchman named Rossaix, one of that large body of his countrymen who had been thrown out of employment by the peace of 1805, and who dispersed themselves over the East in search of a new field for military enterprise. Rossaix was a skilled engineer, and had a design, which he afterwards carried into execution, of entering the service of the ruler of the Sikhs, Maharaja Ranjit Singh.

The conversation which Gardner had at this time with M. Rossaix led him, many years later, to enter the Maharaja's service.

Rossaix himself went to Lahore, and died there of cholera many years before Gardner's arrival, having obtained very lucrative employment.

The party of engineers which now left Cairo was too small to travel safely, and they intended to join a large caravan, organised by some Armenian merchants, which had recently started. After running some risks, Gardner and his companions caught up the caravan a few marches from Jericho, and found that it consisted of about 3000 human beings—"a medley of Asiatics, chiefly pilgrims; a mendicant set, but very sturdy." It was necessary to maintain an incessant watch against them, but, as it proved, unsuccessfully, for the party did not escape robbery—in fact, they were pillaged to such a degree that a small party of Christian, Turkish, and Arab merchants, who had effects which they did not choose to lose, and with whom Gardner and his friends were associated, kept aloof some 300 yards from the main encampment, letting it be known that any prowlers would be fired on.

When near Erzeroum intelligence reached Gardner's French and German friends which decided them on going with him to Astrakhan. They therefore embarked at Trebizond on a Russian craft bound for a small port at the northern base of the Caucasus. From this place Gardner wrote to his brother, who immediately set to work to obtain employment for him under the Russian Government.

Finding that the salaries of mineralogists were very high, and that there was a considerable demand for superintendents (presumably of mines), Gardner applied himself studiously to all the books he could gather together, so that his brother might be able as soon as possible to testify honestly to his acquirements. He was, he says, aided in his studies both by a natural bent and by some training in the rudiments of geology and chemistry happily acquired from his lamented and honoured father. At this period Gardner lived with his brother, and worked and studied under his supervision: he speaks with much gratitude of his fatherly kindness, and recalls with satisfaction the fact that he was able to make himself useful to him.

This settled and promising life was, however, to come to an abrupt end; for when Gardner was on the point of receiving the reward of his labours in the shape of a Government appointment, his hopes were shattered and his home broken up by the sudden death of his brother, who was killed by a fall from his horse on December 14, 1817.

Gardner's first design was to request the fulfilment of the promises of employment for him that had been made to his brother; but far from obtaining his wish, he was disgusted by repeated discourtesies and delays, and, to add to his difficulties, his brother's property was attached in liquidation of claims based on accounts which his death had left unclosed.

After a tedious litigation that detained him nearly a year and cured him of any fancy for the Russian service, Gardner, through the kind intervention of a friend, was allowed to retain about £6000, one-third of his brother's effects. This sum included his own patrimony.

Disgusted with Russia, and disheartened by the loss of his brother, Gardner was about to return to America when he met one day a German named Sturzky, who was accompanied, to Gardner's surprise and satisfaction, by his old travelling companion Dallerwitz. These two gentlemen had left the Russian service, and were about to proceed to the Court of Persia in quest of fortune, and Gardner was easily induced to accompany them. He left the bulk of his fortune in safe hands at Astrakhan, and taking with him a small sum for travelling expenses, started again on his travels. The party left Astrakhan early in October 1818 in a small merchant craft, in which they crossed to the eastern shore of the Caspian Sea, and then, turning south, gradually worked their way to Astrabad.

This was a slow and tedious voyage, and, on landing, the company broke up, Dallerwitz returning to Russia, while Sturzky and Gardner started for Herat. Gardner now proposed travelling through Persia and Afghanistan to the Panjab, having heard while at Astrabad that his friend M. Rossaix was receiving large pay at Lahore.

In the course of the journey to Herat, Gardner and Sturzky fell in with a respectable-looking and intelligent man, with some twenty mounted attendants. He represented himself to be a *naib* or *vakil* (ambassador) from the khan of Khokand, sent from that territory on a political mission to the Courts of Persia and Herat, and now returning to his master. He held out alluring prospects to the travellers if they would accompany him to Khokand. M. Sturzky was at once persuaded to adopt the proposal, and was fully convinced of the truth of the man's assertions. He endeavoured to persuade Gardner to go with him and the *vakil*, and Gardner would have done so but that he fortunately fell ill. Sturzky therefore took a friendly leave of him, and departed with his new ally. This took place within a few miles of Herat, and Gardner entered that city on the following day, and remained there a short time until cured of his fever. He then proposed to visit Khiva, and possibly to rejoin M. Sturzky.

On the 20th January 1819 Gardner was fit to travel, and started off to Ghorian, hearing that a small caravan of petty merchants and Mecca pilgrims, bound for different parts of Turkestan, was collecting there. Losing no time, Gardner covered the thirty-five miles to Ghorian by sunset, but, to his intense vexation, found that he had been misinformed, and that the caravan was really ending, not beginning, its journey. It was bound for Herat, there to rest some time before proceeding eastward. The *kafila* (caravan) was a very small one, and had been no less than eighteen months on the march from Mecca.

Nevertheless, some of its devoted members had still to toil as far as the north-eastern boundaries of Khokand, Kashgar, and Yarkand, and even to the more distant regions of Mongolia.

Gardner returned with the *kafila* to Herat, and having made acquaintances among the pilgrims, determined to remain with them during their stay at Herat, and to travel towards Kunduz in their company. He was now, at the age of thirty-four, about to enter on a career of apparently aimless wandering, which he pursued until his arrival in the Panjab in August 1831, a period of twelve years. Occasionally he settled down for a time, but soon the force of circumstances, or a roving and lawless disposition, compelled him to move on.

We can now leave Gardner to tell in his own language the tale of his first journey in the wilds of Central Asia, on which he started on January 19, 1819.

CHAPTER III.

ADVENTURES AMONG THE HAZARAS, 1819.

SAVAGE HOSPITALITY—THE KHALZAIS (DAI KUNDI HAZARAS)—THE THERBAHS — THE ANCIENT KAFIRS — GARDNER ACQUIRES A FAITHFUL FOLLOWER—THE SLAVE-DEALERS—GARDNER'S "NOM DE VOYAGE"—A GENEROUS HOST—GARDNER'S DANGEROUS ILLNESS—THE KHAN OF KHIVA—A GEOGRAPHICAL PROBLEM—ADVENTURES OF M. STURZKY—GARDNER RETURNS TO ASTRAKHAN.

WE left Herat at daybreak, and as the melting of the snow might soon be confidently expected, the *kafila* took a direct, but little-frequented, road over the snowy ranges of the Western Hindu Kush. We were, in all about 100 persons, bound for various parts of Turkestan, and by general agreement amongst us the city of Kunduz, the capital of the kingdom of that name, then under the sway of Mir Murad Ali Beg, was to be our first destination. Arrived there, or near there, we intended to break off into small parties which could make their own arrangements for reaching their homes. Most of us were provided with rough-coated ponies or mules. The region through which we now commenced to travel was inhabited by the Hazaras, whom we found to be a truly hospitable race. We journeyed along the track that appeared to separate the northern (or hill) Hazaras from the southern tribes, and our daily marches were from eight to ten miles in length, and generally in a north-easterly direction.

The kindly hill Hazaras kept us regularly supplied with fresh bread and milk, and made us welcome to their villages for as long as we liked to stay. I observed, and it was worth observing, that the farther we journeyed from the confines of civilisation the more marked and scrupulous was the punctiliousness with which our wants were met.

We took sixteen marches to traverse the land inhabited by the Hazaras, and in the evening of the fifth day we arrived at a mosque, which served as a serai, or resting-place for travellers, and hinted a wish to stay the night and a readiness to pay for accommodation, food, and forage. Our offer met with polite but sharp resentment: no purchasers could be allowed to rest under their protection. It is considered not only a disgrace but a crime, for which they are responsible to God, if a fellow-creature suffers want under their roof; but these wild Hazaras strictly define the limits of their hospitality, and consider it quite a venial matter to sally forth armed, and to waylay and plunder caravans before they happen to have entered the charmed precincts. But any outrage on a poor and lonely traveller is hooted as a disgrace.

Devotion precedes a marauding expedition. The Hazara invariably recites a prayer in the mosque or at the nearest shrine, and if in the struggle for booty slaughter is probable, he, before striking the necessary but perhaps deadly blow, mutters between his teeth the "kulma," repeating the invocation "Bismilla ill il la." They deem the penal responsibility for the crime materially modified in the eyes of God and man by this propitiatory precaution. In fact, in their eyes it is tantamount to absolution, the booty is regarded as lawfully gained income, and a portion, one-fortieth, is set aside for charity. The omission of the invocation precludes all these benefits; and death, heavy calamity, or some deadly illness is deemed to be hovering over the guilty.

To resume my journey. We proceeded on our

way through thinly inhabited country. The lower Hazara district, the borders of which we skirted, was thriving with grain crops, and we obtained guides and protectors through the district, thereby avoiding adding our slender belongings to swell their prosperity.

These protectors were fakirs, mullahs, or pirs —in other words, men of various religious pretensions. Each conducted us to the limit of his spiritual dominions, and the sanctity of their profession was our only but sufficient protection. They were quite indispensable to our life and property, and were well rewarded by subscription, though they often tried to exact more than we were disposed to afford.

Travelling thus, we traversed, as I have said, the Hazara country for a period of sixteen days. I then left the *kafila*, and turning to the north, with a few companions, I entered the country of the Khalzais,[1] a mountain tribe living to the north of the Hazara region. The history of this race is obscure, but they are supposed to be the

[1] I am very uncertain of the spelling of this name, and have been unable to identify the tribe. They are said, in Edgeworth's abstract of Gardner's travels, to be a section of the Dai Kundi Hazaras. Hardly anything is as yet known of the Dai Kundi country.—EDITOR.

descendants of emigrant Arabs, Mongols, and Tartars. From my notes I take the following description.

The Khalzais are low sized, but stout and active, of a florid complexion, with brown or dark-red hair and beard.

The women are very comely, active in all household pursuits, and not shrinking from holding a spear and taking part in a clan skirmish. The beauty of the women is in repute throughout Afghanistan and the north of Persia, from whence slave-dealers are deputed to kidnap them for the seraglios of the wealthy. Reprisals are often adopted, and expeditions formed by the Khalzais to carry fire and sword into the neighbouring countries. In these expeditions the Khalzais carry off women and children for sale in the slave-markets of Balkh or Bokhara.

The Khalzais are armed with a long straight knife, a short, stout, broad-headed spear, and a matchlock or jezail. Their dress consists of a long loose garment of a coarse woollen texture, manufactured from the wool of their own sheep; a jacket made of roughly dressed skins; a waistband of several folds of cloth; narrower rolls round the legs; raw skin sandals; and a curiously shaped leather hat completes the picturesque costume. In the summer those who can afford to do so, adopt soft trousers.

The women dress in loose trousers, with a short vest of black or blue woollen stuff. Their hair is neatly braided, with long pendent ringlets.

They live in caves, some of which have spacious apartments, calculated to shelter a patriarchal family.

The tribe are devout Muhammadans, and can marry the usual number of wives, but, contrary to custom, they adopt no privacy for them. Notwithstanding, the virtue of the Khalzai female is held in high repute.

From this tribe I passed on to another known as the Therbahs, a tribe of Kafir descent.

The Therbah, who is a half-savage, worships the sun and moon, fire and water, and resembles in some respects the scattered remnants of the Guebers of Persia. The tribe wanders about the sandy wastes south of Merve. They maintain friendly relations with their neighbours the Khalzais, and they understand each other's dialect. They intermarry with the Siah Posh Kafirs, who inhabit the Eastern Hindu Kush ranges, but the pride of the latter tribe does not permit them to give their daughters in return. The Therbah is said to be able to make the journey to the Khawak district, on the border of Kafiristan, in ten or twelve days.

In ancient days the Kafirs are said to have spread over the whole Hindu Kush region, and even far to the west of those mountains, but various invasions worked great changes. Timur passed over the Bamian route into India, and partially destroyed the Kafir races by the sword or by compulsory proselytism. Local traditions affirm that while carrying on an unsuccessful war with the Siah Posh Kafirs he managed to compel 8000 males of other tribes to adopt Muhammadanism. The numerous tribes who follow the Prophet under the name of Hazaras, and the Kemaik races, are lineal descendants of these ancient Kafir tribes. The Therbahs are among them, but have retained their ancient religion. The Therbahs resembled the Khalzais in appearance, and with some trifling exceptions their dress was also similar. Their chief, whose name was Therman Khan, treated me with much friendship and hospitality, and his son Ibrahim Khan attached himself to me also. I passed about a month with Therman Khan, and made several expeditions of exploration, which I should think worthy of record but for the far more exciting scenes through which I was destined to pass.

In addition to two servants who were already in my employment, I here procured two others. One of these was an Afghan or Kohistan lad about eighteen years of age, who had been stolen by an itinerant slave-dealer, bought by Therman Khan as a child, and reared by him. Therman Khan gave me the lad, and he proved a faithful servant and good soldier. I always called him Therbah, in memory of the tribe whence I obtained him, and his history will be found in the following pages.

It being now my purpose to proceed to Merve, a party of Therbahs, under Ibrahim Khan, was ordered by the chief to conduct me to that neighbourhood. In the course of our journey we met with the following adventure, which indicates the species of society into which we had penetrated. We reached a town called Nack, distant some miles from Merve, and there met a party of five slave-dealers from the north. While we were inquiring particulars of the country through which they had travelled, these men opened a shy converse in the Turki dialect with some of our party. When the time for repose came, they sought a private interview with Ibrahim Khan, who in a short time returned to us with peals of laughter, and I was apprised that negotiations had been made for my sale as a slave. The slave-dealers were not convinced that their proposition was declined, and one of them sneaked in and privately thrust five *tillahs* into the hand of Ibrahim Khan: he flung them away, and repeated that I was not merchantable.

At last words grew high and blows were exchanged, and the scuffle ended in the binding in bonds of the five merchants by the chief authority of the place.

They were very near being retaliated upon and made slaves of themselves, but humanity prevailed in the counsels and they were let go—mulcted, however, of everything but a sword and shield apiece, as a just fine for their insolence and violence. After these ruffians had vanished, it transpired that four of them belonged to a body of men whose whole trade consisted of kidnapping children for sale. Eleven *tillahs* of gold, part of the money found on my would-be purchasers, were handed to me. I gave ten of them to Ibrahim Khan when we parted company a fortnight later. From his protection I passed to that of a Turkoman chief, named Shah Mardak, said to be of Mogul origin: he, however, stoutly professed to be a Turkh. He was chief of a small oasis in the sandy tract to the south-east of Merve. He gave me a most hospitable welcome.

I lived with him for some time, moving about in an easterly direction, and eventually left him and made a forced march to Andkhui, where I joined a considerable caravan. This was composed of merchants of various nationalities, the principal of them being a very intelligent man, who passed by the name of Urd Khan. He received me as a guest in his tents, and treated me with great generosity. I had no money left and no prospects at Khiva, his home and the destination of the caravan, save the doubtful assistance that M. Sturzky might be able to afford me.

I have not yet stated that my own travelling name was Arb Shah. I passed as a native of Arabia, and met very few in my travels who could speak Arabic. I explained any deficiency of knowledge of my native language by telling my interlocutor that I came from the opposite corner of Arabia to that with which he was acquainted, having previously taken care to worm this information out of him.

While travelling with Urd Khan I fell dangerously ill with brain fever, and was insensible for two days. We were at the time about ten days' journey from Khiva. Nothing could exceed the paternal benevolence of Urd Khan. He actually conveyed me in a bed made up in a *kajawa*, carried by one of his private camels, and I was balanced by his ladies in the *kajawa* on the other side: they treated me with great kindness.

During my illness we were one day alarmed by twenty horsemen galloping up. Urd Khan, as the selected chief of the caravan, was deputed to deal with them. His tactics were erroneous. Thinking they were but a small party, and calculating on our strength, he told them to be off as "dogs." Off they went and halted suddenly a mile in front, and seemed in a moment to melt away out of sight. We marched on for a few miles, when suddenly a band of some 400 marauding Turkoman horsemen appeared. Urd Khan now changed his tone. As for me, I was dead-sick, and little cared what became of me.

He rode forward and arranged a parley with the chiefs, who condoned his former demeanour to their deputies, as the first batch proved to be. Our lives were to be spared, and we and our women were not to be sold into slavery, the ordinary doom on such occasions, but Urd Khan was to be mulcted of a fine camel and two *kajawas* full of selected merchandise. Then every one had to open his bales, and contributions were levied from us all, in due proportion, under Urd Khan's supervision. My pony was seized; and a rich Jewish merchant, who was among us, was treated with exceptional severity. This he attributed to Urd Khan, and longed for revenge. The depredators affected great indignation at having had to come so far. They had come, they said, twenty *farsangs* on receiving Turkoman telegraphic intelligence of the treatment of their deputies at the hands of Urd Khan.

They do, in fact, communicate with each other with extraordinary speed, and swoop down in numbers, like vultures upon a dead body, when but one solitary bird has originally scented the carrion. We were warned that we should only be safe until noon the following day, and taking the hint, hurried off, and had hardly got across the river Oxus when a body of sixty men, either of the same band or another of like character, halloed to the peasantry on our bank that we were robbers and had despoiled them.

The peasantry were soon up in arms, but fortunately took our view of the matter. The whistling, shouting, shrieking, and signalling on this occasion betokened the state of incessant watchfulness the inhabitants of these parts are obliged to maintain. Aided by the villagers, we were strong enough to hold our own, and moved slowly on. We did not dare to halt, as from the well-known pride of the Turkoman hordes we were in hourly expectation of another attack, and we therefore moved on until within two marches of Khiva. Here a tremendous altercation arose between the Jew and Urd Khan. The Jew wanted to go to Khokand, Urd Khan intended shortly to start for Orenburg, and they were bartering commodities to suit the different markets.

The country we were now in was most inimical to Russians, of whose movements they were very jealous, and the Jew disappeared, and gave out that Urd Khan had a Russian spy with him. I was still prostrate with fever, and indifferent as to what befell me. Urd Khan swore that no harm should touch me, and nobly did that generous and disinterested Asiatic redeem his pledge. He had some acquaintance with the khan of Khiva, and went to see him, and declared that I was too ill to move.

In a great state of anxiety as to my identity, the khan deputed three learned men, who had travelled over half the world, to examine me.

I told them the truth—that I was an American. They were suspicious. One of them, a very enlightened man, thought to pose me by a conclusive and abstruse geographical question, "Could I go by land from America to England?" I promptly answered, "No!" at which, as much delighted at his own superior learning as at my reply, he declared that he was convinced. Americans they considered "Yagistanis," or Independents.

Urd Khan hovered round my couch during this perilous interview, and plied me with incessant gruels, magnifying my deplorable state, and actually managed so well as to get the Jew flung into prison. He then deported me quietly to the home of a friend of his at Urgunz. During all this time I had no resources of my own, and lived entirely on the munificent hospitality of my Eastern entertainer. From this place I wrote to Khokand to M. Sturzky, who wrote me in reply a doleful account of himself. The Khiva people had stripped him of everything, and but for the intercession of a holy travelling *khoja* of great sanctity, he would have been murdered.

He subsequently managed to join me on my way to Astrakhan, after many adventures. He was half-naked, thin, hungry, and ill, but still in good spirits. The hapless man had bought his escape from Khiva at the price of circumcision in a public ceremonial by the fanatical *khoja*, who deemed the wrath of Heaven inevitable had he omitted to avail himself of this happy opportunity of securing the conversion of an infidel.

My health being restored, I dismissed my Therbah to his home, and returned with M. Sturzky, by way of the Sea of Aral, whence I crossed the steppe to Alexandrovsk, where I took ship for Astrakhan.

CHAPTER IV.

WANDERER AND FREEBOOTER IN CENTRAL ASIA.

M. DELAROCHE — GARDNER AGAIN LEAVES ASTRAKHAN — CROSSING THE ARAL SEA—GARDNER APPROACHES URA-TUBE—AN ADVENTURE WITH KIPCHAK — KIRGHIZ — "WHEN AT ROME ACT LIKE THE ROMANS"—A FLIGHT FOR DEAR LIFE—GARDNER A FREEBOOTER—APPROACHES AFGHANISTAN.

GARDNER reached Astrakhan without further adventure, and there had the good fortune to meet a relation and friend, in the person of M. Delaroche, the son of one of Gardner's maternal aunts.

M. Delaroche, who had been a great traveller, had brought with him letters to high Russian authorities, by means of which he purposed to obtain for his relations the remainder of the elder Gardner's fortune, which had been so unjustly attached by the Russian Government.

In this matter he eventually was successful, and was also ready and even anxious to obtain employment for Gardner; but, as the latter quaintly puts it, he had imbibed a prejudice against the Russian method of conducting business, and preferred to remain his own master.

In the course of the year 1820 M. Delaroche left for America and M. Sturzky for Moscow. Gardner took an early opportunity of repaying his debt to the generous Urd Khan, and remained at Astrakhan until the beginning of the year 1823, during which period he apparently spent or lost his small fortune.

He then became restless, and in the month of February again set out on his Asiatic travels.

He could not, he says, rest in civilised countries, and, being free from family ties, was persuaded that he would find happiness among wild races and in exploring unknown lands. Realising, therefore, the scant remains of his fortune, Gardner embarked for the last time on the Caspian Sea. He had determined to lose his identity as soon as possible, and particularly to cast off all connection with Russia—a step that was essential to his safety, as that nation was much hated and dreaded at the period in question by all the tribes and peoples between the Caspian Sea and the city of Khiva.

On leaving his ship Gardner therefore dismissed

his servant, who returned to Astrakhan, and immediately exchanged the Russian furs which he was wearing for the garb of an Uzbeg. This consisted, he says, of a lofty, peaked fur cap; a black *postin* (sheepskin coat); thick wide drawers reaching to the knee; short black boots, with bandages twisted round the leg over them and up to the knee.

There was nothing worthy of note during Gardner's journey across the steppes from the Caspian to the Aral Sea. The ground was familiar to him, and he merely records that he received great hospitality from the various chiefs, and that he resumed (this time for many years) his travelling name of Arb Shah, the convenience of which has been explained.

In spite of the risk, Gardner could not resist sending a message to his friend Urd Khan, to inquire where he was and how he fared. The messenger returned and informed Gardner that Urd Khan had gone to Meshed, and also conveyed a warning from Urd Khan's brother to Gardner that he should not visit Khiva.

Meanwhile Gardner had with great difficulty crossed the Aral Sea: his boat filled with water and nearly foundered. Eventually he and his companions landed on the south-east shore, in a most dangerous swamp at the mouth of a river. There is, he says, a most remarkable formation at this place. The silt of the river forms an immense bed of inert vegetable matter, which presents all the horrors of a quicksand for any unfortunate vessel that founders. No life has ever been known to be saved under such circumstances. Having happily effected a safe landing, Gardner and two or three wanderers who had joined him travelled for a short distance along the bank of the river at whose mouth they had landed, but presently struck off to the east with the intention of reaching Khojend, the home of one of the party. They gave all towns and other dangerous places a wide berth, but on approaching their destination were tracked and apprehended by some scouts, who, however, let them pass unmolested on receiving a satisfactory account of the party from the native of Khojend.

On approaching Ura-tube they made a detour, as the *beg* or *bai* (ruler) of that place was a noted and unscrupulous marauder and robber. About this time Gardner was joined by his faithful Therbah, who had heard of his journey and had followed him up, and also by a remarkable person who was travelling with three or four camels. Gardner suspected this man of being an escaped convict from Siberia, but was uncertain of his nationality —he called himself a Pole, and perhaps was one. He spoke of various parts of Germany and of Transylvania and Albania. He usually spoke French to Gardner, and went by the name of Aga Beg. He showed himself very friendly to Gardner; and it was, in fact, thanks to his information and advice that the party kept clear of the direct road to Ura-tube and Khojend, and went by the Ak-Tagh range, farther to the north.

Barely had they skirted this range when they found themselves in bad company. The adventures that followed shall be related in Gardner's own words.

"We found ourselves," he says, "close upon a large camp of Kipchaks, which was pitched on the banks of the Jisak, a river which empties itself into the Zerufshan. At the head of the encampment was a powerful *beg* or *bai*.

"There was nothing for it but to make the best of things; so we, as the smaller party, sent a deputation to salute the larger. From the date of this *rencontre* the whole destinies of myself and my party were changed, and our horizons were dark with presages of imminent disaster.

"A suspicious cordiality was soon struck up between some of our servants and those of the *bai's* large camp. Pressure was also put upon us by the Ura-tube freebooters, who, on the pretext that we had intruded without leave in their territory, made a demand for fifteen or twenty horses. We had the latter number among our small party, five of which were mine, very fine animals which had caught the eye of the stalwart *bai*, our neighbour. Twenty per cent of all our goods was also demanded, and eight days were allowed us to show our belongings. Nothing is done in a hurry in Asia. It was pretended that similar demands were made on our neighbours the Kipchaks, and their *bai* sent for us to his camp under the pretext of asking our advice. On arriving there he was not to be found, and on our return we found that he had visited our little encampment during our absence. The result of his inspection was soon apparent. Orders came to us that we should move closer to the *bai's* camp. We had to obey, and that very night our horses and camels were stolen under the very noses of our treacherous servants.

"We tracked them to the *bai's* camp, recognised

our property, and demanded their restitution. We were, however, hustled back with volleys of abuse. We then offered to buy them back, but it was of no use.

"Meanwhile, to add to our difficulties, the Ura-tube chief sent an imperative mandate for a contribution of five horses. We had none to give, and grew desperate.

"We swore on our drawn swords to recover our horses and property by stratagem or force, or die for it.

"Aga Beg had two trusty men, as familiar as wild beasts with the intricate ravines about the place, and such ground was homelike to my Therbah. We determined to make a midnight *daur* (raid), recover our horses, plunder as much as we could in reprisal, and escape by the ravines. Hemmed in as we were, we prowled about for two nights, being fired upon once or twice in mistake for wild animals by the camp outposts of the Kipchaks.

"The suspicions of the *bai* seemed at last to be lulled, and the hour came. We entered the camp and carried off twelve horses, including my own five, and plenty of booty, and then made the best of our way south by places in which pursuit was at that hour of night almost impossible. It was a daring deed. We knew that the pursuit would be close and furious, and that the whole country would soon be up. We were at the mercy of Aga Beg's guides, but felt that we could rely on him and them. Our hope was to reach Samarkand, where he had property and a powerful connection.

"Three horsemen of the Ura-tube chief suddenly overtook us about dawn, and with violent abuse ordered us to halt and yield in the name of the Government. On our refusal they threatened to fire, and in self-defence we slew them and fled on, taking their arms and horses, through the tracks most remote from habitations. One night a Turkoman horseman passed near us at full speed, and soon afterwards another came up to us and stopped us. He said he had orders from Samarkand to aid in arresting a desperate band of robbers. We declared that we were in pursuit of them. We might easily have killed him, but agreed that by letting him pass on we might divert suspicion from ourselves.

"It was evidently unsafe to make for Samarkand, as was our intention then; so, wearily but in good heart, we pursued our anxious way towards Hazrat Imam, hoping for shelter there.

"Having reached the Oxus, we hid ourselves

among the rocky banks, and sent a man to the holy place to see what our chances were. He returned with the calamitous news that our party, 'dogs of Mervites,' were proclaimed all over the country, and no one would dare to take us in."

Finding life under such circumstances a trifle too exciting, Gardner and his companions now decided to strike southward and endeavour to make their way to Kabul, there to offer their services to Amir Dost Muhammad Khan, who was at this time establishing himself, by right of conquest and by the will of the people, as ruler of the northern and eastern portions of Afghanistan.

Gardner but seldom mentions dates, and it is difficult to gather from his rapid narrative how long was the period during which he and Aga Beg lived as wandering freebooters. They apparently joined forces early in the summer of 1823, and from the great distances covered during their prolonged flight from the Kipchak marauders, it must have been well on in the year when the party crossed the Oxus at the first practicable spot above Hazrat Imam and headed towards Kabul.

A rough and dangerous mountain country had to be traversed, all authorities to be avoided, and it need cause us no surprise to learn that the condition of the travellers proceeded from bad to worse. Unheedingly they passed the famous lapis-lazuli mines; historic cities were to them but the strongholds of oppression, and, as such, to be avoided.

"Food," says Gardner, "we obtained by levying contributions from every one we could master, but we did not slaughter unless in self-defence."

When near Kunduz, it should be said, they had again been compelled to kill a party of three armed men, who declared that Gardner's party were themselves the robbers whom they professed to be pursuing, and threatened to take them before the ruler of the province.

A guilty conscience is certainly suggested by the following passage, which immediately follows that quoted above: "On coming near Inder-ab (or Anderab) we halted for two days, to rest our wearied bones. We told the same story to all we met, saying, 'Have you seen any robbers? We are in pursuit of a band.'" To this query Gardner says they invariably received the response, "You will find them in Bolor." We shall henceforth become familiar with this name under various forms.

The borders of Afghanistan were at length

reached, but the path to safety and employment under Dost Muhammad Khan was by no means clear.

The reader will be reminded in the next chapter how it was that Dost Muhammad Khan came to be Amir of Kabul, and must further understand that at the time of Gardner's arrival in the Inder-ab valley, that region and the Kohistan (or mountain country to the north of Kabul) was in possession of a rival claimant to the throne. This claimant was Prince Habib-ulla Khan, son of the deceased elder brother of Dost Muhammad Khan. Habib-ulla Khan had for a short time been recognised as ruler of Kabul, but had now been dispossessed by his uncle.

CHAPTER V.

A SOLDIER OF FORTUNE AMONG THE AFGHANS.

THE KINGDOM OF AFGHANISTAN—HABIB-ULLA KHAN AND HIS HISTORY—GARDNER JOINS HIS STANDARD AND BECOMES A SOLDIER OF FORTUNE—AFGHAN TOLLS—THE ROMANCE OF WAR—GARDNER'S MARRIAGE — THE CASTELLO — TRIUMPH OF AMIR DOST MUHAMMAD KHAN—TRAGIC END OF GARDNER'S MARRIED LIFE —HABIB-ULLA KHAN'S RESOLUTION.

THE kingdom of Afghanistan dates only from the year 1747, when Ahmad Khan, hereditary chief of the Sadozai tribe, was crowned King of the Afghans at Kandahar. Ahmad Khan changed the name of his tribe to Durani, and assumed the title of Shah Duri Duran. After a glorious career of conquest he died in June 1773.

Ahmad Shah Durani was succeeded by his son Taimur, who reigned twenty years, and was succeeded by his son Shah Zaman, who was blinded and deposed in the year 1799. Shah Zaman's brother and successor, Mahmud Shah, had no strength of character, and in July 1803 was set aside in favour of Shah Shujah, another brother.

The vicissitudes undergone by this unfortunate monarch are well known, and had resulted in his exile in the year 1811, when the greater part of Afghanistan fell under the dominion of another great clan—the Barakzai—of which Dost Muhammad Khan eventually became the chief. In 1839 the British placed Shah Shujah once more on the throne of Afghanistan, but as soon as the protection of that Power ceased, in April 1842, Shah Shujah was murdered.

His son and successor, Fathi Jang, shared the same fate a few months later, and Dost Muhammad resumed the power whieh he alone could wield effectively. His family has ever since reigned in Afghanistan.

The people of Afghanistan are indifferently called Afghans and Pathans. The former name is by some writers said to indicate the turbulent nature of the people (*fighan* meaning lamentation) —the same Persian word *fighan* means in another sense "idols," and may therefore imply a nation of idolators.

The name "Pathan" is said by Colonel Malleson to embody the idea of strength. "Pashtun" or

"Pukhtun," yet another name of the nation, is said to mean "dwellers in hills."

Gardner and his companions had, of course, no knowledge of Afghan politics, and little anticipated the events which were about to frustrate their intention of seeking employment under Dost Muhammad. Gardner's account of his campaign under Prince Habib-ulla Khan is so spirited, and fortunately so complete, that it follows entirely in his own words.

The history of the internecine struggle between Dost Muhammad Khan and the various members of his family for the throne of Afghanistan has been very incompletely told by historians. The record of the Kohistan campaign, as related in the following pages by Gardner, is therefore valuable as well as interesting.

The happy audacity and confidence displayed by the adventurer on the occasion of his falling in with Habib-ulla Khan throw full light on his character, and enable us to understand how it was that dangers vanished from before him.

At last (says the traveller) we came upon an outpost of the Kohistan region of the Kabul country, and were stopped by a mounted guard.

We demanded the name of the ruler. The guard declared it to be the great Amir Habib-ulla Khan, of Kabul, Kashmir, and Peshawar. We desired to be brought before him. The guard refused, and demanded the usual custom dues. We persisted, and seeing a threatening of an attack, disarmed two of them, but the third escaped and flew for aid. The crisis was now approaching.

In about an hour we heard the trampling and rushing sound of still distant cavalry, and presently the famous but unfortunate outlawed chieftain, splendidly mounted and at the head of fifty picked horsemen, dashed at us. We could see them coming on like a desert-storm for a mile, and I had barely time to order my followers to mount and to place myself at their head, when the cavalcade was upon us. I received them with a respectful military salute. Habib-ulla Khan was enraged at the insult we had offered to his outpost, but amused, I could see, at the attitude of our small band. The moment was come for parley; I ordered my men to sheath their swords, returned my own to its scabbard, and demanded an audience. By this time we were completely surrounded by the chief's party, and I knew that we were in their power, and that nothing but audacity and tact could save us. I enjoined silence, under pain of death, on my men, and then explained myself frankly to the chief.

I told him I was of the New World (he had never before heard of it) and a Christian, and he declared the secret should be inviolable. His first irritation over, it pleased rather than displeased his fine nature that we had refused to comply with the demands of the outpost, and had preferred to fling ourselves on his protection. The affair ended by the generous chief sending then and there a distance of three miles for a sumptuous repast and Kabul vintages wherewith to recruit our famished frames. He then took us with him to his fort, where he recounted to me all his history, his hopes, and his sufferings. He told me how he had been plundered, how grossly his mother had been treated, how his two lovely sisters had been violated by order of his uncle, Dost Muhammad Khan, and how he had slain them at their own request with his own hand, and lastly, how he had fled and become the outlaw I found him.

I sympathised deeply with the brave and persecuted man, whose eyes filled with tears when he recalled the dishonour of his family. The person of the chieftain was as attractive, and his face as handsome, as his stature was gigantic; his prowess in action I have never seen surpassed. His open nature abhorred Asiatic wiles, and thus he had easily fallen a prey to the machinations of his wily uncle, Dost Muhammad Khan.

The Dost at this time had abandoned the follies of his youth and affected great religious austerity, and by these means, and by making grants of land to the *mullahs*[1] in all the Kohistan, the territory still held by his nephew, had succeeded in raising up a religious war against him. He bribed the avaricious and intriguing priests to proclaim Habib-ulla Khan an infidel and a wine-bibber, and was aided by the liberal opinions and jovial habits of the *sardar*.

Being, like Habib-ulla Khan, of a sanguine disposition, and, moreover, being favourably impressed by his appearance and manner, I proffered the services of myself and my followers, which were readily accepted, and I was engaged as commandant of 180 picked horse to be employed in forays into the enemy's country, and in levying contributions on all caravans, especially seizing every morsel of baggage and

[1] Priests.

property that was intended for Dost Muhammad Khan.

Our good friend Aga Beg took leave, and the chief presented the faithful, though mysterious, adventurer with a fine horse, and a safe escort to his destination.

I had one day accidentally noticed a golden or brazen cross hanging from Aga Beg's neck, and asked him in French where his home was, thinking that he might be of that nationality. He replied, with a smile, in that language, that he lived in the mountains of Ura-tube, but gave me no further information, nor did I seek for any. I parted from him with regret, and for ever.[1]

From this date for a period of two and a half years I led a life in the saddle, one of active warfare and continual forays: so successful were we that we had our advanced posts within twenty miles of Kabul, and the Dost dared not show his nose in the whole mountain region.

None of the chief's faithful and ardent followers received any pay. We lived, as I have said, in the saddle, and fed in common, for the good cause

[1] The Pole gave Gardner a curious crystal pipe-bowl as a parting present. This gift was subsequently a source of trouble to the recipient.

of right against wrong which we had espoused. Any money derived from our captures went to pay the general expenses.

We made daily forays, with various results, and Habib-ulla Khan headed us in every struggle, and was the champion of every fight. He seemed ubiquitous in action, and his shout in the charge struck terror into the hearts of our enemies, and seemed to lend double courage and vigour to his followers. There was hardly one of us who was not at one time or other indebted to him for life, and not one who was not ready to repay the debt.

The contributions levied on travellers and traders amounted to nearly 20 per cent. Now the dues of Government (and it was these dues that we affected to levy) ought, by the Muhammadan law, to amount to one-fortieth or 2½ per cent. So, to satisfy our consciences, we detailed to our victims the following rapacious schedule :—

2½ per cent the dues of God;
2½ " for the priests;
2½ " for the poor;
2½ " for the great Amir Habib-ulla Khan;

2½ per cent for prayers of intercession at Mecca;
2½ " for the protection we afforded them out of our dominions;
and the remainder for our expenses (for by this time we had usually got tired of details).

I cannot relate my experiences at length, for the events of one day much resembled those of another, but one occasion is indelibly impressed on my memory.

It was about six months after I joined Habib-ulla Khan that we received information from a trustworthy source in Kabul that Dost Muhammad Khan was about to move in force to the north, but for a short distance only, and not with the intention of attacking us. The politic conduct of his uncle always infuriated Habib-ulla Khan, who longed for an opportunity of settling the family questions in the field.

He now, however, felt that something was likely to happen which would give him an opportunity of dealing a home-blow to his enemy, and so it fell out. We ascertained from our spies that one of the ladies of Dost Muhammad's harem, who had long been absent on a pilgrimage to various shrines, had ended her pious journey at Hazrat

Imam, and was now about to return to Kabul from that place, with an escort of some fifty sowars. The object of her pilgrimage had been to secure the intercession of the priests of all the shrines in her favour, she being unblessed with issue. So anxious was the Dost about the safety of his lady, and of a treasure in gold that she was bringing with her from a source which I failed to identify, that he sent an overpowering body of horse to guard all the Bamian passes.

By a clever ruse, and by making some of our people personate some sowars of Dost Muhammad Khan and misinform other bodies of his troops, we induced the lady's escort to divert their route to the Ghorband Pass, where Habib-ulla lay in wait. We attacked them in front and rear, and they were largely outnumbered, but the escort were true to their trust and made a gallant fight.

Eventually we cut off the camels laden with treasure and those on which the lady and her attendants were carried, and Habib-ulla committed the entire prize to my care, while he covered our retreat.

While so doing he was attacked by a large force of the Kabul cavalry, which had found out what was going on and that they had been deceived. So hardly was he pressed, and so hot was the pursuit, that nothing but extraordinary exertions on our part, and the brilliant courage of Habib-ulla Khan, extricated us.

In the course of the running fight to our stronghold I was enabled to see the beautiful face of a young girl who accompanied the princess. I rode for a considerable time beside her, pretending that my respect for the elder lady made me choose that side of her camel on which her attendant was carried.

On the following morning Habib-ulla Khan richly rewarded all his followers, for he was generous to a fault; but I refused my share of the gold, and begged for this girl to be given me in marriage as the only reward I desired. She was of royal birth on the mother's side, being the daughter (as was at once discovered) of one of Habib-ulla Khan's nearest relatives. He, however, freely and willingly gave her to me, and established me as commandant of a fort near his own abode. There I was very happy for about two years, in the course of which time my wife made me the father of a noble boy.

To return, however, to Dost Muhammad's lady.

She was treated with scrupulous honour and

respect, being given a separate residence with her attendants. Every facility was given her to communicate her whereabouts to her lord, and after negotiations which lasted over two or three months, she was ransomed at the price of 3000 *tillahs* of gold, five horses, three large falcons, and other articles of value. She returned to Kabul with her personal honour untarnished and her private property untouched.

Many of us hoped that after this dignified and chivalrous behaviour to the wife of an uncle who had barbarously outraged the family of Habib-ulla Khan, negotiations might have been entered into and a spirit of amity displayed by the Dost. But it was not to be so. Habib-ulla, far from encouraging any proffer of reconciliation, rather widened the breach by his unyielding pride. He declared that his uncles should humble themselves before him, and not he to them, and he published it abroad that the ransom paid for the lady was the token of their humiliation and the symbol of their admission of his sovereign rights. Neither would the proud youth abate one jot of his claims to absolute dominion, nor lower in any degree his tone of defiance.

The Dost despatched two wily *mullahs*, ostensibly with a view to effect a reconciliation between him and his nephew. These men were kindly and cordially received, but we soon found that they were endeavouring to tamper with our officers, and Habib-ulla assumed a distant behaviour towards them. The *mullahs* were made over to my care as guests. I housed them, and attended with due courtesy to their wants.

When they had resided about fifteen days in my *castello*, which was about a mile and a half to the north-east of the fort of Parwan,[1] Habib-ulla Khan's residence, the leader of the two declared one morning that he had seen a vision during the previous night. A prophet had appeared unto him and declared that it was his, the *mullah's*, bounden duty to convert Habib-ulla Khan and his troops to the right faith. After this announcement he assumed fanatical airs, and stood in one of the principal highways with a Koran in one hand and a rusty pistol in the other, calling on all passers-by to repent, that he might show them the seventh heaven, the everlasting abode of the houris. Being looked on as half-

[1] Parwan or Parwandarrah is a few miles north of Charikar. A British force was defeated there by Dost Muhammad in November 1840.

crazy, not much notice was taken of him, until one day he was seen standing on the top of one of the turrets of my *castello* and beckoning to some armed strangers who had evidently been skulking about the ravines. Signal whistles were soon heard from two or three quarters.

No more ado was made than for the *mullah* to be shot dead forthwith by my *killadar* (fort-warder), and the rest of the party fled precipitately.

I was not at home at the time, but was seated in the presence, receiving orders on some important matter from the chief, when the tidings reached him. He merely remarked, "Let the dead *mullah* be washed and buried, according to the rites of the Faithful." He then wrote to Kabul, explaining how the man had met his death through his own misconduct and treachery. This occurrence naturally was exaggerated and made use of against Habib-ulla Khan and his followers, and the cry for a holy war to the knife became hot and furious. The addition of "saint-killers" was made to the already tolerably complete vocabulary of opprobrious designations used against us by the Dost's party.

Now, as I have already said, the Dost had gained over the priests by large grants of land, most of which lay in the district still held by our party. The time had now come for our enemies, aided by the excited feeling abroad, to make a simultaneous attack on us from all sides, with the object of destroying us if possible, or at any rate of finally driving us out of the country and breaking our power. The Dost employed his whole available force, some 12,000 men, for the work of extirpation. They hemmed us in on the west, south, and east, and for a period of from two to three months there was a series of bloody and desperate fights. We were gradually more and more closely surrounded, and our originally slender numbers were terribly attenuated.

In March 1826[1] the struggle was nearly over. Habib-ulla Khan's force mustered but 180 devoted sowars. Our sole remaining outlets were the Khawak Pass and the Kafir-Ghaur, the latter almost inaccessible and in country unknown to nearly all of us. Well do I remember the occasion of the Dost's final attack. Snow was still lying on the ground in large and deep patches. My troop (which had hitherto escaped fairly well)

[1] It is usually stated that Dost Muhammad overcame the rebellion of Habib-ulla Khan in the course of the year 1824; but the details of the civil war are but little known, and Gardner's date may be correct.

had been reduced in the previous day's fight from ninety men to thirty-nine. The enemy had been most pertinacious, and had followed us until well into the night, contrary to their usual custom. I felt that we were at our last gasp, when an express message reached me from Parwan, which Habib-ulla was defending in person, ordering me to join him at Ghárak-i-Siah, a place so called from a dark ravine beneath it. My heart beat with sad forebodings, too awfully to be realised I must hurry over this part of my history.

I soon learnt that my chief had been overpowered and his fort taken: he himself with the few survivors of the garrison had cut their way through their enemies, and endeavoured to throw themselves into my *castello*. They had, however, been unable to escape from their pursuers, and were sore pressed when I came to their assistance. I reached Habib-ulla Khan about halfway between Parwan and my home, and found him fighting desperately with twelve of his men about him. Cutting my way through the enemy, I reached him, and found that he was badly wounded in the arm. I myself had previously received a ball in my knee.

Habib-ulla Khan, on seeing me, drew me aside

(the enemy having now retired), and, with a stony countenance in which all outward sign of emotion seemed to have been frozen down, told me that all was over with my unfortunate wife and little baby. He then detached half my men, and ordered me to go to my *castello* with the remainder and bring off what was left of the garrison, if any had survived the attack.

On arrival I felt a stern pleasure at seeing the great number of dead bodies of the enemy in comparison to those of the defenders; but our succour was too late—the garrison had been slaughtered to a man.

The silence was oppressive when I rode through the gateway of the fort, and my men instinctively fell back, when an old *mullah* (who had remained faithful to our party) came out to meet me, with his left hand and arm bound up. His fingers had been cut off and his arm nearly severed at the wrist by savage blows from a scimitar while striving to protect my little child. Faint from his wounds and from the miserable recollection of the scenes from which he escaped, the sole survivor, the aged *mullah*, at first stood gazing at me in a sort of wild abstraction, and then recounted the tale of the massacre of all I loved.

The garrison had long and gallantly held their own, though attacked on all sides by an immensely superior force. They had seen Habib-ulla Khan approaching, fighting gallantly, and had for a moment thought themselves saved, but he had been driven back and passed from their sight. The *castello* had then been stormed and all in it put to the sword, with the sole exception of the priest.

After this brief story the *mullah* silently beckoned to me to dismount and to follow him into the inner rooms. There lay four mangled corpses, —my wife, my boy, and two little eunuch youths. I had left them all thoughtless and happy but five days before. The bodies had been decently covered up by the faithful *mullah*, but the right hand of the hapless young mother could be seen, and clenched in it the reeking *katar* with which she had stabbed herself to the heart after handing over the child to the priest for protection. Her room had been broken open, and mortally self-wounded as she was, the assassins nearly severed her head from her body with their long Afghan knives or sabres. The *mullah* had tried to escape with the child, but had been cut across the hand and arm as aforesaid, and the boy seized and barbarously murdered. There he lay by the side of his mother.[1]

I sank on my knees and involuntarily offered up a prayer for vengeance to the Most High God. Seeing my attitude, the *mullah*, in a low solemn tone, breathed the Muhammadan prayers proper for the presence of the dead, in which my sowars, who had silently followed with bent heads, fervently joined. Tear after tear trickled down the pallid and withered cheeks of the priest as he concluded. Rising, I forced myself and him away from the room, gave him all the money I had for the interment of the dead, and with fevered brain rode away for ever from my once happy mountain home.

Habib-ulla Khan saw by our faces that all was over, and, with the same stony expression of despair in his countenance, bade us dismount and take counsel as to our future. His mind, he said, was made up. He would save, by death from his own hands, all his females from dishonour (he had removed them from Parwan some little time before), and then fall upon the enemy and die sword in hand.

[1] To the end of his long life Colonel Gardner was unable to tell without tears the sad story of his Afghan wife and child.

CHAPTER VI.

A FUGITIVE.

GARDNER A FUGITIVE—DESPERATE STRAITS—THE VALUE OF SALT IN CENTRAL ASIA—THE KALENDARS—VISIT TO A KAFIR PRIEST —A KIND RECEPTION—THE KHILTI KAFIRS—HISTORIC REMAINS —DISPOSAL OF THE DEAD BY THE KAFIRS—A RELIC OF THE PAST—FAREWELL TO THE HOLY MAN—AN ATTACK BY ROBBERS —A RACE FOR LIFE—THE ESCAPE—A GOOD SOLDIER—BOLOR— CAPTAIN YOUNGHUSBAND—NOTE ON "BOLOR."

In accordance with his resolution Prince Habib-ulla Khan returned to his stronghold in an inaccessible place near Parwan, and there with his own hands slew his wives and female slaves. He believed that this terrible act was necessary to preserve them from dishonour at the hands of the victorious faction, and his previous experiences certainly justified his belief. The prince's mind became unhinged from his misfortunes, and it is believed that he shortly afterwards died while performing a pilgrimage to Mecca.

Gardner mentions a beautiful act of fidelity on

the part of a Kafir boy, one of the prince's slaves, who had been treated very kindly by him. This boy first begged leave to accompany the prince, and on being told that this was impossible, he insisted on being slain together with the ladies of the royal household.

It would appear that Gardner and seven other wounded men were unable to follow Habib-ulla Khan on account of the severity of their injuries, and this fact undoubtedly saved Gardner's life. Still his circumstances were bad enough, and by some means or other it was absolutely necessary for him and his companions to put as much ground as possible between themselves and the followers of Dost Muhammad Khan.

How they fared shall now be related by Gardner himself. He thus continues his narrative :—

I will not dwell upon the details of my parting from my noble chief and brother, nor will I relate how he carried out his dreadful intention in regard to his family. The days which immediately followed the departure of Habib-ulla Khan seem a wild and sickening dream. I was wounded in the neck and leg, and my companions were all more or less disabled. Our party only numbered eight souls. The greatest danger attended any appearance on our part on the northern plains. There was nothing before us but to plunder to support life.

Our whole property amounted to the value of nine or ten annas in copper coins, called Kohistani *zerubs*. To light a fire by day was certain discovery, and we had to contend against damp clouds and cold sleet.

After making a short march, with great pain and difficulty, we concealed ourselves in a cavity among some rocks, from which we could command a good view of the main passes for nearly two miles. Desperate with hunger, wounds, and privation, we despatched from this place two of our party (having previously sworn fealty to each other on our naked sword-blades) to try and procure some flour or a sheep. They returned without success; but having sworn to stick by one another to the last, all doubts were removed, and we boldly lit a fire and slept in a circle with our feet to the heat. Our *nimchis* and *postins*[1] were our only bedding and clothing.

The night passed, and in the morning, after our

[1] *Postins*=sheepskin coats. The word *nimchi* has a similar meaning: here probably it stands for a sheepskin used as a blanket.

scouts had again sallied forth, we were aroused by three low whistles from our sentinel. A party of six Hindus and two Afghans was slowly approaching, with two ponies loaded with various bundles. It seemed as if they would never arrive!

At last we emerged, and met them with the salute "Salaam Aleikum," and demanded something to appease our hunger, in the name of God and the Prophet. There was a pause. Our numbers were few, but we were desperate and famishing, so without further parley we fell upon the party and disarmed them. The booty miserably disappointed us. We got some snow-preserved fat sheep-tails (*dumba*), some snuff, some dried pepper, some skins, and a big lump of reddish-black salt. We added to our collection a little asafœtida, and half the money belonging to the Hindus, amounting to ten *tillahs*. During the whole time we carefully kept mounted, as is the rule to prevent surprise, and allowed the party to proceed without further molestation. It was evident that, as we hoped, we were supposed to be a mere outpost of a band of professional Turkoman marauders and slave-robbers, of which I, with my fairer complexion, my high black *pirpank*,[1] black *postin*,

[1] Conical hat.

hair-rope girdle, and Turki overall boots, was accounted the chief. They thought themselves well off in not being taken for slaves to the markets of Kunduz, Balkh, or Bokhara.

On returning to our cave we found the mouth nearly blocked up with boulders from an avalanche, which had killed near it some large hyena-like animal. This we considered a godsend, and fell to cooking it. It was disgustingly rotten, but our famished senses cared for nothing, and after dabbing it over with the spices we had just looted, we made a hearty meal of it, half raw.

On the following morning we arose with light hearts expecting the return of our two scouts, who had again gone down towards the plain of Inderab. After our usual orisons, and having posted the necessary look-out on the top of the crags which towered to the height of 1200 or 1500 feet over our head, we proceeded to dress our own and our horses' wounds—for which purpose we ventured for the first time to encroach upon our precious and only lump of salt, part of the previous day's loot. We were reluctant to make use of it in the absence of any of our party, as salt, when scarce, is invaluable to travellers, and in Central Asia it is looked upon as most dishonourable conduct to make unnecessary and unequal use of it.

It was for a similar reason that the day before we had preferred to eat of our half-stinking wolf-meat, instead of at once attacking two fine fat sheep-tails, preserved in snow, which we had captured. Our lump of salt was perfectly round, and polished from the many lickings it had received from the tongues of former owners, and as it would have been considered a sacrilegious act to break off a splinter, we were forced to take some water in the hand and rub the salt in it. With this we washed our wounds, and afterwards applied a dressing of powdered charcoal and clay, which was bound over them and so left for twenty-four hours.

We now turned our attention to procuring a meal for the day without encroaching on our comrades' rations, or on the aforementioned sheep-tails. We finally resolved to collect a quantity of snow mushrooms and edible herbs, sufficient for two or three days, to which we might give a relish by a little salt, a morsel of wolf-meat, or of our fat sheep-tails. What was our consternation to find that during the night rats had eaten through the rope which tied them up, and consumed the whole of them! Nothing daunted, however, we started to collect provisions. Before we had gone far we were recalled by our look-out on the crags. We arrived at our post not a moment too soon, and found ourselves confronted by seven men, all on foot, four of whom were dressed as *dervishes* or *fakirs.* Two of the latter were old men with long red beards, the other two being dressed as *dervishee-kalendars*, with the high cap and *alpha* to suit, thrown over their *postin* vests: all carried the usual wooden bowl, the holy *chob-shereef* or staff of peace, with quantities of bead rosaries and black hair ropes tied round their necks, by which the holy Koran was suspended.

This, as is the custom, they held towards us in both hands as we approached, as a deprecation against evil intentions, and at the same time pronounced the usual fakir's salutation, "Shukur, Shukur Allah," pronounced with a drawling, solemn accent.

Turning away from these men, we brought our spears to bear on their three companions, who were well clothed in Kohistani Afghan costume, and appeared to be fumbling to get their hands on their swords and knives, with the evident intention of resistance. This was speedily overcome, and the most bumptious, who had twice tried to cut off my spear-head, was knocked down, and they were all disarmed. We then proceeded to search them, and were much surprised to find underneath their outer-dress full suits of chain-armour, evidently concealed for the purpose of safe conveyance to Kabul or to some chief in that vicinity.

Although we were but five in number, our scouts being still absent and the look-out man remaining on his post, we resolved to make these men prisoners, and keep them with us till the return of our comrades, and until we had arranged our future movements. So we marched them off to our retreat, and made them assist us in collecting herbs for our day's meal. We took this precaution from dread of treachery on the part of the holy men, of the character of which class we had so many sad recollections. We learned from one of the *fakirs* that the news of the defeat of Habib-ulla Khan had reached the valley of the Kunduz river, and that mounted bands had been collected in that neighbourhood to plunder all weak parties who might be flying from the vengeance of Dost Muhammad, and to protect their own villages from strong parties of fugitives.

We began to feel anxious about the safety of our two scouts, when to our joy they returned on the second day, bringing with them two sheep and some other provisions, carried by three other men, taken in the Inderab valley, two of whom our scouts pronounced to be our lawful slaves, they having been caught in the act of betraying the scouts.

They further told us that one of Habib-ulla's *jamadars*, having been forced to fly from the Ghorband valley, where he was stationed, had crossed the border into Turkestan with fifteen or twenty horsemen; and after safely passing the border fort of Khunjan, had been attacked in the Killaghai Pass by an overwhelming force of the people of that region. The *jamadar* and all his party had been killed or taken prisoners.

This news determined us to break up our present camp, and to make with all speed and secrecy to the famous holy shrine of Hazrat Imam, situated on the south bank of the Oxus, and about two marches north of Kunduz. There we were sure to find sanctuary.

We resolved therefore to start that very night, and to proceed by a bypath mostly used by the

Kafirs, to a place called Pir Nimchu Kafir Ghaur (or the cave of the priest of the Nimchu Kafirs).[1] In accordance with this resolution we started after nightfall, taking our prisoners with us. However, we set them at liberty at the head of the pass, having previously taken the suits of chain-armour from them and deprived them of their arms. I also exchanged clothes with one of the *dervishes.* We then showed them a secure place to rest in, and warned them not to stir till the following day. We subsequently discovered that these men were not travelling in their proper characters, but were nothing more nor less than a band of robbers, and that the bearded old men were merely decoys. In fact, one of our recently returned scouts declared that he recognised in them part of a large body of professional robbers well known throughout that region.

The night was fine and clear, and we went on our way, taking with us the three men our scouts had brought in—one as a guide to the roads and paths, and the other two as our *bonâ-fide* slaves.

[1] Nimchu Kafirs are the descendants of mixed unions between Kafirs and Muhammadans, and are to be found all round the borders of Kafiristan.

After descending a short distance, our path struck off to the north-east for a few miles, and then again to the east, after which we kept our old guide, the North Star, nearly on our right hand for eight or ten miles, when, after passing with some difficulty over a rocky spur of the Northern Hindu Kush, we descended and crossed a small rapid stream, whose banks were thickly wooded. After passing through the underwood, we entered a deep watercourse with high cliffs on either side. This was the Ghaur-i-Kafir, or Kafir's path.

It now became very dark, so we halted on a nice grassy spot, well sheltered in case of rain. We had got over eighteen or twenty miles.

Here one of our party suggested that it would be well if we got rid of our Afghan dress and tried to appear like Turkomans. We immediately set to work, and with some skins which formed part of our booty extemporised Turkomani caps. We then turned the hairy side of our *postins* outwards, and substituting grass ropes for our *lunjis*,[1] we produced a decidedly successful personification of a small band of wandering Turkomans.

[1] *Lunjis*=scarves.

We started again, however, as soon as the light served, and after a fatiguing ride through deep defiles and watercourses, we arrived late in the evening at the Ghaur-i-Pir Nimchu—our destination.

We had sent one of our party in advance to give notice of our approach, and were most kindly received by the holy man. He had with him nine or ten disciples, by whom we were treated with the greatest civility. We and our horses were quickly provided with every necessary, and before we went to rest our feet were well washed with warm water and bran, mixed with sweet herbs.

They seemed to have ample stores of everything, and the best wine of Kafiristan was not wanting. Being all of us very tired, we soon went to rest on soft bear- and sheep-skins, which were spread for us in a large cave.

In the morning we all performed our orisons in company. The *pir* seemed to be of a very advanced age, I should say almost ninety: although somewhat bent and with but dim eyesight, he still possessed considerable vigour and a stentorian voice, and was altogether of a commanding appearance.

He and his race were of the Khilti race of Kafirs, which tribe inhabits the outer ranges and northern crest of the Hindu Kush. There were no inhabitants within a long day's march of this place, and even at that distance they were but few and far between. The old *pir* said that the holy place was originally established by the great kings of Ghor; and he showed me two marble slabs with Arabic characters engraved on them, said to have been presented by two kings of Ghor who reigned at Delhi — viz., Muhammad Ghori, and Shah budin Ghori, first Emperor of Delhi. There was likewise a large slab of green marble, also with an inscription, said to have been presented by Timur in person when he attempted to invade Kafiristan, but got no farther than this point. This memorial was erected in the year 1398.

The aged *pir* said that even in these bad and unholy days he could still, by the grace of God and the Prophet, boast of having a lakh[1] of disciples far and near, and comprising both Nimchus and Muhammadans. We too, feeling a reverence for the holy man our protector, went through the usual ceremony and became his disciples.

[1] A lakh = 100,000.

We now for the first time had our wounds properly dressed; and the good old man presented us with hill-ponies in place of some of our horses, which were worn out. He soon guessed that we were a portion of Habib-ulla's following, and assured us that our misfortunes gave us a stronger claim on him than if we had come in happiness and wealth. He advised us to go to Hazrat Imam, avoiding Kunduz and such noted places, and to travel through Badakshan. We resolved to follow his advice, but fate willed it otherwise.

The old *pir* was remarkably shrewd and intelligent for a man who had never been farther than the Khawak Pass on one side and the sources of the Khalsu on the other.

In legendary and traditional lore he was well informed. According to him Scythia was the original cradle of the Kafir race, and they claim one of the kings of the dynasty of Cyrus as their founder.

I must here mention that at the intercession of the *pir* we exchanged our two slaves with him for some skins and other articles of clothing of which we were in need. Our third prisoner freely volunteered to join our fortunes, and having taken the oath of fidelity, he was provided with a Turkoman dress and arms. The good *pir* also presented me, as a special mark of favour, with a fine leopard-skin mantle and cap to match, the latter about three-quarters of a yard high. But his highest mark of favour was his presenting me with an old and worn-out Koran, which he ceremoniously hung round my neck in the large cave.

I here formally and in his presence assumed command of our small party, each one faithfully promising to give strict obedience to my orders.

On the day of our intended departure our strength received a welcome accession. We had, of course, always had a good look-out kept for us by one of the disciples, as pursuit was quite possible, though improbable. Early on this day the signal was given that a small party of strangers was approaching. This turned out to be five of our old friends and comrades, another remnant of Habib-ulla Khan's following. One of them was very badly and two slightly wounded. They had been under the command of a *naib* or lieutenant named Usbuk Beg, a native of Karategin, a district north of the river Oxus. About a month before our defeat he had a party of about seventy horsemen under his orders, mostly Usbegs and Hazaras, of which we now saw the survivors. Shortly before Habib-ulla Khan's last fight, Usbuk Beg had been cut off by Dost Muhammad's troops and forced to fly towards Kunduz. After being allowed to pass several border forts in apparent friendship, he had been treacherously attacked by large numbers of Kunduz horsemen, when all but nine of his troop were slain or captured. These nine were again attacked in the Inderab valley, and lost four more of their number. Finally, the five survivors reached this place of safety. The soldier who was badly wounded was left to be well cared for by the holy men; and after staying an extra day to allow the others to recruit their strength, we finally started, now thirteen in number.

On taking my leave of the *pir*, he generously placed in my hands a Russian silk handkerchief, in one corner of which were tied up sixty gold Bokhara *tillahs*. Having obtained a guide from our kind host, we each of us bent down and received his parting blessing. We then embraced his disciples, and took leave of them with regret and affection.

They held out every inducement to me to remain with them, promising me certain felicity in a future state, which would, they said, be ensured by having my remains placed on the highest peak of the Hindu Kush. They disposed of their dead in this way, and never by burial. Although Muhammadans, they appeared to have a strange hankering for the worship of fire, water, and the sun. Among other earthly inducements to join them, they promised to place 20,000 brave Khilti Kafirs under my command.

There being no access to their country except by bypaths such as that by which we had travelled, and known to few, Kafiristan may be considered as one huge fortress, well kept by the able hands of its brave inhabitants.

I have not yet described the *pir's* place of abode. It was a collection of caves situated on an extensive rocky plateau about 1000 feet above the ravine below, and with high peaks above it. There was no vegetation whatever, with the exception of a few mossy patches. Most of the caves were immense clefts, not produced by the action of water, but evidently by some great convulsion of nature. Some of them were not less than 100 yards in depth, and from 10 to

50 feet broad, but invariably narrowing towards their farther end. Most of them were stored with grass, firewood, and various requisites for the use of the hermit and his disciples. In one I perceived a copious spring of cool clear water, and the quantities of provisions and stores which were supplied spoke well for the reverence with which the holy man is regarded by his followers.

Had we not expected a hot pursuit from Dost Muhammad's troops, this would have seemed a safe refuge; but I was determined to run no risk of bringing our kind host into trouble.

Setting forth, then, refreshed, strengthened, and encouraged, we travelled in the direction of Hazrat Imam—our first two days' journey being most tedious, for we had to recross the spurs of the Hindu Kush, over and through which we had reached the *pir's* retreat.

I will not weary you by detailing our marches, but must describe a remarkable relic of the past which we observed on the most northern range of these mountains. On a smooth rocky platform, having a slight slope towards the north, was an immense mass of stone, which our guide called the Asp-i-Dheha. This on inspection turned out to be (as I imagined) a unique curiosity, but our guide told us that a similar one existed in the Khilti country. It was a colossal figure of a horse, now lying prostrate on its left side, the head turned to the north. It had evidently at one time been erect, as the stumps of the four feet were still in position: they were part of the platform, and had evidently never been detached from it. I assured myself that there was no joint or cement, and that the entire figure must have been hewn from the solid rock. These four stumps were of different lengths, and the portions of the legs still attached to the horse's body corresponded perfectly with them. It seemed singular that the enormous mass had not been broken in falling, but this was accounted for by its very size and by the hardness of the material—a black flinty porphyrite with beautiful veins of dark red and green running through it. On striking it with my knife it rang like bell-metal.

I should say that its height when erect was about 15 feet to the withers.

One guide related the tradition concerning the horse as follows: "This horse once had wings and could fly; even now it often speaks and implores its master to come and ride it again. The giant, its master, lives far away in the north, in the land of ice and snow. Every night he used to fly down on this horse to meet a beautiful queen of these parts. In the course of time she died, and the giant, coming down as usual and finding her dead, was so overpowered with grief that, alighting from his horse, he cut off its wings. He then took up the mountain and buried himself beneath it. His horse waited so long for him that it was turned into stone, but always remained facing the north, expecting its master's return. Hence it is that it often calls aloud to him, as has been said."

As it was our wish to reach Hazrat Imam with as much secrecy as possible, we resolved to keep to the hills as far as Takht-i-Sulaiman, and afterwards reach our destination by the Lataband Pass. We then hoped to be safe from all pursuit.

We moved northwards, and shortly after leaving the horse met a man armed with a bow and arrows and carrying a shield. He told us that he was a herdsman, and showed us a path which led in the required direction past an old fort called Killa Seth. His home was hard by, and, as he informed us, a day's march from Takht-i-Sulaiman.

As he volunteered to show us the way, he was quickly mounted behind one of our party, and we took leave of our former guide, who had conducted us from Ghaur-i-Pir. Our new conductor informed us that the ruins of the fort were at times infested by a party of Kunduz horsemen, sixty in number, who had recently carried off his goats.

After a long day's ride we came at sunset to the ruins, which stood on a high hill. These consisted of foundations only, half buried in the earth, but were both massive and extensive. Some of the stones, which were cut in an oblong form, must have weighed several tons. We pushed on for a mile or so, and halted for the night in a narrow glen. About a mile from our post was a village, the first we had seen since parting with Habib-ulla Khan. The inhabitants were herdsmen, and confirmed our guide's account of the dangers of the road we had intended to follow. They told us that the Kunduz marauders infested that region, and had taken away many of the inhabitants, making slaves of them and plundering their villages. This information changed our plans, and we turned in an easterly direction. We had started, as usual, at break of day, and rode at a rapid pace, hoping to reach a pass called the Dara Sulaiman before night.

About two hours before sunset we met an Udassi *fakir*, who was, he said, seeking medicinal herbs, and who had just come from Hazrat Imam *viâ* Jerm. He claimed to be a transmuter of metals into gold. This superstition is very common in the East, among the higher as well as the poorer classes.

While he was pointing out to us the direction of the Takht-i-Sulaiman, which, he said, was a long day's march from us, we perceived a considerable body of horsemen moving towards the south, but apparently not approaching us. When about due west of us they suddenly changed their direction and moved on us at a quicker pace. We were now satisfied that they were enemies, and pledged ourselves to sell our lives and liberty at as dear a rate as possible. We now made every effort to reach the pass before them, as, should we succeed, we might hope to withstand their first charge and finally escape in the darkness.

They were about fifty in number, well-mounted, and (as we found) all armed with matchlocks slung on their shoulders, swords, spears, knives, &c. It was now raining heavily, with dark heavy clouds all around us. Galloping for the pass at full speed, we arrived within 600 or 800 yards of it, well in advance of our pursuers, when a small party of five men emerged from the pass and boldly charged towards us in front, loudly ordering us to halt in the name of the Kunduz chief, Mir Ali Murad. We, however, paid no attention to them, when two of them brought their matchlocks down to the present and threatened to fire on my Therbah, who was nearest to them. He immediately charged them, and quickly unhorsed and slew both of them; and our volunteer, who was a capital horseman and spearman, wheeled round upon the others and despatched two. My Therbah immediately afterwards killed the remaining man with his long Afghan knife.

The fray now became general, as the main body charged us, trying to save their comrades. This fortunately prevented their using their matchlocks, and we had reached the mouth of the pass, which we held with desperation. Their overwhelming numbers, however, soon broke our ranks, and they unfortunately got mixed up with us: there was no room for orderly fighting, and it was a mere cut-and-thrust affair.

Soon we had only seven men left out of thirteen, and we slowly retreated up the pass, keeping them off as well as we could. In the pass we lost two more men, one our late volunteer, and were now reduced to five, each of us severely wounded. I myself received two wounds, one a bad one in the groin from an Afghan knife, and the other a stab from a dirk in the chest.

It was now quite dark, and the rain was coming down still heavier than before. However, our enemies followed us no farther, — no doubt the plundering of the dead being their chief inducement to return. We made our way through the pass as quickly as we could in the midst of heavy rain, hail, and lightning, while the roll of the thunder seemed to make the very rocks around us and the ground beneath us to vibrate most sensibly. What with my two former wounds still raw, and my two fresh ones (one of which was bleeding freely), I was soon so weak as nearly to faint in my saddle; while my Therbah was in nearly as bad a condition. We, however, kept up our spirits, and congratulated ourselves that not one of our party had been taken alive or doomed by capture to hopeless slavery.

Thus we proceeded through the whole dark night, the vivid and repeated flashes of lightning alone showing us the way over most difficult ground. About daybreak we arrived at the eastern mouth of the pass, and having cleared it, we left the road and made for the shelter of a secluded glen, where we halted. The rain had now nearly ceased, and we proceeded to collect forage for our jaded horses. We were so utterly wearied that we did not care for food for ourselves, though we had two days' rations of mulberry-bread with us, which had been given us by the holy *pir*. We accordingly lay down in our dripping clothes, indifferent whether we might be traced and again attacked by our last night's enemies. I did not even take the precaution to apply any dressing to my wounds, merely satisfying myself that the bleeding had ceased.

Notwithstanding a drizzling rain which shortly came on, and the keen cutting blast from the hills, we slept nearly the whole day. Whilst I slept my Therbah sat watchful by my side, and no expostulation of mine could induce him to lie down and take rest. Though he spoke in high terms of praise of the bravery of our comrades, and particularly of our volunteer, who had been killed beside him, he never made any reference to his own exploits, and considered it as an insult for any one to allude in his presence to his acts, or draw attention to his wounds.

I may here be permitted to say that, from long association with these rude people, I have in a measure contracted some of their habits and peculiarities—this among others; and though bearing on my body the tokens of my younger and wilder days in the shape of thirteen or fourteen wounds, nothing annoys me more than to be asked how I got this and where I received that. If such a question had been asked me in Turkestan, I should certainly have knocked the man down who questioned me. And I may here say, once for all, that in all the occurrences of my past, misspent life, I was invariably actuated in my inward soul by feelings at once honest and upright, at least so far as my poor senses allow me to judge between right and wrong.

We now deeply repented not having acted on the advice of the old *pir*, and as we considered it useless to attempt to reach Hazrat Imam, we determined to strike off directly to the east, towards the Kokcha river, and thence across the Oxus towards the Shighnan and Bolor ranges, in whose wild fastnesses we felt sure of a safe retreat.

NOTE ON "BOLOR."

The name Bolor, applied by different writers to various regions of Central Asia, has long puzzled geographers. It has even been stated, but quite without justification, that no such place as Bolor ever existed; for it cannot be seriously believed that writers who have been proved trustworthy in all other particulars should have entered into a general conspiracy to deceive the generations of mankind for whom they successively wrote, on this one subject only. Yet so conflicting are the various statements as to the locality of Bolor that an eminent English geographer was driven to form the theory that part of the map of Central Asia had become accidentally semi-inverted: by correcting this supposed error he most ingeniously brought the rival Bolors into one focus.

Without making a wearisome catalogue of all the geographical works in which this mysterious region is mentioned, it may be interesting to notice the following allusions to Bolor by the best known writers:—

1. Hwen-Thsang, who travelled during the years 629 to 645 A.D., visited Bolor twice. He describes the kingdom as lying on the Indus, and in the heart of the Himalayas. In another place he states that it lay south of the mountains that formed the southern boundary of Pamir. In the opinion of Mr Ney Elias, one of the highest authorities on the subject, the Bolor of Hwen-Thsang is now represented by the small States now under the Gilgit agency—viz., Chitral, Gilgit, Panyal, Hunza, and Nagar.

2. Al-Biruni, a writer in the eleventh century, mentions "Balur Shah" as the ruler of a region which General Cunningham identified as Balti or Baltistan.

Mr Ney Elias, however, dissented from this opinion, on the authority of Mirza Haidar, who invaded Bolor in 1530-31 and placed it in the Gilgit Chitral region.

3. Marco Polo says that he travelled through Bolor on his way from the high plain of Pamir to Kashgar. In the opinion of Sir Henry Yule this region would be that to the north of Balti and Kanjut, and included in Sirikol.

4. The name Bolor occurs in various writings of the seventeenth and the first half of the eighteenth centuries; and towards the middle of the latter century it came to be believed, on the authority of certain Jesuit missionaries who entered Eastern Turkestan from China, that the true position of Bolor was to the west of Pamir. This belief is supported by statements in the Chinese Imperial Geography, which mention Bolor as a country east of Badakshan and south-west of Yarkand.

Bolor, in fact, according to the Chinese and the Jesuit geographers, was either Pamir itself under another name, or a portion of the region now known as Pamir. This localisation of Bolor coincides with the geography of Gardner, and is therefore at variance with that of all writers who place this "will-o'-the-wisp" of a country to the south of the Karakorum Mountains. Being unable to reconcile the conflicting statements quoted above, and many others referred to by the various writers on the subject, I appealed for assistance to Captain Younghusband, whose acquaintance with Central Asia need not be dilated on, and in his reply to my letter lies, I believe, the solution of the ancient problem.

Writing from the Hindu Kush frontier on the 16th September 1894,—"I have not," he says, "myself heard the word Bolor used. . . . In these countries ranges of mountains seldom have a name. We, for instance, call the mountains round me here the Hindu Kush; but not a single native of these parts has ever heard that name applied to them. Mountain-people look upon mountains as the usual state of affairs on this earth, and don't give a name to the mass of mountains amongst which they live, any more than the inhabitants of a plain country give a name to the plain. An outside traveller has therefore to invent a name to apply to the mountain-range which he visits.

"We have unearthed Hindu Kush and applied it to the whole range, although I believe it is in reality the name of a single pass only; and in the same way Gardner may have applied the name Bolor.

"I have talked over the matter with Lieutenant Cockerill, an officer who has been travelling round the frontier this summer, and he suggested that very possibly Bolor may be merely a corruption of the Persian word *bálá*—upper or above.

"This word is pronounced by the people of Badakshan (and by Afghans too, I believe) very broad—"baw-law." Upper Chitral is often spoken of as Chitral Bálá, and in this way a passing traveller may have thought that the upper part of Chitral was named Bálá—Baw-law—Bolor. Or again, the upper regions anywhere might be called Bálá. A traveller from the plains of Badakshan going to the Pamirs might say, 'I am going up above, I am going *bálá*,' and a stranger might think that *bálá* was a name. This is far-fetched in a way, but in the default of any other theory it is worth thinking over."

It is indeed well worth thinking over, and is to my mind the only approach that has yet been made to a reconciliation of the conflicting statements as to the cloudy land of Bolor.—H. P.

CHAPTER VII.

THROUGH BADAKSHAN.

THE KOKCHA RIVER—THE KUNDUZ CHIEF—SLAVE-DEALING—TRAVELLING COMPANIONS—SOME BADAKSHAN HISTORY—THE RUINS OF ANCIENT ZARUTH—THE KAFIR EMPIRE OF EARLY TIMES—DIFFICULT TRAVELLING—ATTACKED BY WOLVES—UNDESIRABLE ACQUAINTANCES—THE THERBAH'S FINGER—RETRIBUTION—THE CHIEF OF SHIGHNAN—JUSTICE TEMPERED BY MERCY.

HAVING somewhat recruited ourselves and our horses by a few days' halt in the glen, we set off north-eastward in the direction of Jerm, and, I think, after two or three marches we entered the Kokcha valley and crossed that river eight or nine miles north of Jerm. Thence we struck for a ford on the eastern branch of the same river, north of Yomal, and between that place and Khairabad. We crossed the river and journeyed on some fifteen miles, where, for the first time since leaving the Khawak Pass, we ventured to approach some scattered villages, which we observed at the base of a high mountain-range running north and south. These mountains appeared to be of considerable altitude, and many of their peaks were topped with snow.

We were deceived by the height of these mountains, for on approaching the villages we found that, although in a rocky situation and surrounded by ravines, they were at a distance of some miles from the actual base of the hills. With the exception of three or four huts, all these habitations were deserted. A few poor families lived apart from each other, and appeared to be in the lowest state of poverty and wretchedness. All this misery was caused by the oppression of the Kunduz chief, who, not content with plundering his wretched subjects, made an annual raid into the country south of Oxus, and by *chappaos* (night-attacks) carried off all the inhabitants on whom his troops could lay their hands. These, after the best had been selected by the chief and his courtiers, were publicly sold in the bazaars of Turkestan. The principal providers of this species of merchandise were the khan of Khiva, the king of Bokhara (the great hero of the Muhammadan faith), and the robber *beg* of Kunduz.

In the regular slave-markets, or in transactions between dealers, it is the custom to pay for slaves in money; the usual medium being either Bokharan gold *tillahs* (in value about 5 or 5½ Company rupees each), or in gold bars or gold grain. In Yarkand, or on the Chinese frontier, the medium is the silver *khurup* with the Chinese stamp, the value of which varies from 150 to 200 rupees each. The price of a male slave varies according to circumstances from 5 to 500 rupees. The price of the females also necessarily varies much, from 2 *tillahs* to 10,000 rupees. Even double the latter sum has been known to be given.

However, a vast deal of business is also done by barter, of which we had proof at the holy shrine of Pir-i-Nimcha, where we exchanged two slaves for a few lambs' skins! Sanctity and slave-dealing may be considered somewhat akin in the Turkestan region, and the more holy the person the more extensive are generally his transactions in flesh and blood.[1]

The few wretched families at present residing in the hamlets where we halted were mostly *Tajiks* and farmers, with some few labourers and petty

[1] *Note by Colonel Gardner.*—I subsequently knew at Mooltan a most respectable Lohani fruit merchant who was proved by his own ledger to have exchanged a female slave-girl for three ponies and seven long-haired, red-eyed cats, all of which he disposed of, no doubt to advantage, to the English gentlemen at that station.

traders, most of the Uzbegs being in their tents among the hills pasturing their cattle. The inhabitants treated us with all hospitality, so we resolved to stay here for a certain time, to rest. During our stay three strangers arrived direct from Jerm and Yomal. They informed us that the latter place was a long day's march west or south-west of us. On becoming acquainted with these men I discovered that one of them was a respectable Syad named Mir Ali Shah, who had a servant with him; both were well armed, and with handsome weapons. The third person was, curiously enough, a Hindu named Jey Ram, of respectable appearance and well armed. These people appeared to have travelled much together. They were both well-educated men, and could read, write, and speak fluently Persian, Turki, Pashtu, and Arabic. The Hindu had further some colloquial knowledge of the languages of Kafiristan, as he had formerly travelled in that country with some other Hindus.

They appeared to be intimate with the courts and chiefs of Turkestan and Afghanistan, and Mir Ali Shah had held some position of trust under Dost Muhammad shortly after the death of Sardar Azim Khan, the father of our late chief Habib-ulla

Khan. The Syad was a great traveller, and had been to Shikarpur, Lahore, and Peshawar, and had also made a pilgrimage to Mecca, and visited all the places of note in Persia. Jey Ram had been to many places in Russia, as far as Moscow.

They appeared to have been travelling for pleasure during the last two years under the ostensible character of *hakims* (doctors), to which they added astrology and fortune-telling. I invited them to stay with us as our guests as long as it might suit them to do so. They dressed our wounds and those of our horses with such skill and success that my Therbah declared that they had been sent by God for our succour. By their advice we remained in these villages for eighteen or twenty days to recruit our strength, as they stated that the country through which we proposed to travel was so difficult that we should be obliged to leave our horses behind and proceed on foot. They further said that they themselves were now on their way to those countries, and that on reaching the Oxus they intended to sell their horses and do likewise. They intended to remain during the winter in the Darra Darwaz, and in the following spring to visit Yarkand. Our present residence was called Zaruth Nao.

While resting here these men related to us the legends and traditions of the country round, particularly concerning the treachery of Shah Sultan Shah, a former ruler of Badakshan, who had murdered a Kashgar prince when the latter had fled for refuge to his country when Kashgar had been invaded by the Chinese.

The prince was enticed into Badakshan by false promises of friendship, and then put to the torture to force him to give up his jewels and treasure. Finally he was put to death by being cut up, limb by limb, in the presence of his wives and children. God had, however, punished this cruel act by means of the prince's grandson, who instigated the chiefs of Balkh and Kunduz to attack Badakshan, and having caused himself to be placed at the head of their troops, had avenged his grandfather's murder by the conquest and almost total depopulation of Badakshan. Even now his descendants were the chief instigators of the yearly raids into this unhappy country.

The Syad informed me that Faizabad, which stands on the north of the junction of the two main branches of the Kokcha river, has always been considered the capital of Badakshan, but that since the invasion of the country its importance has gradually decreased, notwithstanding its extensive iron-smelting trade and silk manufactures, and that Jerm may now be considered the most prosperous place.[1]

Badakshan is the garden of the East, and the only obstacles to its prosperity are the constant depredations of the Kunduz chief. He is prevented by the difficult nature of the country from extending his forays north of the Oxus, except occasionally towards the north-western boundaries of Badakshan.

While remaining at Zaruth Nao we started one day to see the ruins which existed in the neighbourhood, and after riding over a most difficult country for about seven miles, came to a semicircular platform of bare rock about 300 or 400 yards in circumference, in the centre of which were the ruins of Zaruth. Nothing, however, now remained but large masses of hewn stone, all of a black colour and flinty nature, which were strewn about in all directions. In the midst of these ruins was piled up an immense cairn of loose stones, contributed by visitors; and, as was the custom, each of us

[1] About three years after this history was related to Colonel Gardner, the Kunduz chief made an organised raid into Badakshan and totally destroyed Faizabad.—H. P.

added one or two more to the heap. There was another cairn at the entrance to a cave, which was at the base of the eastern face of the neighbouring cliff. Having washed our hands (as in duty bound) in the spring-water close by, we entered the cave in single file, the mouth of it being only about 2 feet or 2½ feet broad; its height was about 20 feet.

However, as we advanced it gradually widened for about 15 yards, at which distance from the entrance were its largest dimensions—namely, about 24 feet in width. The roof was here so high that we could not perceive it in the darkness. The cave continued with these dimensions for about 20 yards farther in a straight line, and then turned and grew narrow towards the north, and ended in a cleft a few yards farther on.

The floor consisted of the bare uneven rock, but the walls on each side were well polished to the height of 6 or 7 feet, on which space were to be seen the mutilated remains of idols, which had been originally cut out of the rock in pretty high relief. They were, however, so mutilated that only one or two could be distinguished as having limbs, and the faces of all were smashed.

At the farther end of the cave there was a small spring of water, near which was a very remarkable echo, which appeared to reverberate through other spacious galleries.

The story of this place (called Sheheid Ghaur-i-Zaruth), as told me by the Syad, was that formerly the whole of Badakshan was held by the Kafirs, and the Kur Kafirs held the northern part of the range now called the Koh-i-Kojah-Muhammad; other tribes held the whole of the ranges south of the Oxus, through which country numerous caves and ruins are to be seen to attest to their former power. From the reign of Sultan Mahmud of Ghazni[1] (A.D. 1000) down to Khusrao (A.D. 1150), the last of the Ghazni dynasty, constant raids had been made into Badakshan in order to destroy the Kafirs and annex their country; but it was not until Muhammad Ghori conquered Delhi and founded the Muhammadan Government of India (A.D. 1193) that the country called Kafiristan was broken up, and the name of Badakshan bestowed on that part from which the Kafirs were driven.

At this time a holy man from Mecca headed the Ghazis in a religious war, and slew 300 or 400 Kafir priests in this very cave. All the idols were

[1] The Ghaznivide dynasty existed from A.D. 962 to 1186, but did not possess an independent sovereignty until A.D. 999, when Mahmud threw off his allegiance to the Court of Bokhara.—H. P.

then destroyed, and on the ruins of their place of worship the Mecca *pir* built a masjid to commemorate the heroic deed he had consummated. This done, the holy man took up his abode there, and his successors held sway until the days of Timur—some 200 years.

This monarch attempted to complete the subjugation of Kafiristan, but was foiled. The Kafirs, in retaliation, issued from their fastnesses and made a successful raid to the north and west. They came to this place, slew the *pir* of that day with, it is said, 500 followers, and razed his masjid to the ground. The Syad told me of numerous other caves in the neighbourhood even more extensive than this one, but the roads to them were very dangerous at this time of year from constant avalanches.

Having halted about twenty days at these villages, and being now pretty well recovered from our wounds, we started and took a north-easterly direction, to get through the Khojah Mahomed range, by the pass called Kafir Ghesh Durrah, from two large stone idols cut out of the solid rock, and representing the Kafir deity Ghesh (the Earth) and his wife Dizane (the producer of all things). The road was so bad that we were obliged to lead our horses over it. It was far more difficult than the Khawak Pass, though at about the same altitude—the ascent and descent being far more precipitous.

Darkness came upon us, with rain, sleet, and snow, when we were at the top of the pass. We passed a most wretched night under some rocks, and were nearly frozen from the intensity of the cold and the bitter wind, which blew keenly. We started early the following morning, and after travelling for four days over most difficult, almost impracticable country, and after traversing another pass at least equally elevated as that just described, we arrived at the southern branch of the Oxus, just opposite the junction of the Shakh Dara river, which flows into it from the eastward.

During the entire march of four days we only met two or three solitary Badakshani herdsmen; and though we saw some few ruined villages off the road, we did not come across a single inhabited one,—a significant proof of the present state of desolation of this part of Badakshan.

We found the bridge over the river destroyed, and only some rope-crossings left—which, as we had horses, left us nothing for it but to make a bridge or raft.

The inhabitants of this region had fled into the fastnesses to escape a grand raid, which was daily expected, and we could get but little assistance. Finally we managed with incredible difficulty to bind blocks of ice together with straw ropes, which when covered with grass formed a means of crossing for us and our horses. I should mention that in all my misadventures I had religiously kept the horses which I stole in reprisal from the Kipchak chief. They were excellent animals, and though some had been killed and others left behind, I still had five of them. As I have said, that was the number of survivors of my party after the attack of the Kunduz robbers, and we certainly owed our lives to the excellence of these horses, which I was anxious to keep as long as possible in so dangerous a country. From the reports of the guide whose services we managed to secure, we made out that we were about seven or eight marches from the ruby mines. I was most anxious to visit them, but my Therbah and Jey Ram remonstrated, and begged me to wait until we reached the fort of the chief of Shighnan, from which we could proceed to the fort of Gharan, in the immediate vicinity of the mines. There he promised us a cordial reception.

After crossing the river we passed a miserable

night, without food or a light for our pipes, with the keen wind blowing down upon us from the snowy heights of the Bolor Mountains and the Pamir steppes.

The next morning I was still more importunate about the ruby mines, fearing to lose the opportunity of a lifetime, and eventually I prevailed. So, having shifted our camp to a more sequestered spot, and leaving the remainder of our party with strict orders to lie close, the Syad, the Therbah, and myself started off, armed with stout spears. We wandered through rock and precipice, and after weary toil were brought to a standstill by a deep, swift torrent. We managed to wade through it by tying our three selves together — separately we should certainly have been carried off our feet.

Having reached the other side we strode on exulting, hoping to reach some outlying hamlet; but on attaining the summit of a hill, at least 13,000 feet above the level of the sea, we were disappointed to find more journeying in store for us. Night was approaching, and we had brought no food with us. Just then we came upon an exciting wild hunt. A quantity of wild sheep tore past us, hotly followed by wolves. My Therbah promptly shot one of the sheep, but two wolves turned and disputed our right to it. We shot the nearest wolf, but others came up and hovered round. Now we were in a fix, for we had no materials for a fire, and jaded as we were, had the prospect of a night's skirmishing with hungry wolves, leopards, hyenas, and jackals. The Syad was better off, as he sustained himself by his unfailing resource of opium.

We buried our sheep under a pile of stones, and leaving the Syad to watch, the Therbah and I set out in search of fuel. After some trouble we collected a miserable bundle of tufted shrub and animal dung, and returned just in time to save our raw material. The Syad was musically snoring under the influence of his opium, and a wolf had dragged our sheep from underneath the stones and had nearly eaten one of its legs.

I was behind the Therbah, having gone farther away to secure a tall shrub I had remarked at a distance, and was nearly eaten by a pack of wolves, for just as I hurried up and shot the first depredator, the main body threw themselves alike on his dead body and on me. I tried to force my way through them, but one of them gave me a sharp nip, and the taste of blood made him set up an unearthly screech, which, being taken up by the others, proved my salvation, for my friend the Therbah hurried up, shouting and firing into the midst of them. At this they slowly and sulkily retreated.

We then proceeded to warm, rather than roast, the new flesh at our scanty fire, at which the Syad expressed great disgust, and asked what crime he had committed to be asked to eat raw meat. The Therbah and I had not spoiled our appetites with opium, and fell to; immediately afterwards the former fell asleep. The Syad then, somewhat recovered from the effects of the opium, convinced me, after a long argument, of the danger and fruitlessness of attempting further to find the ruby mines.

The next morning we commenced the return journey, and had just reached the stream which had given us so much trouble before, when we heard a sharp whistle, and saw two men peering down on us from a rock about 150 yards above us. The Syad gave a friendly salute, and went forward to meet them, and presently returned with them. As will be seen, a pleasant acquisition they proved!

One was a stout active greybeard of about sixty, the other a tall strong young man of about twenty. Both carried long heavy matchlocks with wooden forked props attached, and matches lit, and each had a sword and shield loosely slung over their shoulder. Seeing this, the Therbah and I, unperceived by them, loosened our weapons.

They accosted us in a friendly way, and seemed astonished at our double-barrelled muskets, and at the intelligence that they killed at 800 yards. They declined to make a close inspection of such terrible weapons. They told the Syad that they were servants of the Kunduz Beg, and had been with some others in search of falcons for the prince. They were very officious in offering aid in crossing the stream to the Syad, begging to carry his garments and boots for him.

The Therbah and I did not like the appearance of things, and declined assistance. The strangers were very reverential to the Syad, kissing his feet. We had now approached the brink, and the Syad, after breathing a short "Bismillah, Illah, Illah," descended the bank, entered the stream, and had got half-way across when off started the two strangers with his boots and clothes,—the Therbah and I, who had kept our eyes on them, in hot pursuit. The Therbah dropped his gun to lighten himself, and we gained on them rapidly. I covered them with my weapon, when they dropped the clothes. We speedily recrossed the ford, not knowing how many more marauders might be about, when "bang" went a matchlock, and a ball struck the ground at our feet. A second shot went through the Syad's *pirpank* (a high, conical, black lambskin cap), a third took off the top joint of the second finger of my poor Therbah's left hand. The ball struck him while waving his arm to me to fire. Feeling that there was no help for it, I took steady aim, fired, and rolled over the elder robber, who fell down the *khad* (declivity). The younger one rushed away, yelling to his comrades. We went our way, looking constantly round, and presently we saw three or four men gathered round the dead or dying robber. A few dropping shots were sent after us, but luckily we escaped scot-free to our camp.

When I awoke next morning I was surprised to see three strangers telling some long yarn to the Syad's servant and to the Hindu, Jey Ram. I feigned sleep, and heard them say how they belonged to the great *beg* of Kunduz, were out on an expedition in search of falcons, had been set upon by a desperate gang of robbers the evening before, their leader shot dead, and they themselves robbed of all their money. They showed the matchlock of the victim of my double-barrelled gun.

I soon identified in one of the strangers the younger of our two assailants, and the man I had seen fire the shot that took off the Therbah's finger. I resolved on the capture of these men, who, with their listeners, thought me buried in profound slumber. I contrived to give a signal to my trusty Therbah, and suddenly sprang upon the men, and with his aid overpowered them in an instant.

I bound and secured the younger worthy, and when the Therbah presently recognised him, I had much difficulty in preventing him from at once avenging his shattered hand.

The Syad appeased him by saying that the fellow would be sold next day as a dog of a Kafir at the fort in Shighnan, to which we now proceeded.

In the evening we arrived there, and were received with much kindness by the *bai*, or chief. He came out to meet us, attended by two or three followers, and with a present of two goats, some melted butter, floor, and firewood, all very acceptable. The old man welcomed us to his dominions, and loudly praised their beauty. He identified our prisoners with a gang of professional robbers from the Jerm district, whose chief was the man I had killed, and who had been pillaging and murdering for the last three years. He said that they must, according to the custom of the country, be either sold in slavery or suffer death. The good old *bai*, though of the blood royal, did not disdain to sit up half the night with us, squatted on the ground in true patriarchal style, armed to the teeth with sword, dagger, and buckler. We had not a cloth among us to spread on the greensward, little being left to us beyond our good horses and arms, and our scant clothing.

The night passed away, and next morning we heard that the young robber had made a clean breast of all the transactions of his gang. We were summoned to the presence, and the young miscreant, after a solemn adjuration, repeated his confession before us. He told a tale of murders and robberies in which he had taken part during the last eight months, and offered to show where the booty was buried. He was sent off under escort, and soon returned with every item he had mentioned.

The *bai* then assumed a judicial air, no further evidence of guilt was deemed requisite, and each member of the conclave was called upon for his vote as to the punishment. At the same time three *mullahs* or *khojas*, who were in special attendance, opened each his Koran and pored over the statutes with great gravity. Two men were sent out to ascertain the wish of our party. After the votes were all given it appeared that, with one dissentient, who was for pardon, it was unanimously decided that all should be sold into slavery for life. Mine was the dissentient, but powerless, voice.

The *bai* then summoned a person of high official standing, whose dress proclaimed him to be no less than the Court barber. A solemn prayer was offered by the head *khoja*, after which the long hair of the prisoners was cut by the above functionary within an inch of their scalps.

They were then proclaimed for public auction, and knocked down to the *bai* himself at the low figure of 18 *tillahs* of gold-dust a-head.

After this their hair was close shaven to the

scalp. The *bai* then rose and took hold of the young man who had confessed by the arm, put his hand upon his head, and declared him penitent. He then ordered him to be his personal attendant. The young man at once prostrated himself, and the *bai* being now seated, he placed his head underneath the heel of the chief. The *bai* then raised him up, and he was forthwith released and a freeman. The other two, who were doomed for slavery, were sent away in custody of four or five armed men, who were instructed where to meet a slave-dealer who would take possession of them.

CHAPTER VIII.

AMONG THE KIRGHIZ.

BEAUTIES OF KAFIRISTAN—TITLES OF THE SHIGHNAN LADIES—METHODS OF OBTAINING GOLD FROM THE RIVERS—VISIT TO A KIRGHIZ ENCAMPMENT—A BENEVOLENT RULER—DRESS AND APPEARANCE OF THE KIRGHIZ—A VENERABLE FAKIR—VISIT TO THE RUBY MINES—WAIT FOR THE WEDDING—A DISAPPOINTMENT—CONSOLATION—WANDERINGS IN THE PAMIRS—A ROBBER CHIEF—A RIDE FOR A WIFE—A TRAGIC OCCURRENCE.

ALL the prominent points of the Shighnan valley are studded with *castellos.* The control of the *bai* over his subjects was very limited. Bands of depredators amounting to 200 or 300 men would at times cross the Pamir steppes and plunder the Tash-Kurgan district and others in an easterly direction, going as far as Yarkand and Kar-galik. But now, in consequence of the wide-reaching ascendancy of the Kunduz power, the Shighnan clans are rather the plundered than the plunderers.

We proceeded on our journey through the valley, amid the usual varieties of mountain country, and encountering the usual difficulties with practical skill. Every effort was being made to procure by bribery a respite, at least, from the dreaded raid of the Kunduz ruler. Everything obtainable was being collected — gold-dust, horses, leopard and lion skins, falcons, fine greyhounds, &c. Most of the inhabitants, especially women and children, had for the last two or three months been removing all their chattels into the mountain fastnesses to the north of Shighnan, and had even crossed the boundary range into Roshan and Darwaz.

All the houses and hamlets I saw in Shighnan were well kept, especially when the presiding female was of Kirghiz extraction, or from Wakhan, Chitral, or Kafiristan. The beauty of the women of the last-named region is proverbial in Asia; hair varying from the deepest auburn to the brightest golden tints,[1] blue eyes, lithe figures, fine white teeth, cherry lips, and the loveliest peach-blossom on their cheeks.

All along the westerly part of the Shakh Dara

[1] Sir Henry Rawlinson, speaking at a meeting of the Royal Geographical Society in April 1881, said that, forty years previously, while at Kabul, he had seen a Kafir slave, the most beautiful oriental lady that he ever saw. She was the only lady he had ever met who, by loosening her golden hair, could cover herself completely from head to foot as with a screen."—H. P.

valley were traces of former habitations, once populous and happy hamlets. Here and there were clumps of mulberries, apricots, peaches, cherries, walnuts, and poplars. But for the feverish excitement of a life of perpetual fear of invasion, nothing could be more charming than the rustic society of these mountains. Polygamy, of course, prevails, and each *bai* or baron numbers his seven or eight partners of his existence.

The first four wives had titles which signified (1) the original; (2) the beauty; (3) the handmaid; (4) the pet. Here, as in Turkestan, the females are by no means secluded: each and all were free to come and go as the mountain breezes. Far different is it with the females in the Afghan families of Kabul and other large cities.

In the families among whom I was now sojourning connubial honour and felicity were the rule. I remember that one day the Syad and myself were paying a social visit to the old *bai*. In our position of guests we enjoyed the privilege of entering the sacred precincts of the harem, and we found the old man submitting to a pretty sharp slipper-beating at the hands of two beauties, who had taken this mode of avenging themselves for an imaginary breach of fidelity!

The population generally were herdsmen or farmers, but they added to their income by gold-washing in the rivers and by occasional plundering expeditions. There are three different methods of obtaining gold from the rivers. The first is to wash the river-sand at certain well-known spots, particularly at the inner angles of curves, where the strong current of the main stream causes swift reverse eddies, and allows the gold scales and particles to subside together with quantities of deep purple and black ferruginous sand, in which alone gold is found. This operation is lucrative in the Upper Oxus and several other rivers. The proper season is after the rains, and when the snow-floods have subsided and left the rivers at their lowest. Sometimes as much as four *tillahs'* weight of gold is collected—about 120 grains. This, when rubbed up with a little mercury, forms a still amalgam. It is then taken home and separated from all impurities. The mercury evaporates through an application of heat, and the residuum of pure gold is stored in the hollow shank-bones of large birds, such as herons, cranes, &c. The second method, in vogue principally in the neighbourhood of Hazrat Imam, consists in the formation of a sort of gold-trap of fleecy sheepskins, which are laid down in the bed of the river at chosen spots. They are held in place by heavy stones, and care is taken that the natural inclination of the wool faces the stream, so as to keep the entire growth of the wool freely flowing in the water. After two or three days' immersion the fleeces are carefully taken from the river and sun-dried. Without hazarding a suggestion that the fable of the Argonautic expedition of the Golden Fleece may have derived its origin from the immemorial practice just described, it is certain that the possession of these golden fleeces is the cause of severe skirmishes, as armed parties frequently rush upon the men left to watch, and sometimes bear off the prize, leaving its guardians dead on the riverside. The third method is to scoop out little holes in the sand in suitable places, and rubbing the sand in the hands, to pick out the grains of gold by aid of a keen eye. This is principally practised by the nomad tribes to the eastward of the Pamir steppes, in the regions of Khotan, Chiang, &c.

To return to our sojourn with the *bai.* We became pleasantly intimate, and one day he proposed to take the Syad and myself on a trip to visit a Kirghiz encampment. My Therbah attended us. Starting at daybreak, we arrived after a scramble of eight hours through ravines and over rocks. The encampment was pitched on a strangely chosen spot. Not a tree was to be seen. There were wild mountain flowers in abundance; and a purling stream fringed with willows wound through the tents pitched on either bank.

Not only the males but the females of the encampment met our small cavalcade a mile out, and favoured the *bai* first, and afterwards the rest of us, with many embraces. There were about eight families. The peculiar warmth of welcome was chiefly attributable to the presence of the *bai*, whom they honoured as their chief. This voluntary allegiance arose from the fact of the chief being able to some extent to protect them. Some forty families in all of the Kirghiz owned the *bai's* sovereignty, of whom about twenty had been subject to his father. To each family was granted an allotment of land on the slopes of the western base of the Pamir steppes. Here they soon shook off their former nomadic habits. When the snows melted they used to go with their families to visit their old friends in the higher Pamir steppes, but faithfully returned to their new settlement in the fall of the year to reap their crops. The uniformly conciliatory policy of the patriarchal *bai* reconciled them to a stationary life. He never imposed on them a tax higher than the time-honoured fortieth part of all produce. Any further contribution was entirely voluntary. The *bai* told me that there were some fifteen chieftains in the same position as himself along the district of the Bolor ranges and the western skirts of the Pamir steppes, and that they all acted in a similar way to their Kirghiz settler subjects. In all there were about 30,000 souls who had divested their allegiance from the Court of Khokand to the petty Bolor chiefs. The whole of the nomad Kirghiz tribes of this region were formerly subjects of the king of Khokand, but had been driven into rebellion by the extortions to which they had been subjected. The Khokand authorities were truly rapacious, and each official in turn exacted dues from the unhappy nomads.

The personal appearance of the male Kirghiz is peculiar. He wears a coarse skin or woollen garment tightly girt round the waist with leather or woollen ropes; a woolly or fur cap. The features are pure Tartar: small, deep-sunken eyes, depressed forehead and nose, and high cheek-bones. When fully accoutred with the heavy rude matchlock over his broad shoulder, the Kirghiz, though squat and low in figure, presents, with his robust frame and ruddy cheeks, the type of a resolute mountaineer. The women of the encampment, while bearing traces of their Tartar descent, were much the more pleasing-featured portion of the community. They had light-brown hair, blue eyes, and rosy cheeks and lips.[1]

Each family had its sheep, protected by fierce hill-dogs; and the headmen owned camels and rugged ponies.

The women were uniformly modest and virtuous, active and good-natured in the performance of their household duties.

There were in camp some beautifully shaggy-maned Khazak ponies, with bushy and glossy hair all over their heads and bodies, almost con-

[1] Colonel Gardner was rather an enthusiast on the subject of female beauty. As recent travellers in the Pamir region have described the appearance of the women in less favourable terms, I will add the testimony of Captain John Wood, who visited that part of the world in December 1837: "If unable to praise the men of the Kirghiz for their good looks, I may, without flattery, pronounce the young women pretty. All have the glow of health in their cheeks, and though they have the harsh features of the race, there is a softness about their lineaments, a coyness and maidenly reserve in their demeanour, that contrast strongly and most agreeably with the uncouth figures and harsh manners of the men."—From 'A Journey to the Source of the River Oxus.'—H. P.

cealing their eyes, and reaching to the ground; also some splendid Shahbaz hawks, collected as a propitiatory offering to the Kataghani robber-chief. I accompanied the *bai* when he went to present these gifts, which seemed to give great satisfaction.

On our way we visited the famous ruby mines. To reach them we had to diverge southwards. Before starting we were treated to a sumptuous repast served on wooden trays, on which were spread handsome tablecloths. Everything was served by fair hostesses. We had *kababs* and *pillaos*, both sweet-spiced and saline, with fresh cheese-curds, washed down by draughts of fine though somewhat acid Kafiristan and Chitral wine. Nor was fine, fat, snow-preserved wild mutton wanting. We had horn spoons and ladles to help ourselves with.

The presents for the dreaded chief consisted of lion and tiger skins, large red-deer antlers and horns of markhor and ibex, some fine furs, a few bags and bones full of gold-dust, some musk-glands, and a few rubies of inferior quality.

Having taken leave of our hosts and hostesses with outstretched hands, muttering a short prayer after the head *mullah*, we mounted and started off towards a lonely hamlet where we were to pass the night before going to the mines.

Here dwelt a solitary fakir of venerable aspect, with long white locks and eyebrows, and evidently of an advanced age. He was seated on the only mat in the place, outside his hovel, absorbed in reverie. All his worldly property seemed to consist of some earthen pots of grain placed in a hole dug in the middle of the hut. He was evidently one of those hermits of the mountains who relinquish the world and all its cares. He was a remarkable man, for he had visited Turkey, Asia Minor, Arabia, Persia, Turkestan, and Afghanistan; had seen Constantinople, Bagdad, Erzeroum, Mecca, Medina, Ispahan, and Teheran. Moreover, he was known to be the owner of a remarkable ruby, and the old *bai* was most anxious to become its possessor. He made most urgent entreaties for the gem, but for some time the fakir sat perfectly unmoved. The *bai* declared that by means of this ruby only could the robber-chief, whom he was on his journey to propitiate, be induced to spare the lives, property, and honour of all the innocent families around. At last the fakir quietly arose, and lifting the plank that covered a hole in the hut, after a little fumbling produced the gem. Having motioned us with a dignified gesture to be seated, he proceeded quietly to unfold a bit of rag, then with much grace placed the jewel softly in the hands of the *bai*, bestowed on him his blessing, expressed his hope that the offering might produce the anticipated result, and then relapsed into a silent reverie. The *bai* offered him a sum of money, but the old man gently declined it, but desired that the allowance of grain, which it appears was made him, should be somewhat augmented, in order that he might be able to relieve wayworn and destitute travellers. This was at once agreed to, when the fakir motioned to us to leave his hut, whereupon we departed.

On examining the gem I found a small Zoroastrian altar cut in high relief on the centre of the oblong face of the stone, and round the altar a double cordon of letters of the same kind of characters that appear on the Scytho-Bactrian coins which are found about Balkh, Bokhara, &c. The stone was very valuable, from 150 to 200 carats in weight—a pure lustrous gem. It was salaamed to by the *bai* and all his followers.

The ruby had been found about the time of Timur by an ancester of the fakir in a cave near the famous shrine and Kafir city of Esh or Oosh in the Bolor ranges.

On the following day we took leave of the holy man and proceeded to the mines. They consisted, somewhat to my surprise, of cave-like burrows about 1000 feet above the river. They were cut in soft, decayed, sandstone stratified rock, which both above and below alternated with a species of mountain limestone, also in strata. There was a thick, whitish, and in parts yellowish, saline-like crust formed on the sides of the cuttings, which exuded from the limestone rock, and which was in many parts strongly marked with green, yellow, and dirty-white spots, giving evidence of the presence of iron or copper oxides. The upper part and roofs of the burrows were utterly neglected and in ruins. After wading diagonally through the slush we emerged. Around were old dismantled forts which once commanded the passage of the river and the entrance to the mines. It was said that there were copper, antimony, and lead mines in the vicinity, but that they had not been worked since the days of Timur. In my wanderings I lost no opportunity of inquiring about the various mines which existed in the regions which I visited, but I never found one which seemed likely to repay attention.

After leaving the ruby mines I returned with the *bai* to the valley, which he made his head-quarters at this time, and stayed with him about two months. I had intended to proceed to Yarkand, but the *bai* dissuaded me from going there without protection. Moreover, the *bai*, who was at least sixty-five years of age, desired us to witness his approaching nuptials.

The bride was a fair young Kirghiz, with a rich dowry of camels, ponies, sheep, hounds, hawks, &c.

Early in the morning of the wedding-day all the *bai's* male subjects gathered round the fort gateway in their gaudiest attire of various skins and furs thrown over dirty and tattered woollen garments, and armed to the teeth. Most of them had spears in their hands, a large, heavy, forked matchlock slung over their shoulders, with sword and shield, and perhaps the handle of a long hatchet-like knife sticking out from the waist-band. Some wore gay heron-plumes in their head-dresses, all were mounted on Kirghiz camels or ponies. The most comical addition to the dress was a flag stuck on a pole tied to each man's back, which waved high over his head.

There was a monster kettle-drum, horn trumpets, and a nondescript brass wind-instrument, a few stout male singers, and some dancing-boys got up in female attire.

When the old *bai* came forth from the fort, with the bridecake of mulberries and a wreath of flowers, there was a general greeting of "Salaam Aleikum," and the instruments set up a tremendous discordant braying, which set the camels scampering about the plain. The motley cavalcade then started up a ravine, and every one commenced firing salutes of blank cartridge.

When we had come within a quarter of a mile of the Kirghiz encampment the *bai* sent a formal deputation of some of his followers, with wreaths of flowers in one hand and the sword in the other, to demand the bride; but lo! imagine the uproar and disappointment when it was found that the fair one had absconded with her mother, and that her father had started with some twenty horsemen in hot pursuit. The end was tragic. On the father overtaking the fugitives they refused to surrender, and a bloody fight ensued. The enraged Kirghiz chief killed his own wife and daughter, and after a brief and bloody struggle not one of the eloping party survived. They were thirteen in all, and the eleven men of the party laid fifteen of their opponents low, besides wounding the chief himself. We returned in sadder mood to partake of what should have been the marriage-feast. As if to drown the past in oblivion, the night witnessed deep potations of the beloved kumiss, and before morning the *bai* was consoled by marriage with a lovely girl of fifteen, daughter of one of the Kirghiz' headmen.

Shortly afterwards we took leave of the *bai*, although warmly pressed by him to settle down as honoured members of his principality, and went on to visit another chief, whose abode was called Bolor Kash.

We had been invited to pass the remainder of the summer with this chief, and were received with all due honour and courtesy. It was about the end of August 1826 when we arrived at Bolor Kash, but I was anxious to push on, and cut our visit down to three or four days. I found in this village, as in all other Kirghiz communities, an old witch, who was the oracle of the place. She was at once genealogist, news-monger, astrologer, historian, exorciser, match - maker, doctor, and divine.

While staying here I was distressed to hear that the presents offered by my friend the head *bai* of Shighnan had not been considered sufficient by the rapacious *beg* of Kunduz, and his wrath was feared.

Travelling in these regions was extremely difficult, and at one time we took seven days to cover forty miles.

During our journey we came upon a lonely hamlet where a near relation of the ruling prince of that region had betaken himself. He had unfortunately killed a favourite courtier of the ruler, and had to fly for his life.

He had assumed the title of Shah Nawaz Beg, and was trying to carve out a principality for himself. He had already made a fair beginning by the subjection of a community of five Kirghiz families. Travelling on, we came to more hamlets, until at the end of September we crossed an unnamed river and arrived at the fort of the ruler against whom Shah Nawaz Beg had revolted.

The Syad and Jey Ram, who were previously acquainted with the prince, went ahead, leaving us some 500 yards outside. We were soon summoned, and passed up a steep ascent of some 300 yards, and into a kind of domestic chapel—a small mosque—and thence into a private bath, where we performed our ablutions. Thence we proceeded to the mosque, where we performed our evening orisons, which we had scarcely concluded when we were summoned to the presence of the potentate. He was seated in state on some coloured felts, with a large dirty-looking bolster to support his back. Round the walls of the room, which were wattled, were squatted kinsmen and courtiers armed to the teeth.

On our arrival the ruler arose; and we exchanged the usual hearty salutations, and he favoured each of us with warm embraces. Tea, wine, and kumiss were freely distributed, and the king entered into easy conversation with us, lamenting with strong emotion a recent disastrous affair in which some of his followers had been murdered. He aimed his remarks pointedly at some of our party, knowing that they would not fail to pass them on to those for whom they were intended.

We stayed a fortnight with the prince, and then moved on about nine miles, to the northern Bolor ranges, where we sojourned a month in a cave, occasionally used as a shooting-lodge. We found game as plentiful as the population was scanty, the great wild sheep being the favourite quarry.

Our intention now was to go up towards the Ustum valley, south of the Alai ranges, and about mid-way between the Terek Pass and Lake Karakul; but winter approached, and a noble robber-chieftain, Shah Bahadur Beg, to whom we had been introduced, would have detained us hospitably. However, we were anxious to push on, and prevailed over his objections and started. Shah Bahadur Beg's residence was the fort of Ták, or Kurghan Ták, distant about two and a half days' good marching from the fort of Bolor Kash, and north or north-west of it. The intervening country is monotonous and sparsely inhabited.

After a week's travelling, aided by some of Shah Bahadur Beg's retainers, we met a party of travellers, who declared that the passes were all closed by snow; so we were obliged to return, not, however, without extracting blackmail (which was readily paid) of 10 per cent from these and other wayfarers.

On our way back to the Shah's stronghold we fell in with a party of thirteen Kirghiz families who had been compulsorily summoned by him to arrange a marriage dispute. It seemed that a fair young damsel, daughter of the Kirghiz *bai*, had been betrothed and sold for various considerable sums to a number of different suitors. It was settled now by the elders and priests that all the young suitors had an equal right to her, that the lady should ride with a slung bow, and that whoever caught her should be the lucky swain.

Accordingly she appeared: a lovely girl, with a heron's plume stuck in her high fur cap gracefully waving over her fair forehead; a red leathern girdle round her waist; and a small light bow slung over her arm. She also held a few arrows. She then chose a fleet horse and started off at full speed, hotly pursued by her suitors. The excitement of the chase was vivid. She was long seen waving the bow over her head in the distance, until a turn of the plain round a mountain spur hid the headlong party from our sight. Had she escaped and returned to camp in possession of the bow, she would have been considered as freed from all engagements; but it was not to be so. After a long chase the young lady returned, flushed and tired, without her bow, and somewhat abashed. Shortly afterwards we saw the triumphant suitor describing a figure of eight on horseback on the very spot whence the lady came again into our range of vision, and brandishing the fateful bow aloft.

Then the elders and priests arose, and with pipe and tambour played the conquering hero into camp. Before an hour had elapsed the nuptial knot had been tied. The bride now for the first time loosed her virgin tresses, which were formerly plaited over her neck; and then the wedding banquet commenced.

The wedding-cake, of pulverised mulberries, was cut into substantial lumps by young female attendants, whole roasted sheep were chopped up, and sour kumiss was handed round. Then came a ball, and all danced and gambolled until the bleating of the lambs in the encampment, and the general stir of animal life, warned us that the grey dawn was breaking.

Alas! it ushered in a melancholy day. Although not one of our party had slept a wink amid the joyous revelry of the night, we were up and off at sunrise, and had not proceeded more than four or five miles when of a sudden Shah Bahadur Beg himself unexpectedly and mysteriously appeared before us, with a strong body of followers. He welcomed us courteously, and then rapidly disappeared on some expedition, the object of which we could not divine. The mystery was soon terribly solved. In the evening the Shah returned from his raid; with him were some seven or eight Kipchak Kirghiz elders and females, and to our grief we recognised the beauteous heroine and bride of yesterday's revels, strapped to the chief's back, on his horse. Earnest were our intercessions for the prisoners, and so far as the rest of them were concerned, they were successful, for the Shah graciously released them.

As to the unhappy girl, our prayers were fruitless. The Shah declared that he had had the misfortune that day to kill both her parents, her brothers, and her husband, and that he was therefore bound to constitute himself her protector. Sadly we accompanied the Shah to his home.

Nothing reconciled the girl to her fate. She stabbed herself to death before the Shah two days afterwards, with a dagger which she had evidently concealed for the purpose.

We wintered here with the Shah, and in the spring of 1827 took our departure, resisting all the inducements of our host to stay. He considered that, with women, wine, good horses, good guns, good dogs, good falcons, and with a *castello* on the top of a crag in Yagistan,[1] all that life could offer was at our feet.

[1] "Yagistan" means "the independent country."

CHAPTER IX.

A REMARKABLE JOURNEY.

THE GARDEN OF EDEN—THE AKAS AND THE KEIAZ—GARDNER LEAVES PAMIR—CROSSES THE YAMUNYAR RIVER NEAR TASHBALYK—THE YAK—YARKAND—THE TWO CITIES—LEH AND SRINAGAR—THE GREAT EARTHQUAKE—GARDNER'S JOURNEY THROUGH GILGIT AND CHITRAL—THE STRATEGIC IMPORTANCE OF CHITRAL—SECOND VISIT TO KAFIRISTAN—GARDNER TRAVERSES AFGHANISTAN AND IS IMPRISONED AT GIRISHK—VISIT TO KABUL—FAREWELL TO THE THERBAH—GARDNER ARRIVES IN BAJAUR—SYAD AHMAD THE REFORMER—HIS HISTORY—DEATH OF THE SYAD—GARDNER BECOMES CHIEF OF ARTILLERY AT PESHAWAR AND CONCLUDES HIS TRAVELS.

GARDNER passed the winter of the year 1826 with the hospitable robber-chief Shah Bahadur Beg, and set forth in the spring of 1827 on his journey to Yarkand.

In addition to Jey Ram the Hindu, and Mir Ali Shah, the Syad, Gardner's party included the Syad's servant and Gardner's own four attendants, or eight persons in all.

The party determined to travel northwards at first, so as to strike the trade route from

Samarkand to Yarkand; and with this object they journeyed through Karategin to the valley of the Surkhab; then turning eastward they went by the great Alai valley or plateau.

This is a region considered by many to be no other than the site of the Garden of Eden and the birthplace of the human race. In contrast to most of the regions round about, the Alai valley is very fertile. Gardner stated in after-life that the wild fruits there were equal to the garden fruit of Kashmir.

At this point the only Afghan who remained of the party which originally followed him from the Kohistan declined to go any farther east, and took his leave.

Gardner gives a curious account of the inhabitants of the Karatagh and Aktagh mountains, who were, he says, the descendants of the ancient Kafir race who inhabited this region.

Although no subsequent traveller, whose experiences have been published, has as yet confirmed Gardner's account, his statement is too curious to lose, and may even hereafter be proved to be accurate. Dr Sven Hedin is stated to have discovered a previously unknown tribe very similar to Gardner's Akas.

The mountain-ranges known as the Aktagh and Karatagh are considerably to the west of the place in which Gardner now was; but he states that the Akas, as he calls these wild tribes, lived also in the mountains bordering the Alai valley, and that they were the original inhabitants of Kashgar.[1] At the time of his visit they were entirely confined to the mountains.

"The Akas," says Gardner, "and other mountain tribes of the great Kashgar population, pretend, like all the people of Great Kashgar, to great antiquity, and are probably the aborigines of these mountains (Aktagh), from which they take their names.

"Very few Akas have ever embraced Muhammadanism, and these few are a tribe to the north of and about the Terek Pass. They go by the name of Grums, a degraded and little respected tribe.

"The other Akas are an independent and fierce race, of predatory habits, and prove themselves to

[1] Gardner mentions the Alai and Trans-Alai ranges by name, and appears to apply the name Aktagh to some range near them. The mountains in this region are so named in Arrowsmith's map of Central Asia, the only one that Gardner could have seen at the period when he dictated his recollections to Mr Cooper and Sir Henry Durand: this seems to explain his mistake.

the surrounding Muhammadans to be of obstinate and warlike character. A continual and bitter warfare exists between them, much resembling that between the Kafirs of the Hindu Kush and their Afghan and Chitrali neighbours.

"All the Akas that the Muhammadans make captive in their raids are invariably sold as slaves.

"The Akas are of low stature, but well made and hardy; manly, fierce, and savage in manner. They are generally dressed in skins. Their women, though of fair complexion, are not entitled to be called good-looking, being of coarse features except in one curious tribe called the Keiaz.

"This tribe live in small communities in the most inaccessible peaks of the mountains, and number some 7000 souls in all. They lead the life of wild beasts, living in holes and dens dug out of the crags. They subsist chiefly by hunting, in which they are very expert, and so barbarous are they as seldom to use fire to make their meat more palatable. If the tales told by their Muhammadan neighbours are to be relied on, the Keiaz are not content with the raw flesh of wild animals alone, but sometimes devour the bodies of their enemies who fall into their hands.

"Among the mountains and valleys that I passed through on my way to Ausgess resided these Keiaz. They, like the Akas, were generally clothed in the skins of wild animals that they slew in the chase. They were armed only with a small bow and a spear. They adore rude idols, large masses of curiously shaped stone or rocks. They mix very little with the Akas, by whom they are considered a barbarous people; but the latter admire their women, frequently take them captive, and make them slaves or even wives.

"The Keiaz marriage rites are simple: the lover lays his bow at the feet of the lady; if she lifts it up, kisses and returns it, she is his wedded wife. By taking her husband's bow and flinging it on the ground before him, she can divorce herself, and she may secure a husband by unslinging his bow from his shoulder. I heard, however, that these practices, though existing and considered sacred, were seldom resorted to. The Keiaz, in their funeral ceremonies, much resemble the Akas, who sometimes burn their dead, and sometimes bury them in a sitting or erect position, but never place them in a horizontal position in mother earth.

"Sometimes, again, they lay their dead in deep water-holes, or allow them to be washed away by the torrents into which they fling them.

"The Akas and Keiaz had various divinities, but also worshipped obscene figures."

The MSS. concerning Gardner's journey from the Pamirs to Yarkand are so incomplete and confused, that I have experienced great difficulty in tracing his route. Among other places mentioned in connection with the Akas and Keiaz are a fort and valley named "Ustum": the valley is stated to have been a very large one, running east and west, and at the eastern extremity was a second fort, named Uskumbak.

This second fort was said to be eighteen days' march south-west of Kashgar, and the Ustum valley may therefore be the exit from the Pamir plateau now known as the Gaz defile. Gardner had therefore, apparently, turned southward again from the Alai plateau, and had passed near Lake Kara Kul, thus travelling by the old trade-route from Samarkand to Yarkand. Possibly, however, Gardner left the Alai valley by the more direct road of the Terek Pass. This pass is a very long one, and is divided into two marches. The second march ends at a place called Egrushtam — a name not unlike Ustum, which Gardner in another paper spells "Rustam."

Gardner states that he and his companions halted a few days at Uskumbak, as was the regular custom of small parties of travellers by this route, so as to unite with another party, and so make up a caravan of sufficient strength to brave the perils of the great desert of Kashgar. Three merchants had already joined him, and by the accession of a party of seven stragglers at Uskumbak, natives of Yarkand, who were desirous of going thither, Gardner's party was brought up to seventeen and provided with guides: he therefore went on his way without further delay.

From Uskumbak Gardner and his companions marched in three days to another fort called Dunchu (or Dunchai), which was four long marches south-west of Tash-balyk, a large town on the north bank of the Yamunyar river. They heard that during this three days' journey water was only procurable at one spot, and that at the middle of the second day's march. They therefore carried water with them, slung in skins under the horses' bellies. On arriving at the spot where water was promised, they found it extremely salt and bad, in small pools, but were obliged to make the best of it. On this day, all along the road, they met herds of yaks, which Gardner describes as follows:—

"On this day all along our march we met with large herds of various species of deer, antelope, &c., and some small herds of what the Akas named 'ansak,' but which the Yarkand men called 'yak,' a large animal resembling a cow. These yak, of which there are two or three species, are found in great numbers to the north, and were very numerous also throughout the whole of the desert to the south. Early this evening we put up at some dried-up reservoirs, in some of which, however, a little muddy brackish water still remained, round which numerous footprints of deer, antelope, and yak proved that they resorted to this place for water. The Mogul merchants told me that a certain tribe of Chinese Tartars venerated those yaks to such a degree as to make the wounding or killing of them punishable with death. The animals which I saw between this place and Yarkand had cylindrical horns curved outwards, very long pendent hair, and horse-like tail: the largest specimen I saw here very much resembled an English bull in appearance, and the footprints of some were larger than those of any bull. The head was somewhat short, crowned with two round horns, which tapered from the foot upwards and terminated in sharp points.

"To the wandering tribes of Tartars these animals are most valuable, but more particularly to the tribes called at Yarkand the Kizl and Alai Kirghiz, who wander about in large or small *obahs* or camps, and drive the animals from place to place in summer towards the Pamir. They are an easy mode of conveyance, furnish good, warm coverings and wholesome food. They are never employed in agriculture. Tents and ropes are manufactured from their hair, and many dress themselves entirely in the skins.

"The yaks' tails have been held in high estimation for ages throughout India as objects of pageantry and parade, and no man of distinction stirred abroad or sat in his durbar at home without two or three "thrusters - away of flies" attending him. The Chinese and some of the Chinese Tartars sometimes dye yaks' tails of a reddish black, or some other colour, and wear them as tufts in their bonnets or on their horses, often accompanied by a peacock-feather, the emblem of royal dignity or high station. The yak is one of the most timid of animals, and very swift: when chased by horsemen and dogs, and on the point of being overtaken, it hides its hindquarters in some bush and there waits for its enemies, imagining, perhaps, that if it could conceal its tail, which it considers perhaps as the object they are in search of, it might escape unhurt."

On the third day after their departure from the Pamir plateau, Gardner and his companions reached the town of Dunchu (or Dunchai), having, he says, to wade the Yamunyar[1] river to reach it, the town standing on the south bank of the river.

From Dunchu they journeyed to Yarkand in twenty-one days, making one halt only to visit a great mound with caves, which Gardner calls Mahu or Mahusang. He states that mephitic vapours arise here from clefts in the ground, and also that the mound apparently covers the site of an ancient city. Gardner's description of Yarkand is briefly given in Mr Edgeworth's abstract in the following words :—

"Reached Yarkand. It consists of two cities, one inhabited by the Muhammadan population, the other by the Chinese garrison. The gates are closed at night. The population number

[1] The existence of this river was for a considerable time doubted by geographers : it is, however, correctly named by Gardner.

80,000 to 100,000 souls, and there are 15,000 soldiers in the garrison. There is a Muhammadan governor, named Khan Ali Jan. The Chinese governor is named Shun Teth. Green and black tea, packed in vellum, shawls, wool, porcelain, and chrysoprase beads are among the principal articles of trade."

Gardner remained three days at Yarkand and then went on his way southward, reaching Kargalik on the second day. Thence, going south steadily, he arrived in thirty days at Leh, the capital of Ladak. In the course of this journey he traversed the Karakoram Pass, but says little about it, no doubt because it was really much easier travelling than many passes which he had already traversed. The diary of his journey is given in Mr Edgeworth's abstract, but is not sufficiently interesting to merit transcription. Sir Henry Durand mentions that Gardner travelled from Yarkand to Leh as a pilgrim, wearing the hadji dress. Arrived at Leh, he was sent with five or six others to collect pilgrims from Khoten and other places to the eastward, and while on this errand he saw the Pangkong Lake.

Having collected the pilgrims, Gardner returned to Leh, and went thence to Srinagar, the capital of Kashmir. Shortly before he arrived there a terrible earthquake occurred, which killed 11,000 or 12,000 people. The stench from the corpses was frightful, and the survivors were afraid to bury them. In consequence a kind of plague broke out in a few days, people fell to the earth with vertigo and nausea, and their bodies turned black. The natives fled in all directions. Diwan Kirpa Ram was at this time governor of Kashmir for Maharaja Ranjit Singh, having recently succeeded his father.

At the time of Gardner's arrival at Srinagar that city was still under the influence of Afghan merchants and soldiers, and from some of them Gardner heard a false report that his former leader Habib-ulla Khan was once more in the ascendant, and the adventurous soldier decided at once on joining his old chief. Accompanied only by Jey Ram the Hindu, by his faithful Therbah and three other Muhammadans, he made an astonishing journey from Srinagar through Chilas and Bunji (where he crossed the Indus) to Gilgit, and thence to Chitral. Of this journey Sir Henry Rawlinson writes in his "Monograph on the Oxus":[1] "Gardner actually traversed the Gilgit valley from the Indus

[1] Journal of the Royal Geographical Society, vol. xlii.

to the Snowy Mountains, and finally crossed over into Chitral, being, in fact, the only Englishman up to the present time [1872] who has ever performed the journey throughout."

Gardner subsequently wrote voluminous reports on the importance of Chitral to India, both as a trade-route between that country and Central Asia and as a weak spot in our military position. He was, however, in advance of his time, and his words fell upon deaf ears. Later days have seen a wiser policy adopted; and those who have witnessed the very recent occupation of Chitral by England, and of Kafiristan by the Afghans, without understanding the military advantages of both moves, may be enlightened by the following note, written by Gardner about thirty years ago:—

"It is said that when Amir Dost Muhammad Khan was invading Kunduz and Badakshan in 1850, the large body of troops which had been sent from Kabul *viâ* the Khawak Pass [the route followed by Gardner himself] had met with but slight success. There appeared no prospect of thus reducing these distant regions to subjection until a body of from 2000 to 3000 irregular cavalry, with four or six guns, I know not which, were sent up from Jalalabad by the Chitral caravan-route, and crossing the Baroghil Pass into Wakhan, swept to the westward, *viâ* Kala-i-Panj and Ishkashem, meeting no resistance until they arrived at Jerm.

"The chief of Badakshan, seeing himself thus unexpectedly attacked both in front and rear, went with the leading inhabitants of his province and tendered his full submission to the Afghan ruler.

"This body of troops then continued its march, and in a similar manner compelled the surrender of the chief of Kunduz, who had previously made a noble and successful defence against the Kabul army.

"May it not be suggested that what happened on the above occasion may be repeated in the reverse way, and that Afghanistan may fall to Russia if attacked in like manner; that is, that while one army was knocking at the time-honoured gate of Bamian, another might steal its way down the Chitral valley, and suddenly dash on the astounded and probably weak garrison of Jalalabad."

Gardner's prophetic lines show at any rate that as a student of "the great game of Central Asia" he was in the front rank.

From Chitral he sent his followers and baggage down by river to Jalalabad, while he himself for the second time entered Kafiristan and travelled along the Kamah or Kameh river. He was accompanied by a priest, and was well treated, his only difficulty being to escape from the hospitality of his hosts.

The full diary of this visit to Kafiristan and of Gardner's journey from Pamir was lent to Sir Alexander Burnes, and was destroyed when that unfortunate officer was murdered at Kabul and his house pillaged.

All that remain by way of record of this most interesting passage in Gardner's adventurous life are some disconnected notes and allusions. Some of the notes are written on the margin of various printed pages concerning Kafiristan.

Among the allusions are two references to the fact related by the Kafirs to Gardner—that two Europeans had lived in their country about the year 1770, and had, according to one story, died in captivity, and, according to the other, been murdered by the Kafirs, under the supposition that they were evil spirits. These unfortunate Europeans were probably Roman Catholic missionaries.

A geographical note by Gardner is of interest. On a statement by Captain Raverty concerning the Kashkar, Chitral, or Kunur river, and an unnamed river which Captain Raverty says joins it at Chigar-Serai, Gardner says:—

"The river called the Kameh or Kafir-Ab rises east or south-east of the Kotal-i-Dara [Dorah Pass on modern maps] in the north of Kafiristan, and flowing at first south-west, bends down to the south-east and joins the Chitral or Kashkar river near Chigar-Serai. Thence those united streams or rivers are known as the Kunur river, and fall into the Kabul river at or near Jalalabad."

The Kameh river does rise as stated above; it does bend slightly westward, and then to the south-east. The statement illustrates Gardner's knowledge of a country into which no white man but himself had then penetrated. Concerning the tribes of Kafiristan enumerated by Raverty, Gardner writes:—

"These are the names of the principal valleys as well as of the tribes, the main valley being the Kameh, down and along the upper portion of which the Kam or Kameh tribe inhabit."

This statement also has been confirmed by the recent writings of Sir George Robertson; but no one but Gardner could have made it at the time when it was written by him.

Leaving Kafiristan by Chigar-Serai and Jalalabad, Gardner journeyed towards Kabul, but on approaching the capital found that he had been misinformed about Habib-ulla Khan, who was now said to have perished while on a pilgrimage to Mecca. Dost Muhammad was all-powerful, and it was no part of Gardner's plan to place himself in the lion's jaws, though as a matter of fact he was eventually compelled to do so.

Gardner now contemplated returning to Persia, and marched *viâ* Ghazni and Kilat-i-Ghilzai to Kandahar. At this city the Sardars, Dost Muhammad's brothers, who governed the province, sent for a crystal hookah, Gardner's most valued possession, which had been given him by his mysterious friend the Pole of Ura-tube; they also demanded from him and his followers (a band of Khaibari outlaws who had attached themselves to him) a ransom of a lakh and a half of rupees.

Gardner arrived at Kandahar early in the spring of 1830, and after a time occupied in reasoning with the Sardars, he obtained permission from them to take leave and proceed to Herat. This permission was conveyed in an official letter written in Persian, and was evidently couched in terms of double meaning, for on reaching Girishk and presenting the letter, Gardner and his followers were treacherously seized while at dinner, and were cast into the subterranean dungeons of the castle. After a few days the Khaibaris and the Therbah were released; but Gardner was kept for nine months a prisoner beneath ground.

Now was shown his remarkable influence over those who from time to time became his followers —for none of the Khaibaris would desert him, but went round to the priests, exciting sympathy in his behalf. These faithful men eventually obtained Gardner's release, but with extreme difficulty, and by means only of the whole party promising not to go to Herat, and stating in writing that they had been well treated.

The head of the party of Khaibaris was one Ghulam Rassul Khan of Ali Masjid, and this man actually proposed to re-enter Kandahar and force the Sirdars to give them some money to help them on their way. So bold a proposal delighted Gardner, and the attempt was accordingly made, but without success.

Ghulam Rassul Khan now obtained the dress

of a *shahzada*,[1] in which Gardner was dressed; and certain men who were at variance with the Sirdars gradually joined the party until their number reached forty armed and mounted men. With this following Gardner set out towards Kabul. He had thus escaped from most imminent danger, from a long and apparently hopeless captivity, and found himself at the head of a strong body of men, several of whom had shown extraordinary fidelity to him. All that he now wanted was money, and accident or design soon placed within his grasp the means of obtaining a supply.

Between Kilat-i-Ghilzai and Kabul Gardner's party met a *kafila* or caravan bound for Kandahar, and belonging to merchants trading under the protection of the Kandahar rulers. Gardner, who with his men had halted as soon as the approach of the caravan was signalled by his scouts, pretended that he also was proceeding to Kandahar, and joined the *kafila*. As soon as a favourable opportunity arose he seized and bound the merchants, thus anticipating them in their intentions with regard to him; then, taking the bull by the

[1] Probably meaning a prince of the ex-royal family, of whom there were a great number.

horns, he made straight for Kabul, with the intention of throwing himself on the mercy of Amir Dost Muhammad Khan.

The party rode night and day, so as to outstrip the messengers of the Kandahar Sirdars, and riding direct to the Bala Hissar or palace, Gardner and Ghulam Rassul Khan presented their arms, horses, and spoil to Dost Muhammad and asked for a private audience. They then told their story to the warlike chief, who heard them patiently, agreed that they had been badly treated by his brothers, and had done rightly in taking the law into their own hands. He declined to take anything from them, but would not allow them to remain in his territory. The Amir then gave Gardner a safe-conduct to the territory of Mir Alam Khan of Bajaur, whom Gardner decided to visit. This chief had already treated him kindly when he passed through Bajaur on his way from Kafiristan to Afghanistan a year previously.

When leaving Kabul Gardner lost the services of his faithful follower the Therbah, who had shared so many dangers and hardships with him, and had done nobly in keeping up the fidelity of the Khaibaris during Gardner's long captivity at Girishk. The Therbah now returned to his own home, and Gardner once again became a lonely man, with no resource but his own stout heart and ready wit. Never had these two allies stood by him better than in his bold action at Kabul, where he had countless enemies. In the words of Sir Henry Durand, whose narrative has been closely followed in this chapter, "Gardner seems to have been indebted for life, and that many a time over, to his cool audacity, which never failed him for a moment, be the strait what it might."

Gardner obtained permission from the Amir to remain a few days at Kabul, and left that city towards the end of January 1831. He was, he says, disappointed at having failed to establish himself in a military career under that great leader of men, but for many reasons he was glad to leave Afghanistan. There were too many Afghans whose fathers and brothers had met him in battle to make a residence in a country where blood-feuds were a sacred duty even moderately safe from treachery and violence.

Moreover, neither Gardner's admiration for the Amir, nor gratitude for the protection he had afforded to the fugitives, could blind Gardner to the iniquity of Dost Muhammad's conduct towards

Prince Habib-ulla Khan. Finally and principally, Gardner adds, he hated every Afghan of the dominant faction for the death of his innocent wife and son.

The period of Gardner's wanderings was now approaching a close; but before he could enter the Panjab, the country which, with its then dependency, Kashmir, was thereafter to become his home, he had to traverse the most dangerous of all regions —that from Kabul to Peshawar—the very home of battle, murder, and sudden death.

It was, however, he writes, with a light heart that he retraced his footsteps from Kabul to Jalalabad, and thence to Kunar and Bajaur, where he was again kindly received by the ruler, Mir Alam Khan.

His adventures in those troubled regions may now be related by himself:—

I arrived at Bajaur at the moment that a certain Muhammad Ismail had arrived from the fanatic chief Syad Ahmad with a demand for aid from the *mir*, as from all neighbouring Muhammadan chieftains. This Syad Ahmad was a remarkable man, who gave much trouble for some years to Maharaja Ranjit Singh.

Some four years prior to my arrival at Bajaur he had raised the green standard of the Prophet in the Eusafzai hills, between Peshawar and Attock, and proclaimed a religious war against the Sikhs. Syad Ahmad belonged to a family of Syads in Bareilly, and commenced life as a petty officer of cavalry in the army of Amir Khan, the great soldier of fortune. After preparing in India for the religious war which he desired to wage, Syad Ahmad entered Afghanistan; but finding no enthusiasm there, he proceeded with several hundred followers to Punjtar in the Eusafzai hills, and made that place his headquarters. This, as I have said, was early in the year 1827.

After various vicissitudes the Syad actually became in 1830 master of the city and district of Peshawar, from which place he ousted Sultan Muhammad Khan. This prince was a brother of Amir Dost Muhammad Khan, and at this time ruled Peshawar as a tributary of Maharaja Ranjit Singh, the sovereign of the Panjab.

This success of the Syad proved his ruin, for the Maharaja immediately occupied Peshawar in person, and determined to destroy the reformer once and for all. He intrusted the task to his son, the Shahzada[1] Sher Singh, whose operations were at first unsuccessful.

Syad Ahmad had two faithful and trusted followers, the Maulvis Abdul Hai and Muhammad Ismail, and these men strained every nerve to obtain assistance and reinforcements for their master.

When Muhammad Ismail arrived at the Court of Mir Alam Khan the latter was in doubt what course to adopt. The religious enthusiasm of his people, and their hatred of the infidel Sikhs, impelled him to make common cause with the Syad, but at the same time he had substantial reasons to maintain friendly relations with Ranjit Singh, and more especially with the Wazir (or Prime Minister), Raja Dhyan Singh. The influence of the latter was very great throughout all the mountain regions on the northern boundaries of India.

In this difficulty my arrival, with my trusty band of Khaibaris, was very welcome to the *mir*, and no doubt combined with his former friendship to elicit the warm reception which he gave me.

[1] The recognised sons of Maharaja Ranjit Singh bore the title of *shahzada* or prince.

He was wary enough to say nothing of his intentions to me for three or four days after my arrival, until my attention was attracted by an impassioned address which I heard Muhammad Ismail deliver to a large assembly of the wild Eusafzai mountaineers. The enthusiasm which he aroused suggested to me that I might do worse than join the Syad his master, as I saw a good opportunity of getting together such a body of followers as would make my services valuable to any ruler to whom I might subsequently offer them. Therefore, when Mir Alam Khan proposed to me to take command of those of his followers who desired to array themselves under the sacred banner of the Syad or Khalifa as he now styled himself, I fell in readily enough with his wish.

In a few days I marched towards Balakot, the headquarters of Syad Ahmad, at the head of some 250 well-armed and warlike mountaineers, all burning with religious zeal and with the desire to work their will in the rich city of Peshawar. For rich it seemed to them, though at that time its prosperity was at a very low ebb, it having been for so many years bandied about between the Sikhs and Afghans.

On the march I heard a curious story concerning

the Syad, which may or may not have been true. In either case it did not appear to lessen the respect in which the narrator evidently held the holy man.

At some period of his career, said my informant, Syad Ahmad was in the service of Sirdar Pir Muhammad, chief of Kohat and one of the Barakzai[1] brothers. The Syad was then young, active, energetic, and a first-rate swordsman and horseman. One day he and another man applied for pay towards their expenses, and received a written order for some 30 or 40 rupees on a village a few miles from Peshawar. They went to the village in company and received the money; but when returning they quarrelled as to its division, the upshot being that Syad Ahmad slew his comrade. Then, taking all the money, he hastened to Peshawar. At the gateway of Sirdar Pir Muhammad's house in that city he found a swift horse standing, ready saddled and bridled, according to custom. This horse he forcibly seized, and fled on it across the Kabul river to Bajaur. There he immediately began to preach a holy war against all unbelievers. It did not appear to distress my religious enthusiast to believe that the great Khalifa, the Defender of

[1] That is, one of the brothers of Dost Muhammad Khan.

the Faith, the glitter of whose sword was now to scatter destruction among the infidels, was identical with the thief and murderer of the story.

However, as it turned out, we set out to join the holy standard just an hour too late, for the Syad and his faithful *maulvi* were slain, fighting bravely side by side, before we could join in the fight. They were taken by surprise at a place near Balakot and surrounded by a large party of Sikhs, who had crossed the river Indus on *massaks*, or inflated skins. In his anxiety to rejoin his master Muhammad Ismail had left me and my force a march behind, and, owing to the mistake or treachery of a guide, we took longer than was expected in coming up.

I well remember the scene as I and my Eusafzai and Khaibari followers came in view of the action.

Syad Ahmad and the *maulvi*, surrounded by his surviving Indian followers, were fighting desperately hand to hand with the equally fanatical Akalis of the Sikh army. They had been taken by surprise and isolated from the main body of the Syad's forces, which fought very badly without their leader. Even as I caught sight of the Syad and *maulvi* they fell pierced by a hundred weapons.

Those around them were slain to a man, and the main body dispersed in every direction.

With some difficulty I kept my party together, and withdrew to the hills, showing so bold a front to the Sikhs that they did not dare to follow us far. The Eusafzai mountain-passes always gave the Sikhs cholera, as Avitabile[1] used to say.

I was literally within a few hundred yards of the Syad when he fell, but I did not see the angel descend and carry him off to Paradise, although many of his followers remembered afterwards that they had seen it distinctly enough.

I remained two nights at Panchthar, where I rested my men after their exertions, and divided the booty between them. The death of the Syad broke the only link that held his followers together, and in the retreat many of the parties from different regions fell upon one another for plunder. My Khaibaris and Eusafzais were equal to the best in this matter, and cut down several of the Hindustani fanatics[2] who had joined them for protection,

[1] General Avitabile, Ranjit Singh's Italian governor of the Peshawar district. See Appendix.

[2] The Hindustani fanatics were the Indian followers of Syad Ahmad. Their descendants give trouble to the present day, and took a prominent part in the recent Frontier war.

and whose clothing or equipment seemed to them a desirable acquisition.

Having rested my men, and given leave to my faithful Khaibaris to return to their homes, I returned to Bajaur, where I was kindly welcomed by Mir Alam Khan. It was while in comparative ease and security, and habited as a Mussulman, at Bajaur, that I managed to jot down the rough records of my wanderings. As a devout man I carried the Koran suspended from my neck, and in its leaves I deposited my scraps. After a time the holy book got so bulky that I had to devote my tobacco-pouch as a receptacle for my writings. No one would ever touch the Koran of a neighbour, and had any interference been attempted or suspicions aroused, I should have represented my scraps as additional prayers.

My stay at Bajaur was not a long one, as during the summer I received an invitation from Sultan Muhammad Khan[1] to enter his service as chief of artillery. This prince had been reinstated as governor of Peshawar when, as I have related, Maharaja Ranjit Singh came to his assistance in the previous year. Sultan Muhammad Khan took

[1] Brother and enemy of Dost Muhammad Khan.

great interest in artillery, but I taught him all that he knew about the subject.

Gardner's travels had now come to an end. Except for the period of his imprisonment at Girishk, he had been constantly on the move since his final departure from Astrakhan in February 1823, a period of eight and a half years.

Few men have undergone such perils and have travelled such long distances through unknown countries.

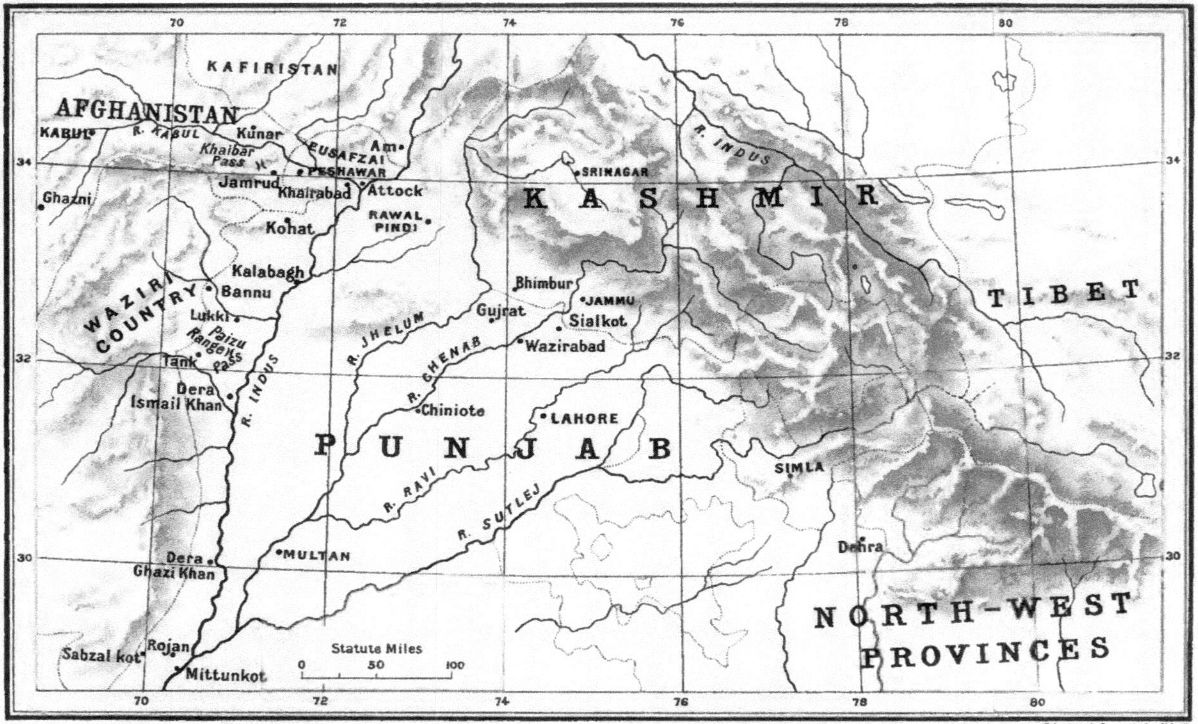

John Bartholomew & Co., Edin^r.

CHAPTER X.

ADVENTURES IN THE PANJAB.

PESHAWAR—MAHARAJA RANJIT SINGH—GARDNER ENTERS HIS SERVICE—VISITS ON THE WAY—DR HARLAN AND GENERAL AVITABILE—GENERALS VENTURA AND COURT—RAJA DHYAN SINGH, THE PRIME MINISTER—GARDNER'S *DÉBUT* AS A GUNNER—HE BECOMES AN INSTRUCTOR — CAMPAIGN ON THE INDUS — OPERATIONS IN BANNU — THE SIKH - AFGHAN WAR OF 1835 — FINAL CONQUEST OF PESHAWAR BY THE SIKHS—GARDNER OBTAINS COMMAND OF THE JAMMU ARTILLERY — RANJIT SINGH'S LAST CAMPAIGN — A RAPID MARCH—THE REBELLION OF SHAMAS KHAN.

It may be as well to repeat, for the information of those unfamiliar with Eastern history, that Peshawar, so long a bone of contention between the Sikh and Afghan nations, was now practically a portion of the Panjab.

Sultan Muhammad Khan, though nominally an independent sovereign, was to all intents and purposes a vassal of Ranjit Singh.

It was, in fact, not very long after Gardner's arrival at Peshawar that the Maharaja compelled Sultan Muhammad to join his Court, and replaced him as governor of Peshawar by a succession of Sikh *sardars*, who, proving incapable of managing the turbulent people of Peshawar, that "nest of scorpions," were succeeded finally by the iron-handed Avitabile.

Gardner thus describes his entry into the Panjab:—

I went to Peshawar in the month of August 1831, and remained there until the spring of the following year, 1832, when a letter was received by Sultan Muhammad Khan from Maharaja Ranjit Singh[1] desiring my services. I myself would

[1] Ranjit Singh, who became Maharaja of the Panjab, was born in the year 1780, and at the age of eleven succeeded his father as chief of one of the least important of the twelve confederacies which at the time composed the Sikh nation. One by one the confederacies fell before the talents and ambition of Ranjit Singh, who then turned his attention to those portions of the Panjab that were in possession of neighbouring rulers. Multan was captured in 1818, and Kashmir in the following year.

The only Powers that the Maharaja now had cause to fear were the British and the Afghans, and with the object of facing them on equal terms Ranjit Singh set about the task of raising a large army, formed on the European system. With this object in view he gave employment to a considerable number of foreign officers, of whom the most important were Generals Ventura, Allard, Court, and Avitabile; Colonels Gardner and Van Cortlandt. The skill and tenacity with which the Sikh army fought the British in two desperate campaigns show with what success these officers and their assistants served Ranjit Singh.

have preferred to remain at Peshawar, but Sultan Muhammad dared not refuse the Maharaja. I regretted leaving him, as he had treated me kindly and honourably, making me daily a guest at his table, and giving me a liberal salary.

On taking my leave of Sultan Muhammad he bestowed a number of gifts upon me, including an excellent horse and a sum of money.

I was directed to travel under the care of the Maharaja's *daroga*, or chief of the stud, who was then at Peshawar, collecting the annual tribute of horses. Some delay, however, occurred in his setting out on his journey to Lahore, as none but the best Persian or Turki horses were accepted in tribute, and I took advantage of the opportunity by again visiting my friends Mir Alam Khan of Bajaur, Futteh Khan of Panchthar, and Paindah Khan of Am, on the right bank of the Indus.

Thence crossing to Torbela, I went down to the fort of Attock, where I met the *daroga* with his horses. His escort consisted of some forty well-armed Sikh horsemen; but notwithstanding, he had been attacked at night between Peshawar and Attock by 300 or 400 Afridis, and four of his horses had been taken from him.

On our way from Attock to Rawal Pindi we

were again attacked by 400 to 500 Ghakkars near the Margali Pass, with a loss on this occasion of two horses and five men.

After this nothing of import occurred until the party arrived safely at Gujrat. Hence the *dar-oga* started direct for Lahore, while I and my servants remained a few days with Dr Harlan,[1] then governor of the district. Then, crossing the Chenab river, I went to Wazirabad, where I remained four or five days the guest of General Avitabile,[2] the governor. It was unfortunate that a sore animosity existed at the time between these two governors. However, I received letters of introduction from both, and went from Wazirabad to Lahore, where I met Generals Ventura [3] and Court.[4]

[1] Dr Harlan was an American adventurer who obtained employment at different times under Ranjit Singh and Dost Muhammad. He was thoroughly unscrupulous and a man of considerable talent. His 'Memoir of Afghanistan' is worth reading.

[2] General Avitabile was governor of Wazirabad before he was made governor of Peshawar. He greatly beautified the town of Wazirabad.

[3] General Ventura was an Italian officer of high character in the service of Ranjit Singh. He was much honoured and trusted by the Maharaja, and commanded the "Fouj Khás" or model brigade of the Khalsa army. General Ventura eventually became governor of Lahore.

[4] General Court was a French officer of artillery, a most honourable and estimable man of considerable professional skill.

For biographies of all the above officers see Appendix.

After a few days' delay I was presented at Court by General Ventura and the Prime Minister, Raja Dhyan Singh.

I presented my letters from Syad Jan, chief of Kunar, and from Mir Alam Khan of Bajaur, both of whom were on friendly terms with the Maharaja. I also had letters from the three Barakzai brothers, Sardars Sultan Muhammad of Peshawar, Pir Muhammad of Kohat, and Syad Mahmud of Hashtnagar.

On the day of my presentation to the Maharaja, and while I was waiting outside the Shalimar Gardens, an incident occurred which is described in the work called 'Adventures of an Officer,' by the great and good Sir Henry Lawrence (afterwards my well-known and honoured friend).

A certain Nand Singh, an officer of the Maharaja's cavalry, rode his horse intentionally against me and endeavoured to jostle me into the ditch, which was deep and filled with running water. I touched the rein of my good steed, gave him half a turn, pressed him with my sword-hand the veriest trifle on the loins, and in an instant Nand Singh and his horse were rolling on the ground. I calmly expressed a hope that the fallen man was not hurt, and was treated with much civility during the remaining time that I was kept waiting.

Shortly after I was summoned to the Maharaja's presence, and was graciously received by that great man. Much as I had heard of the insignificance of his appearance, it at first startled me; but the profound respect with which he was treated, and the extraordinary range of subjects on which he closely examined me, speedily dispelled the first impression.

The Maharaja was indeed one of those master-minds which only require opportunity to change the face of the globe. Ranjit Singh made a great and powerful nation from the disunited confederacies of the Sikhs, and would have carried his conquests to Delhi or even farther had it not been for the simultaneous rise and consolidation of the British empire in India.

At the time of my arrival at Lahore the Maharaja was in want of an instructor of artillery, M. Court being employed principally as superintendent of the gun-factory. He was a very amiable and accomplished man, as was General Ventura.

A few days after my audience Raja Dhyan Singh, the Prime Minister, showed me the two guns that had been presented by Lord William Bentinck, the Governor-General of India, to Maharaja Ranjit Singh. Dhyan Singh pointed out to me the shells and fuses in the tumbrils, and asked me if I could explain their use or fire them. I found in one of the tumbrils, inclosed in a bundle of fuses, a small printed slip of paper giving instructions as to the time of burning, time of flight, &c. Having read this, I told Dhyan Singh that I hoped to be able to fire them and to satisfy him as to my knowledge of their proper use. I, however, asked to be allowed to cut and burn one fuse first, which at his desire I did in his presence. The result agreeing with that shown on the printed slip, there seemed to be no further difficulty.

Accordingly one of the guns, with its tumbril, &c., was given over next day into my charge, and I was ordered to get ready to fire three or four of the shells at different distances in the presence of Maharaja Ranjit Singh. I took a few soldiers in hand, and in a few days' time all this was done with a degree of success unexpected even by myself, the shells bursting exactly as required at 600, 800, 1000, and 1200 yards.

This occurred in the presence of the Maharaja and his entire Court, and all seemed pleased, especially the Prime Minister Raja Dhyan Singh, who ever after acted as my patron and steadfast friend. His brothers Raja (afterwards Maharaja) Gulab Singh and Raja Suchet Singh also befriended me.

In consequence of my success as an artillerist I received a considerable present, and was enrolled in the Maharaja's service with the rank of colonel of artillery, and was placed in full command of a camp of eight horse-artillery guns, two mortars, and two howitzers. I was likewise deputed to teach most of the principal officers attached to the artillery, at the head of whom were General Sultan Muhammad and several colonels, all of whom as my *shagird* (pupils) were directed to present me with a *nuzzar* or douceur of 500 to 1000 rupees.

For two or three months Maharaja Ranjit Singh witnessed with much interest their firing of shell, shot, canister, red-hot shot, &c.; all receiving presents from his Highness according to their proficiency and merits. The presents ranged from 500 to 5000 rupees, and were usually paid, half in gold and silver, and half in *Pashmina* shawls,[1] &c.

This mode of treatment proved, of course, a strong incentive to the Maharaja's officers, who worked hard, early and late.

I should mention that on meeting my countryman Harlan I resumed the character of a *wilayati* or foreigner, and resumed also the name of Gardner, which I had abandoned for so long that it sounded strangely in my ears. The Sikhs usually called me "Gordana."

Thus matters continued for three or four months, when I was ordered to proceed with my park of artillery, to which was added a force of 800 regular infantry and 400 "Ghorcharahs," or irregular cavalry, to join General Ventura. The General had previously been despatched with his force of about 6000 men to subjugate and annex Sabzal-kot and Rojan, both on the right bank of the Indus below Mittun-kot. This object, after some trouble, having been effected, I received an order to march with all speed with my force of artillery, infantry, and cavalry *viâ* Dera Ghazi Khan and Dera Ismail Khan to join the Sikh

[1] Commonly called "Kashmir" shawls.

force, then in Bannu, under the command of Sardar Tara Singh. Accordingly I went, finding considerable difficulty at and on each side of the Paizu Pass, from bad roads and an almost complete lack of water.

On reaching the fort of Lukki, to the north of the Paizu Pass and on the river Gombela, I found Tara Singh hard pressed by the Bannuites, he having but 2000 Sikh irregular cavalry and four small guns with him, without any infantry. He found himself obliged to act on the defensive against some thousands of well-armed and mounted Bannuites, assisted by 4000 or 5000 wild mountain Waziris on foot. However, in the course of about four months we managed to cut down, burn, and destroy all the grain crops, and to level and destroy the forts, villages, gardens, fruit-trees, orchards, &c., of all the most refractory, and of those who refused to pay their fixed annual stipend or revenues. This effected, we returned to Lahore viâ Kalabagh on the river Indus.

In such expeditions I served the Maharaja for some three years, and early in 1835 I was marching south when, at Wazirabad or Ramnagar, I found the whole Sikh army, with Ranjit Singh at their head, in full march towards Peshawar. Here

Tara Singh, with and under whom I was still serving, halted on the banks of the Chenab for a day or two for instructions. Having received them, we changed our front and marched westward, and soon took up our respective positions in the advancing Sikh army. On arriving at Peshawar we found Amir Dost Muhammad with 40,000 or 50,000 of his own troops, and about 60,000 to 80,000 Ghazis, encamped at and about the mouth of the Khaibar Pass.

The "Francese Compo,"[1] or French division of the Sikh army, then personally commanded by the four French and Italian generals—Messieurs Allard,[2] Ventura, Avitabile, and Court — and having a strength of 20,000 to 22,000 men, marched towards Hashtnagar, and thence slowly and cautiously made its way westward and southwestward with the object of turning the left flank of the Dost's army; while the remainder of the Sikh army, commanded by Ranjit Singh himself, and 60,000 to 80,000 strong, horse and foot, threatened Dost Muhammad's centre and right flank.

[1] This was the camp name of the "Fouj Khas," or model brigade.

[2] General Allard was a French officer who died in Ranjit Singh's service. See Appendix.

The good, kind, and polite old Fakir Azizuddin,[1] with his younger brother Nuruddin, *Chefs Diplomatiques* of home, foreign, and private affairs, Head and Grand Ministers of State to Ranjit Singh, were, as peacemakers, day and night, backward and forward, parleying direct between Ranjit Singh and Dost Muhammad. They certainly performed this duty at great personal risk, as serious and heavy cannonading and skirmishing took place every day from morning till night between the two armies.

The firing and fighting took place along the whole front, and there being but two and a half or three short miles between the armies, and the Afghan position being on rising ground, every movement on either side was plainly visible to the other. Thus matters proceeded for about a month, when the entire Sikh army, with the French division, were ready to advance and make a simultaneous attack on the Afghan position.

Ranjit Singh ordered pay to be issued to the

[1] Fakir Azizuddin, Foreign Minister to Maharaja Ranjit Singh, was a very remarkable man. He originally gained influence over the Maharaja by his skill as a physician, and subsequently impressed his master by the wisdom of his advice. Sir Lepel Griffin, the highest authority on Panjab history, considers Azizuddin to have been one of the ablest and certainly the most honest of all Ranjit Singh's courtiers. His brother Nuruddin was also much respected.

whole army without delay, and accordingly all arrears, with one month's pay in addition as a present, were issued to all the troops with such celerity that the entire 100,000 men were paid off in the course of about four hours. A general advance and attack along the whole line was ordered to commence at four o'clock the next morning. This was done, but the Sikhs had not advanced above 1000 yards when the words "Fled! Fled!" were loudly vociferated by the whole army, proclaiming that the bird had flown. In fact, Dost Muhammad, with all his troops and Ghazis, had retreated during the night into the Khaibar, and when day broke not even a single tent or Afghan was to be seen.

The Sikh army was halted, and encamped on their advanced ground for two days, and Fakir Azizuddin returning from his mission on the evening of the second day, the camp was broken up on the third, and the whole army retired on Peshawar. After five or six days' rest Maharaja Ranjit Singh with his army marched back to Lahore, leaving Sirdar Hari Singh Nalwa as governor of Peshawar. By this one month's sparring, coquetting, and skirmishing with Dost Muhammad, Ranjit Singh gained his long-wished-for object, the undisputed occupation and mastership of the Peshawar valley. But still it could not be called a bloodless victory, for the Sikhs daily lost from 100 to 150, or even 200 men: the Afghan loss must have been much greater, the Sikh artillery being far more numerous than, and superior to, that of the Afghans.

The cavalry charges—in bodies of from 2000 to 5000 men on either side—were usually very serious and bloody affairs; and the Sikhs daily lost many lives at the merciless hands of the Ghazis, who, each with his little green Moslem flag, boldly pressed on, freely and fairly courting death and martyrdom. They only became shy of thus advancing when they had seen the bodies of dead Ghazis burnt in heaps; for in their wild fanatical simplicity they believed (as they do even now) that if their bodies are thus burnt, instead of going to heaven they inevitably go to the nether regions.

On recrossing the Indus at the fort of Attock the Sikhs unfortunately lost a full boat-load of regular infantry; and the rear and flanks of the Sikh army, both in going to and returning from Peshawar, were, as was always the case, harassed by the Ghakkars. This tribe inhabits the range of hills westward of Rawul Pindi, and claims to be of Persian descent. Their legends speak of a former great Ghakkar dynasty.[1] Parties of the Sikh army were also constantly attacked by the Afridi tribe, which inhabits the hills between Attock and Peshawar.

On reaching the Jhelum river the army was, to some extent, broken up, a large part of it being dispersed on various duties. A body of 5000 or 6000 men were sent to Bannu, as it was stated that the Waziris had collected in large numbers, and were about to unite with the Afridis of Kohat, and with the Khaibaris, for the purpose of attacking Hari Singh, and, if possible, of retaking Peshawar.

The three former Barakzai chiefs of Peshawar had gone to Kabul with their brother, Dost Muhammad; but a short time afterwards Maharaja Ranjit Singh sent for them, and honoured them and treated them well at Lahore, though I do not know how he induced them to go there. When I reached Gujrat a *sardar* or general named Amir or Mir Singh, with two strong battalions of infantry, 500 Sikh irregular cavalry,

[1] In the year 1205 the conqueror Muhammad Ghori was killed by the tribe of Ghakkars.

and my camp of artillery, was ordered to follow and join the force already sent to Bannu. We accordingly marched down the left bank of the Jhelum, crossed over at Khushab, and marched thence *viâ* Towana and the sandy desert road to Kalabagh, where we crossed the Indus. Thence we marched to Bannu by the Esau-khel road, and then joined the main body. We found the Bannuites usually quiet and amenable, willing peaceably to pay their annual tribute; but the hill Waziri tribes, particularly those of Kunigaram, gave us no rest day or night for the three or four months that we remained at Bannu. We received strict orders not to enter the hills, and therefore could not punish them as we desired; but the dread of our doing so, and our daily threatening to do so, prevented them from going towards either Kohat or Peshawar, as otherwise they might have done. Moreover, they soon heard that the Barakzai *sardars*, the former chiefs of Peshawar, had gone to Lahore and were well treated there; and this news kept them quiet for a time. So, receiving the annual tribute without further trouble, we all returned to Lahore.

After a short time I went with my camp to

Amritsar for the Dasahra festival, for which occasion the whole of Ranjit Singh's army was yearly collected in camp. It was about this time that the Prime Minister, Raja Dhyan Singh,[1] took me from Maharaja Ranjit Singh's service and placed me in full command of his own and his brothers' artillery, which was attached to the already organised Jammu contingent of 7000 to 8000 men.

The artillery portion of the contingent, now placed under my command, consisted of six nine-pounder and six six-pounder horse-artillery guns, four mortars, four howitzers, and two three-pounder mountain-guns, twenty-two pieces in all, besides some camel-guns, all well found and in good order. With this camp, and attached to the Jammu contingent, I marched with Ranjit Singh and his whole army about the early spring of 1837 from Lahore to Wazirabad, and thence down the left bank of the Chenab, *viâ* Ramnagar to Chiniote. So far, this march was supposed to have for its object the settling of some differences between Diwan Sawun Mull,

[1] Sir Herbert Edwardes states in his 'Life of Sir Henry Lawrence' that Gardner married a native wife, given him by Raja Dhyan Singh out of his own house.

governor of Multan, and Raja Gulab Singh, ruler of Jammu. However, we halted some time at Chiniote, where at first rumours, and afterwards authentic news, reached us that Sardar Muhammad Akbar Khan, Dost Muhammad's son, had come from Kabul with 20,000 to 25,000 Afghan troops, had passed through the Khaibar, and was now devastating the plains of Peshawar up to the very walls of the city; and that the Sikh governor, Sardar Hari Singh Nalwa, though undoubtedly an experienced and remarkably brave soldier of acknowledged skill, could make no head against him. Soon afterwards news arrived of Sardar Hari Singh's death, he having fallen bravely at the head of his Sikh troops under the sword of the Afghans.[1]

Ranjit Singh, now aroused to action, issued immediate and strict orders for the whole army to reach Peshawar as quickly as possible by forced marches, each commander choosing his own road. The Prime Minister, Raja Dhyan Singh, a remarkably brave and active man, reached the fort of Jamrud, near the Khaibar, with 10,000 to 12,000 irregular cavalry, on the morning of the seventh day from Chiniote; but

[1] Battle of Jamrud, April 30, 1837.

he unfortunately found that Muhammad Akbar Khan, hearing of the rapid and near approach of the whole Sikh army, after doing all the injury he could, had on the previous day fled back towards Kabul. On the morning of the ninth day Raja Gulab Singh,[1] at the head of his contingent, all intact, reached Khairabad, opposite and west of Attock; and during that day the bulk of the Sikh army arrived, and were crossing the river pell-mell and in no small confusion and uproar.

While Raja Gulab Singh with one contingent was passing westward through the Gidar Gali Pass about noon, he received written directions from his brother at Jamrud not to advance towards Peshawar, but to cross the Kabul river and enter and overawe both the upper and lower Yusufzai country,—these tribes, emboldened by Muhammad Akbar Khan's temporary success and firebrand raid, having become refractory and inclined to mischief. This order, though apparently simple to obey, really gave Raja Gulab Singh and our whole contingent plenty—nay, handfuls—of work night and day for six months: for the

[1] Brother of the Prime Minister, and subsequently Maharaja of Kashmir.

artillery it was a regular life in the saddle. During the Yusufzai campaign Mian Udam Singh,[1] Raja Gulab Singh's eldest son, almost daily achieved such prodigies of valour as to call forth the unstinted admiration and applause, and often the amazement, of the whole contingent. If Raja Suchet Singh,[2] his uncle, was too reckless, dashing, flashy, and fiery before the enemy, Udam Singh also was rash and impetuous to a dangerous degree.

Meanwhile trouble had arisen in Gulab Singh's own dominions. Raja Dhyan Singh had an orderly or servant of good family, belonging to one of the hill tribes south and south-west of Kashmir and Punch. This man, Shamas Khan by name, whom the Raja had treated with considerable kindness, spread a false report throughout the whole hill-country (while the brothers were busily engaged) that both Gulab Singh and Dhyan Singh had been killed in battle. The entire population of these hill regions were thus encouraged to rise in armed rebellion,

[1] It will be seen that this brave young soldier was killed with Maharaja Nao Nihal Singh on the 6th November 1840.

[2] Raja Suchet Singh was the third of the Jammu brothers, of whom Dhyan Singh and Gulab Singh have already been mentioned.

and by stratagem and treachery most of the hill forts about there were seized and the garrisons massacred.

This untoward news of course made Raja Gulab Singh anxious to return and regain his sovereignty, and the Yusufzai region being now settled and peaceful, the Raja with his contingent crossed in the autumn to the left bank of the Indus at Bazar-ki-Patan, some miles above Attock, and marched thence direct to Kahati, near the Jhelum, north-west of Rawul Pindi. Leaving his artillery here, Raja Gulab Singh with the remainder of the contingent entered the hills, while another body of troops moved up quickly from Jammu. After some desultory warfare the rebellion was crushed and subdued in about three months, when the whole contingent again returned to Lahore. I had not been long there when news arrived that the Sikh force in Bannu had been obliged to retire across the Indus, and had suffered great loss. On this Raja Suchet Singh with Prince Nao Nihal Singh, son of Shahzada Kharak Singh, with a large Sikh force and the Jammu contingent, were ordered to proceed to Bannu without delay.

Our contingent, under Raja Suchet Singh, reached

Kalabagh by forced marches, and thence went on to Bannu carefully,—the Sikh force under their prince[1] joining us a day or two after. For two months or more we had severe fighting with some thousands of Waziris and Bannuites united. However, we levelled and burnt all the refractory Bannu fort-villages, and beat the Waziris back into their hills, and even well punished and dispersed them. This done, we marched by the Paizu[2] Pass to Tank, to punish the Nawab of that principality—he being the cause and instigator of all the late troubles in this quarter; but previous to our arrival he had fled to one of his strongholds some twenty or twenty-five miles within the Waziri hills. Thither our contingent, with Suchet Singh at its head, quickly followed him. Our way led through ravines, and up along the bed of the Tank river, until we reached a considerable plain, in the centre of which stood the fort of Sarwarghur. However, we found that the Nawab had fled on to Ghuzni or Kabul the day before our arrival. We therefore quickly retraced our steps to Tank, and there annexed the whole of the principality; but we certainly had

[1] Nao Nihal Singh. [2] Now called "Shaikh Budin."

considerable hard work and some severe fighting, both going to and returning from Sarwarghur. The Waziris crowned the heights on each side of us, and disputed every inch of the road.

The object for which we had been sent being, as far as practicable, effected, the whole force marched back to Lahore.

CHAPTER XI.

"THE LION OF THE PANJAB."

EARLY DAYS OF THE SIKH ARMY—RANJIT SINGH'S GURKHAS—THE MAHARAJA AND HIS PADDLE-BOAT — GULAB SINGH AND THE TREACHEROUS MERCHANT—THE JOCOSE *CHAUDRI*—A CAMEL-LOAD OF FLATTERY—CHARACTER OF GULAB SINGH.

In addition to the foregoing record of his campaigns in the service of Maharaja Ranjit Singh, which was written by Colonel Gardner himself, and has been left, as far as possible, unaltered, I have found various disconnected anecdotes concerning the great Maharaja and Gardner's later master, Maharaja Gulab Singh of Jammu and Kashmir, which may amuse and possibly instruct the reader. They also are given in Gardner's own words.

The following description of the early days of the Khalsa army is of undoubted interest, and presents a vivid picture of the homely and simple dealings of Ranjit Singh with his soldiers :—

In the early part of Ranjit Singh's career there was no such thing as money payments. The soldiers received patches of land, and were called *puttidars*. It was considered ignoble to take money payments: a ready-money soldier was held in contempt. It was in 1809, when Lord Metcalfe, then a young political officer from Delhi, was deputed to Amritsar, that Ranjit Singh first set his keen eye upon disciplined and regular soldiery. It so happened that a dash at Metcalfe's encampment was made by some of the redoubted Akalis.[1] The small escort of red-coated Purbias rallied round Metcalfe, and so astonished the Akalis by their unwonted appearance and bold front that they turned and fled. Ranjit Singh was not slow to learn the lesson taught, and he looked about to find any one who could teach drill. One Drounkal Singh appeared, who proved to the Maharaja that he knew the bayonet exercise, &c., and was immediately employed by the Maharaja to make a commencement with some twenty or thirty men. The old troops took umbrage, and resented the innovation: the idea of money payments, too, was abhorrent. Ranjit

[1] The Akalis were a fanatical band of Sikhs who corresponded to the Ghazis of Muhammadan nations.

Singh was not the man to be turned from his purpose. He used to favour the new men in every way—used to send for them in a morning, distribute food from his own table to them after their parades, with which he affected to be highly pleased, and administered *backshish* to each with his own hand. The sight of the money was too much for the remainder of the army, who now no longer held aloof from the new discipline and regular payment. Ranjit Singh attempted a further innovation in introducing the Sepoy cap instead of the turban: this the army would not stand, and mutinied. The wily Maharaja bided his time, and did not press the point. He had about 1200 Gurkhas in his camp. Turning to the Sikhs, he said he would not force the caps on those of his own faith and nation, especially considering the inconvenience which the long hair they were obliged to wear might cause them; but ordered them to surround the Gurkhas when they went for their pay, and secure a promise from them that they would wear the caps. At this time the camp of the Maharaja was pitched on the great plain of Govindgarh, outside Amritsar. The sturdy little Gurkhas got wind of the conspiracy, and went for their pay with loaded muskets. On receiving their pay they commenced returning, and met three battalions of Sikhs marching down upon them, with the intention of which they had been forewarned. They halted and said, "Let us pass, or we open fire,—we are armed and loaded: you would not wear the cap; no more will we." So far from the Sikhs carrying out the Maharaja's orders, they rushed up and embraced the Gurkhas, and a great fraternisation followed. Still Ranjit Singh, though obliged to overlook these acts, did not swerve from his purpose; and he managed to effect his end adroitly, by ordering the drill-instructor, Drounkal Singh, to wear the cap himself, and to enlist in future no recruit without previously taking agreement from him to wear it. This man, Drounkal Singh, afterwards became a colonel, and has descendants possessed of good property all over the country.

Great man though he undoubtedly was, it must be remembered that the Maharaja was quite uneducated. He looked upon his European officers as men of universal talents, and it was his regular habit to compel them to undertake duties in addition to those on which they were specially employed. Thus Avitabile and Ventura, originally engaged as military instructors, were appointed governors of provinces, but were still required to perform military duties; Harlan, though nearly always employed in civil duties, held in addition the command of troops; Honigberger, who was a doctor and nothing but a doctor, was compelled to superintend a gunpowder manufactory, and was pressed to accept a civil government.

The following anecdote, recorded by Colonel Gardner, tells of yet another profession that was once forced on General Ventura:—

Ranjit Singh's Paddle-boat.

Having heard of steamers, Ranjit Singh desired to have one; and believing that a foreigner could do anything, asked General Ventura if he was a good blacksmith, and desired him, without waiting for a reply, to make him a steamer at once. The General protested, but it was as much as his position was worth. Ranjit said he was a fool, and General Ventura promised to make one, and boldly asked for 40,000 rupees. He came to me and begged my aid. I read up all I could about paddle-boat building, and succeeded in turning out a wondrous sort of two-decked barge with paddle-wheels to be worked by hand. I may mention that when the 40,000 rupees were sent by the hands of the *bais* (the personal attendants of Ranjit), they demanded 15,000 rupees out of it. We knew it was better not to murmur but to give it, as people of that sort were not to be offended. Ranjit Singh clapped his hands, as was his wont, in ecstasy with the boat, in the sides of the lower decks of which I had made port - holes which bristled with swivel-guns. This boat was launched on the Ravi, but with the utmost efforts of the exhausted wheel-turners would not go more than 10 yards or so up the stream. However, Ranjit Singh was delighted. I had built fore and aft cabins, and he filled them with nautch-girls, and there was a great *tamasha*. He sent us 20,000 rupees in addition, of which the *bais* took 5000: the cost of the boat could not have been more than 2000. This was the first and only steamer built for the Sikh monarchy. Ranjit Singh was quite satisfied with the fact of the boat moving up the stream, however slowly, without sails or oars: he had equalled the achievements of the West in science, and that was all he desired. The picnic was not unaccompanied by strong drinks, and I received at the end of the celebration a further present of a shawl and 3000 rupees.

Maharaja Gulab Singh.

Scarcely less interesting a figure than the great Maharaja himself was Maharaja Gulab Singh of Kashmir, into whose service Gardner finally passed after the death of Ranjit Singh. The following anecdote shows Gulab Singh in one of his more gentle moments, for, as is told in another place, he could be very terrible to his subjects when it seemed fit to him to strike terror into their hearts. "The utmost reverence and submission," says Gardner, "attended the invocation of his name."

"A travelling merchant had been robbed by three thieves, who had just completed their act of spoliation when their victim in despair uttered the cry, 'Dooai Maharaj!' (Succour, oh king!) Immediately on hearing these words the thieves reflected, and decided to restore all their booty. In doing so they stipulated that the merchant in return should never reveal the circumstance, and this he promised. Proceeding on his journey, he disposed of his property in the various markets, and, faithless to his word, went straight to the Maharaja Gulab Singh and complained of having been robbed. As is usual in these dominions, a hue and cry was sent all over the country, and, as is almost invariably the result, the thieves were captured and brought before Gulab Singh. They admitted the robbery, but on being asked by his Highness if they had anything to plead in extenuation of the crime, they recounted the facts, —how at the mere sound of the invocation to the Maharaja's name they had returned the booty, stipulating only for silence. On hearing this the Maharaja, who had taken the precaution of securing from the mouth of the complainant the list of property stolen, sent to the bazaars where the robbers declared the goods had been sold. They were produced; the perfidy of the merchant was proved; he was sentenced to lose his property, which was handed over to the robbers, who were pardoned. The purchase - money was restored to the buyers, and the merchant was thrown into prison for nine months.

"I was seated in durbar when this occurred.

"Gulab Singh used to enjoy a little opium occasionally, and his tongue never failed to become amusingly unloosened afterwards. Often when *nazars* were presented he used jokingly to return them. One day the *chaudri* of a very turbulent neighbourhood, called Deva Buttala, below Bhimbur, presented a rupee, which Gulab Singh returned with polite jocularity. Many a time had the incorrigible Deva Buttalaites received chastisement for their bold depredations. In such repute, indeed, was their character held, that recruits from this part were more in request than almost any other in the Panjab. The *chaudri* asked, in reply to repeated inquiries from Gulab Singh as to not only his own immediate personal welfare, but that of every one of his relations (and this with great affected interest), whether he might detail the exact truth. 'Go on,' says the Raja. 'Well,' rejoined he, 'there is no period of my mind when I suffered less anxiety, and was so completely at my ease!' 'How so?' cries Gulab Singh. 'Why,' said the *chaudri*, 'I can now keep open house, for I have nothing in it to steal. Formerly I had the trouble of locking the door upon my cooking utensils, but I am spared all trouble now about thieves. For which I thank God,' said the *chaudri*, pretending gratitude to the Disposer of events. Gulab Singh was highly amused at the man's readiness, and gave him a quantity of brass cooking-pots, and 20 rupees, cautioning him to lock his door again.

"In those days a patriarchal simplicity obtained. With the advance of European ideas (call it civilisation if you will) a greater distance came to be observed between the sovereign and his subjects; and the respectful familiarity on one side, and jocular condescension on the other, are not to be found except in remote tracts.

"Gulab Singh had a knack of flattering and saying something personally pleasing to all who appeared at his durbars. One day he loaded a *chaudri* with the most fulsome compliments, till at last the elated recipient, affecting a look of artlessness, asked permission to say one word ('urz kurna'). 'By all means,' says the Raja. 'Unfortunately, sire, I forgot to bring my camels, horses, and mules here to carry away such a load of praises, and fortunately, too, as they must have sunk under the pleasing burden. Instead, have the kindness to give me something personally substantial, which, although really inferior in value to your Highness's approbation, I could yet take away in my hand,' and he held it out. Gulab Singh and the whole durbar were delighted at the humour of the man; 50 rupees were at once sent for, and a dress of honour, which the man carried off, and he was called always afterwards, 'the untwalla chaudri' (the camel-*chaudri*).

"Gulab Singh used to go round and visit peasants' houses personally, and, often incognito, ask about their crops, pat their children, and make himself pleasant in a thousand ways, not forgetting to leave substantial tokens of his visit."

Character of Gulab Singh.

The following study of Maharaja Gulab Singh, written by Gardner, and included by Colonel Carmichael Smyth in his 'History of the Reigning Family of Lahore,' is worthy of perusal. It presents an interesting picture of that very remarkable statesman, missing only one trait—the intense pride taken by Gulab Singh in his very dubious descent from the ancient reigning family of Jammu,—a pride which, in the opinion of that shrewd observer Sir Herbert Edwardes, was even more powerful than the avarice which seemed to most people Gulab Singh's guiding impulse:—

"The character of Gulab Singh in the early

days of his power was one of the most repulsive it is possible to imagine.[1] Ambitious, avaricious, and cruel by nature, he reduced the exercise of his cruelty to a system for the promotion of the objects which his ambition and avarice led him to seek. He exercised the most ruthless barbarities, not in the heat of conflict or the flush of victory only, nor in the rage of an offended sovereign against rebellious subjects: he deliberately committed the most horrible atrocities for the purpose of investing his name with a terror that should keep down all thoughts of resistance to his sway.

"To turn to smaller traits; he is an eater of opium, he tells long stories, offers little, promises less, but keeps his word; has a good memory, and is free and humorous with even the lowest and poorest class of his subjects. The partaker and companion of their toils and labours, seeming to be their diligent and careful instructor and father, their intimate village brother, their free, jocose, humorous neighbour, their constant

[1] It is a most remarkable circumstance that, in spite of the publication of Colonel Gardner's extremely candid account of Maharaja Gulab Singh's character and career, the latter apparently felt no ill-will towards Gardner, but retained him permanently in his service.

visitor; yet, with all this, in reality a very leech, sucking their life's blood, the shameless trader of their sons and daughters; the would-be great merchant of the East, the very jack-of-all-trades, the usurer, the turn-penny, the briber, and the bribed. With all this he must be accounted the very best of soldiers, and, for an Asiatic and an uneducated man, he is an able, active, bold, and energetic, yet wise and prudent commander. He is anything but strong-headed and hot-blooded; prudently making slow, resolute, and judicious movements, thinking more of his resources, reserves, &c., than is the wont of Orientals. Looking more to the future and its wants and requisites than to the present or the past, slowly he proceeds, feeling his way as he advances, quick in taking advantages, relying much on his subtle political talent, and looking on arms as his last resource. In the field of battle he is self-composed, prudent, and watchful to the last degree; but at the breach, storm, or charge, he freely, though reluctantly, expends his men, while himself just the man to be at their head if required. Generally, however, he is the cool and able commander in the rear."

CHAPTER XII.

INTRIGUE AND ANARCHY.

DEATH OF RANJIT SINGH — AMBITIOUS PROJECT OF THE DOGRA BROTHERS — MAHARAJA KHARRAK SINGH — MURDER OF SARDAR CHET SINGH — DEPOSITION AND DEATH OF KHARRAK SINGH — THE VENGEANCE OF HEAVEN — DEATH OF NAO NIHAL SINGH.

MAHARAJA RANJIT SINGH died on the 27th June 1839, and, in the words of Sir Lepel Griffin, the six years which followed were a period of storm and anarchy, in which assassination was the rule and the weak were ruthlessly trampled under foot. The kingdom founded in violence, treachery, and blood did not long survive its founder. Created by the military and administrative genius of one man, it crumbled into powder when the spirit which gave it life was withdrawn. The death of Ranjit Singh was, in fact, followed by a rapid succession of crimes and tragedies such as have rarely been paralleled in history, save in the darkest period of the downfall of Rome, or in the early days of the French Revolution.

Colonel Gardner thus tells the tale:—

In the old age of the Maharaja there was a person whom he especially took into favour, and whom he loved like a son from his birth. This was Hira Singh, the son of Raja Dhyan Singh. Ranjit Singh could hardly bear the boy to be out of his sight, and he from infancy was sedulously taught to call the monarch *taba* (papa). As Hira Singh approached manhood the army also yielded its affection to the Maharaja's favourite, and so it came about that this senile love of the old Maharaja, aided by the inclination of the powerful army, suggested a dream of greatness to his uncles the Dogra brothers, and led to the successive deeds of violence by which it seemed to them that their ambitious design might be gratified. This dream was that Hira Singh, the heir of their family, or at least the most promising of its rising generation, might eventually succeed to the throne of Ranjit Singh. Those to be swept away were the male members of the Maharaja's family, and all those ministers, advisers, and chiefs who would not join the Dogra party.

A glance at the table (Appendix) will show that in the course of a very few years this programme was carried out in all its essential features; and I will now relate how it was that all these murders were brought about directly or indirectly by the Dogra brothers, Dhyan Singh and Gulab Singh, for the eventual aggrandisement of their family in the person of Hira Singh. The two brothers played the awful game with deliberate and unswerving pertinacity, and the narrative will explain how their schemes were carried out, and how Dhyan Singh and Hira Singh were themselves overwhelmed in the torrent of blood which they had caused to flow. When Ranjit Singh's death opened to them the field of action, the veil of futurity hid these events from their eyes: their only thought was that the way to the throne had to be cleared of all obstacles, and at the same time an outward show of fealty to the Khalsa, and of loyalty to the sovereign line of succession, had to be maintained. The slightest suspicion might have been fatal, yet prompt action seemed to be the least dangerous course, and the first blow fell quickly.

. . . .

Ranjit Singh when on his deathbed summoned to him his only legitimate son, Shahzada Kharrak Singh, and proclaimed him his heir, with Raja Dhyan Singh as Minister. Now Kharrak Singh was a blockhead, and a slave to opium: at the time of his accession to the throne of Lahore he passed his whole time in a state of stupefaction. His chief adviser was a *sardar* named Chet Singh, and this man had the courage to set himself forward as a rival to the all-powerful Dhyan Singh, and was also so rash as to make known his intention of having the Minister assassinated. Matters came to a climax in October 1839, but little more than three months after Ranjit Singh's death; and being, as I was, the commandant of Raja Dhyan Singh's artillery, and high in his confidence, I was closely connected with the events which I am about to describe.

It must be remembered that Dhyan Singh and his brothers had been created Rajas by Ranjit Singh, and that in the latter years of his reign they had become nearly independent, gratitude and the additional power that Dhyan Singh's office of *wazir* conferred upon them being the links that bound them to the service of their old master and benefactor. After his death they became entirely independent, and maintained a large force of troops of their own race (Dogras).[1] Sardar Chet Singh, the chief adviser of the new Maharaja, endeavoured to obtain the support of General Ventura and the other foreign officers, and was aided by the ill-feeling which had long existed between Ventura and the Minister. By the 8th October things had reached such a pitch that the murder of the whole Dogra family had been decided on, and Chet Singh was rash enough to say in durbar to Dhyan Singh, "See what will become of you in twenty-four hours."

Raja Dhyan Singh, who was a man of inflexible resolution and imperturbable serenity of demeanour, smiled politely and replied, "Your humble servant, sir; we *shall* see." He had for some time past prepared the way for his intended action by spreading rumours that Chet Singh was a traitor, and in the pay of the British Government. As such rumours gain

[1] "The Dogras are a branch of the Aryan invaders of India who settled in the hill country between the Panjab and the Himalayas.

"They are divided into castes, and the Dogra Rajputs (who rank next to the Brahmans) rose to power with the brothers Dhyan Singh and Gulab Singh, and are a ruling and fighting caste.

"Jammu is about the centre, as it is the capital of the country of the Dogras."—Drew's 'Northern Barrier of India.'

credence in proportion as they are detailed and minute, he noised it abroad that Chet Singh had engaged to place the Panjab under the protection of the British, to pay 6 annas in every rupee of revenue to them, to disband the Khalsa army, and to turn all the *sardars* out of their command.

The time to move had now arrived, and he betook himself as soon as the durbar was over to the zenana of Kharrak Singh (to which he had the right of admission by favour of the late Maharaja), and secured an interview with the Maharani, the mother of Prince Nao Nihal Singh. This lady was well aware of the weakness of her husband, and Dhyan Singh easily persuaded her that the success of Chet Singh would result in the entire supremacy of that *sardar* and the foreign officers, and the reduction of the royal family to a cipher. Prince Nao Nihal Singh was at this time a spirited, ambitious youth of eighteen years of age, the only descendant of Ranjit Singh who showed character and ability. His wife was summoned to the secret conclave in the zenana, and subsequently the prince himself was called in. It was agreed that none could be more devoted to the family of Ranjit Singh than the Dogra brothers, and that the only obstacle to general tranquillity was the traitor Chet Singh. The arrangements decided on were the death of the latter, the retirement of Kharrak Singh from active public life, for which neither his inclinations nor his mental endowments fitted him, and the regency of his son, Nao Nihal Singh. The prince fully and cheerfully agreed to a programme which was to lead to his aggrandisement.

The next step was to ascertain the feelings of the Sikh *sardars* of the French brigade. Dhyan Singh found them entirely with him, and secured a promise of their co-operation. Lastly, the concert of the powerful Sindhanwalia family was necessary. Chet Singh, prompted by General Ventura, had already sought alliance with them, assuring them that the Dogra family were in correspondence with the British with a view to the disinheritance of Ranjit Singh's descendants and their own elevation to power. Raja Dhyan Singh's policy—viz., placing Nao Nihal Singh on the throne—was sufficient answer to any doubts the Sindhanwalias might have felt as to the loyalty of the Dogra family, and their aid was at once promised.

Finally, Dhyan Singh gave instructions to the army, which was now completely at his orders, to remain perfectly quiet all night. I received orders that loaded guns were to be placed at nightfall at all the gates of the palace, and that whatever occurred, whatever thunders there might be at the gates, every one was to feign sleep. Raja Dhyan Singh asked me if I would like to accompany him, and of course I accepted the invitation. The party consisted of about fifteen: the three Raja brothers — Gulab Singh, Dhyan Singh, and Suchet Singh—in addition to Prince Nao Nihal Singh; then came the heads of the Sindhanwalia family, then two trusty noblemen called Rao Lal Singh and Rao Keshur Singh, and myself. The ladies of the zenana had promised to leave us free entrance to the building where the Maharaja and his Minister slept.

It was near midnight when we entered the palace, and no sooner had we left the gate through which we had been admitted than a voice accosted us, "Who is it?" Dhyan Singh replied, "The Maharaja goes to-morrow to bathe at Amritsar, and we are to make the necessary preparations." This was the concerted answer. We reached another and inner gate, which noiselessly opened on a whispered order from Dhyan Singh. Without uttering a whisper, we stealthily crept our way in the dark up a flight of stairs, over a place called the Badshah-i-Takht, and thence to the immediate vicinity of the royal apartment. Here Gulab Singh and Dhyan Singh held a whispered consultation, the purport of which I could not catch. At this moment a man started up, and seeing us, called out and tried to run off. Suchet Singh shot him dead, and was himself instantly almost knocked down by a tremendous cuff on the ear dealt him by his brother, Gulab Singh, who cursed him under his breath for his imprudence. On looking over a parapet we saw two companies of the Maharaja's guard. Dhyan Singh quickly went down the staircase to the place where they were stationed, and was accosted by the subadar in command, who said, "Why did you fire?" I had followed Dhyan Singh, and stood immediately behind him. He simply showed his right hand (on which he had two thumbs) and put his finger to his lips. On seeing the well-known peculiarity the subadar whispered, "Lie down," and the whole of the two companies noiselessly lay down at full length and pretended sleep. The subadar then pointed with a mute gesture to the room of the doomed man, the door of which had been left ajar. There was a light in the room. Dhyan Singh approached and entered it, followed by the whole party. Lo! there sat Maharaja Kharrak Singh on his bed washing his teeth. The adjoining bed, which belonged to Chet Singh, was empty. When asked where his Minister was, Kharrak Singh simply replied that he had gone out on hearing a shot fired.

Perceiving a fierce sort of half smile light up the faces of the Dogra brothers, he begged that Chet Singh's life might be spared, and would have proved very restive had not his own son and some four or five Sikhs held him down while we proceeded in search of the fugitive. Two torches had to be lit, and on entering the room where we expected to find the Minister it appeared to be empty: it was very long and narrow. Lal Singh, however, called out that he saw the glitter of a sword in one corner, and there cowered the wretched man, his hand upon his sword. We were armed only with daggers. The eyes of Dhyan Singh seemed to shoot fire as his gaze alighted and fixed itself on his deadly foe. Gulab Singh was for interposing to do the deed of blood himself, fearing for his brother (who was a short man) in the desperate defence he counted on; but Dhyan Singh roughly shook him off, and, dagger in hand, slowly advancing towards his enemy, said, "The twenty-four hours you were courteous enough to mention to me have not yet elapsed." Then with the spring of a tiger the successful counter-plotter dashed at his enemy and plunged his dagger into his heart, crying out, "Take this in memory of Ranjit Singh." Dhyan Singh then turned round to his party, his face radiant with gratified purpose, and courteously thanked us for our aid.

We then, in token that this was entirely a State proceeding, prostrated ourselves at the feet of Maharaja Kharrak Singh, and subsequently at the feet of his son, Nao Nihal Singh. The latter had been most actively and fully occupied in trying to pacify his father, whose rage was uncontrollable. It was only by the intercessions, prayers, and explanations of the Maharani and the other ladies of the zenana, added to those of his son, that he could be brought to understand the political necessity of the doom that had been meted out. The night's work done, we all returned quietly to our camps. A general sensation of relief was felt on all hands at the death of Chet Singh: not the slightest animosity was awakened by it, and the opinion was openly breathed by all, "Now all will go straight."

Chet Singh having been dealt with, the Dogra brothers turned their attention to Maharaja Kharrak Singh, and experienced no difficulty in removing him from their path, aided as they were by the ambition of his son, Prince Nao Nihal Singh. Immediately after the death of Sardar Chet Singh, Kharrak Singh was deposed. His actual reign had been limited to a few months, and he was not long permitted to survive its termination. It is stated that the deposed Maharaja lingered for some nine months after his deposition, during which period he was gradually poisoned by his physicians, with the connivance of his son and successor. Kharrak Singh cherished the greatest affection for this unnatural son, and in the agony of death called for Nao Nihal Singh in order to pardon him: the young prince, however, visited his father once only during his long illness, and that on the day before his death, and even then treated him with the greatest brutality and insolence. The next day, November 5, 1840, Kharrak

Singh breathed his last at the early age of thirty-eight.

The vengeance of Heaven soon fell on Maharaja Nao Nihal Singh. On the day following Kharrak Singh's death his body was burnt in accordance with the Sikh custom, and two of his Ranis and eleven of his slave-girls were burnt with him. The new Maharaja stood for a time by the blazing pile, which had been erected in the open space opposite the mausoleum of Ranjit Singh; but, either ill or impatient, he would not remain as etiquette demanded until his father's body had been consumed by the flames, but went to a bathing-place about 120 yards away to perform the ceremony of ablution. He was attended by the whole Court, and five elephants were in waiting; but as it would have been considered irreverent for him to ride past the funeral-pile on his return, the elephants were sent back to wait at a little distance. I was present at the commencement of the ceremony of cremation of Maharaja Kharrak Singh, and when the torch was applied was standing close by in attendance on Raja Dhyan Singh. Before the new Maharaja left the spot I was directed by Dhyan Singh to go and bring forty of my artillerymen in their fatigue dress: I was not told, nor have I ever ascertained, what they were wanted for. When I returned, the catastrophe had just occurred.

Maharaja Nao Nihal Singh had passed through an archway on his return from bathing, and just before entering it he took the hand of his constant companion Udam Singh, the eldest son of Raja Guláb Singh: the two young men entered the archway together. As they emerged from it a crash was heard; beams, stones, and tiles fell from above, and the Maharaja and Udam Singh were struck to the ground. The latter was killed on the spot, and Naó Nihal Singh was struck to the earth. He was injured in the head, but presently attempted to rise, and cried out for water. The Prime Minister rushed up, and, it is said, pushed aside the dead body of his own nephew, reserving all his devotion and care for the young king. Nao Nihal Singh was carried into the palace, the doors were closed, and admission denied to all. Several of the principal *sardars* begged to see the Maharaja, among them the Sindhanwalias, relations of the royal family: in vain did Nao Nihal Singh's mother, in a paroxysm of rage and anxiety, come and beat the fort gates with her own hands—admittance even to the fort there was none, still less into the Maharaja's apartment. None of the female inmates, not even his wives, were suffered to see him.

The palki-bearers who had carried Nao Nihal Singh to his palace were sent to their homes; they were servants in my own camp of artillery, and were five in number. Two were afterwards privately put to death, two escaped into Hindustan, the fate of the fifth is unknown to me. One of the palki-bearers afterwards affirmed that when the prince was put into the palki, and when he was assisting to put him there, he saw that above the right ear there was a wound which bled so slightly as only to cause a blotch of blood about the size of a rupee on the pillow or cloth on which Nao Nihal Singh's head rested while in the palki. Now it is a curious fact that when the room was opened, in which his corpse was first exposed by Dhyan Singh, blood in great quantities, both in fluid and coagulated pools, was found around the head of the cloth on which the body lay. Be this as it may, when the doors were thrown open the Sindhanwalias found the young Maharaja dead, Dhyan Singh prostrate in affliction on the ground, and Fakir Nuruddin, the royal physician, lamenting that all remedies had been useless.[1]

Thus perished Maharaja Nao Nihal Singh on the day following the death of his father.

[1] It was at the time commonly believed that the death of Nao Nihal Singh was brought about by the Dogra brothers, but it is at least equally probable that it really resulted from an accident. Syad Muhammad Latif, the author of 'The History of the Panjab,' points out very sensibly that had the fall of the parapet been foreseen, some other companion than Udam Singh would have been chosen for the doomed prince. Dhyan Singh himself also appears to have narrowly escaped being crushed, his arm being severely contused. This certainly points to an accident.

CHAPTER XIII.

THE DEFENCE OF LAHORE.

THE RIVAL CLAIMANTS—SHER SINGH PROPITIATES THE ARMY—DEFENCE OF THE FORTRESS — GARDNER'S DEFENCE OF THE GATEWAY—TERMS OF PEACE—MURDER OF THE MAHARANI AND ACCESSION OF THE MAHARAJA SHER SINGH.

WITH Nao Nihal Singh expired the legitimate line of Ranjit Singh. All that remained to thwart the ambition of the Dogra brothers were Sher Singh and the other princes whom Ranjit Singh had from time to time, for reasons of his own, chosen to acknowledge.

Sher Singh, the eldest of the princes, was very popular with the army, and would in ordinary course have now succeeded to the throne; but to further their deep-laid plot, the Dogra family set up a rival claimant in the person of Maharani Chand Kour. This lady was the widow of Kharrak Singh and mother of Nao Nihal Singh, and she based her claim to the throne on the assertion that a widow of Nao Nihal Singh would in due time give birth to an heir. Chand Kour claimed the regency of the kingdom pending the birth of her grandchild, and her pretensions were by no means without the support of precedent among the Sikhs. Still further to complicate matters, and with the intention of eventually destroying both claimants, the Dogra family now pretended to be divided among themselves. Raja Gulab Singh and his nephew Hira Singh espoused the cause of the queen, while Raja Dhyan Singh declared for the party of Sher Singh, who assumed the title of Maharaja.

Sher Singh remained for a time at his estate of Batala, but by the end of the year considered himself strong enough to assert his claim, and marched on Lahore at the head of a small body of troops. This took place early in the month of January 1841, and on the approach of Sher Singh, Chand Kour, Gulab Singh, and Hira Singh threw themselves into the fortress of Lahore. The Dogra troops of Gulab Singh were on this occasion all placed under my immediate orders, but in the event of a battle it was arranged that Gulab Singh himself should take supreme command, while I should devote myself to my especial charge, the artillery. Until the actual fighting commenced Gulab Singh could better aid our side by giving his full attention to diplomacy. I must mention that Dhyan Singh did not accompany Sher Singh to Lahore, but withdrew for a time to Jammu, the capital of the Dogra dominions.

On approaching Lahore Maharaja Sher Singh summoned the whole Khalsa army to join him, and in his proclamation made use of a traditional Panjabi expression, which may be translated "five brothers." The meaning of this term was that every soldier was to take four relations with him on the campaign, to share in the pillage that would ensue. Such was the ancient custom of the Khalsa army, and the magnitude of the assembly on this occasion may be imagined: to the very horizon the plains and the hills were one blaze of camp-fires. To strengthen his influence with the army Sher Singh made great concessions to them, giving them leave to execute lynch-law, and do all that they thought fit for their private enemies. To this flagrant weakness may be attributed the mutinies and violence which occurred during Sher Singh's reign, and particularly the atrocities inflicted on the detested pay officials.

I should mention that previous to our throwing ourselves into the fort of Lahore, Gulab Singh's Dogra troops, under my command, were encamped at Shadera, across the Ravi. We had been casting guns in the garden there, and those guns which were unfinished I buried before moving into Lahore. They were not discovered. The situation was critical. At the utmost our force did not exceed 3000 men, and against us were probably not less than 150,000 men, with 200 pieces of artillery, encamped on the plain of Mian Mir.

The revolution had awoke the country, and was about to sift the husks from the wheat—separate the good and bad; and the whole Manjha[1] was astir. Gulab Singh knew well that the troops had been bought over, but adhered bravely to his determination to defend the Maharani to the last. Being of an acquisitive turn of mind, no doubt the fact that the "Koh-i-nur" and the whole of the State treasury were in the fort had due weight with him. The army and the population, which

[1] "The Manjha" was, strictly speaking, the country in the neighbourhood of the cities of Lahore and Amritsar; but the term had a wider significance, and was used to distinguish the Sikhs who lived north of the Sutlej from the "Malwa" Sikhs, who lived south of that river. The Malwa Sikhs preserved themselves from coming under the sway of Ranjit Singh by placing themselves under British protection.

flocked in hundreds of thousands, were eager for plunder. The first thing to be done was to see whether the Sikh *sardars* were with us. All swore heartily to be faithful; and Tej Singh was the most fervent in his protestations of loyalty. Now the city guard was composed of portions of the regular army; Dogras only held the fort. A largesse of two lakhs of rupees was distributed among the city guard in order to secure their fidelity. Every preparation for the crisis was made that ingenuity could devise, and for two days we were hard at work, but still there came no move on the part of Sher Singh. At last on January 13th one of the most tremendous roars that ever rose from a concourse of human beings drowned our voices, distant as it was, and warned us that the man had arrived. Sher Singh had indeed come, and planted his flag and pitched his camp on the high mound called "Budha ka awa." The whole of his troops then thundered a salute, which continued for two hours, amid shouts of "Sher Singh Badshah! Dhyan Singh Wazir! death to Chand Kour and the Dogras!" We were shut up in the fort, and two days elapsed amid the most portentous buzz of voices from the moat outside, while Sher Singh made preparations for attack. My women and all the others, excepting the queen, had been hidden previously in disguise in various parts of the city. Another deafening salute, which lasted for more than an hour, announced to us that Sher Singh had been enthroned by the army, and that obeisance was being made by the commanding officers. The poor queen was so sick with terror at the uproar made, no doubt to overawe us, that she caused another lakh of rupees to be given hurriedly to the doubtful city troops of the regular army, who held the gates of the city. With the hour, as, I must say, is ever the case in critical periods, came the man; and nothing could surpass the calmness, the forethought, the activity, and the mental resource of Gulab Singh, or his sedulous consideration for the terrified queen. His determination never failed him. He had a knack of seizing occasion for action with such rapidity of vision, combined with such immutability of purpose, that those of his actions that appeared most questionable were justified by the bright results by which they were always attended. Every *sardar* solemnly swore fealty again on the Granth.[1] We had blocked the archways

[1] The sacred book of the Sikhs.

leading to two gates of the fort with carts and waggons, and had planted two guns loaded to the muzzle with grape at each of the upper forts, Dogra soldiers lining the parapets of the walls above. The night after Sher Singh's investment passed in comparative silence, which to us was as full of portent as the former noise. Resistance, indeed, seemed useless in the teeth of such odds. As the morning dawned the whole army arose and surrounded the city. Every gate was immediately opened to them by the soldiers, who, having pocketed three lakhs from the queen, had made an equally profitable bargain with Sher Singh. Destruction stared us in the face: we had red-hot cannon-balls ready to blow ourselves and the whole city into the air, if the worst came to the worst. Two heavy siege-trains of forty guns each were laid against the fort, while no less than eighty horse-artillery pieces were drawn up on the broad road immediately in front of us on the city side, which position they were peaceably allowed to take up by the treacherous troops.

The tops of the minarets of the Badshahi mosque swarmed with marksmen, who fired direct into the interior of the fort. General Sultan

Muhammad and Imam Shah commanded respectively the right and left wings of the army. As with the city troops, so with the *sardars*, especially the important Sindhanwalias, all forsook us. The treachery of Tej Singh was so conspicuously and pointedly base, he having prayed us to leave the gates of the upper fort open for the *sardars*, that we all swore to a man to kill him if fate put him in our way. The gates of the outer wall leading into the Hazuri Bagh having been opened, Sher Singh entered in person and took shelter in a *tykhana*.[1] Gulab Singh was now summoned to surrender. Every moment we expected to see the spark of a port-fire and to hear the crash of the cannonade. Gulab Singh's keen eyes peered anxiously through the openings: still there was no noise, and not a musket fired. I then sidled down the archway to look through the chink of the Hazuri Bagh gate, which I had blocked up with carts, and saw fourteen guns deliberately loaded, planted within 20 yards, and aimed straight at the gate.

The Dogras on the walls began to look over, and were jeered at by Sher Singh's troops. The little fort was surrounded by a sea of human

[1] Underground room.

heads. Gulab Singh made contemptuous replies, and roared out to Sher Singh, demanding that he should surrender. There was a brief but breathless pause, and I had not time to warn my artillerymen to clear out of the way when down came the gates over our party, torn to shreds by the simultaneous discharge of all the fourteen guns. Seventeen of my party were blown to pieces, parts of the bodies flying over me. When I had wiped the blood and brains from my face, and could recover a moment, I saw only one little trembling *Klasi*. I hurriedly asked him for a port-fire, having lost mine in the fall of the ruins. He had just time to hand it me, and I had crept under my two guns, when with a wild yell some 300 Akalis[1] swept up the Hazuri Bagh and crowded into the gate. They were packed as close as fish, and could hardly move over the heaps of wood and stone, the rubbish and the carts, with which the gateway was blocked. Just at that moment, when the crowd were rushing on us, their swords high in the air, I managed to fire the ten guns, and literally blew them into the air. In the pause which followed I loaded

[1] "Akalis," literally "Immortals," the fanatical Sikhs, corresponding to "Ghazis."

the guns with the aid of the three of my artillerymen who survived, and our next discharge swept away the hostile artillerymen who were at the fourteen guns outside, who had remained standing perfectly paralysed by the destruction of the Akalis. Then Sher Singh fled, and grievous carnage commenced. The Dogras, always excellent marksmen, seemed that day not to miss a man from the walls. The whole of the artillerymen round the field-pieces in front of us strewed the ground. In the Hazuri Bagh we counted the bodies of no less than 2800 soldiers, 200 artillerymen, and 180 horses. And now the whole park of artillery opened upon us that day, and for the three days following, tearing the walls of the fort to rags. They mounted their heavy guns on high houses, the walls of which they pierced to command the fort. Many a time did Sher Singh attempt a parley; but Gulab Singh knew his countrymen too well to believe any protestations. He said, "Wait until Dhyan Singh comes." At last that noble Minister did arrive, furious, as it seemed, with Sher Singh for his rashness; and after protracted delay, the firing on both sides was finally subdued. Our bombardment was over, and the brothers arranged terms of peace. Our little force was to quit the fort with honour, and betake itself to the old encampment on the other side of the river. It was decided that while Chand Kour should be recognised as titular head of the State, and as such should receive a personal allowance of twenty lakhs of rupees per annum, the posture of public affairs and the temper of the army were such that a man was required as king. Sher Singh was therefore chosen Badshah, and Raja Dhyan Singh kept his original place as Wazir and War Minister.

Dhyan Singh then arranged for an interview between his brother and the new monarch. During the siege we had been up to our knees in State jewels and gold mohurs; but as our lives were not worth a moment's purchase, no one had possessed himself of aught. Gulab Singh, however, had secured the "Koh-i-nur" about his person. (Chand Kour would have swallowed it if she had got hold of it.) And now came a masterpiece of acting on the part of Gulab Singh. He presented the "Koh-i-nur" with much *empressement* to the reigning sovereign, and took great credit for saving the royal property. In return he obtained a firman for twenty lakhs' worth of villages west of Bhimbur, and was recognised as guardian of the Maharani Chand Kour. He had not, however, lost the opportunity of securing about two millions of treasure in his honourable hands from the fort, which spoil was securely conveyed to Jammu.

Thus ended the memorable defence of the fortress of Lahore. The poor Maharani did not long survive, dying a miserable death by the hands of slave-girls, bribed by Sher Singh, who dropped a great flagstone on her head while she was lying in her bath. This brutal act incensed the Dogra brothers; but they were pacified by the reversion of the landed property of the murdered queen, which property is in the possession of their family to this day.

Thus on the 18th January 1841 Sher Singh became Maharaja indeed, and for the space of a year and a half nothing of great importance befell him. He was brought into close connection with the British, owing to the course of the Afghan war, and gave free passage to their troops through his dominions, thus carrying out the policy of Maharaja Ranjit Singh. His army, however, got more and more out of hand, and Sher Singh strove in vain to lay the spirit of insubordination which his unwise concessions had aroused. Murders of commandants and other officers constantly occurred, and the sound advice of Dhyan Singh was rejected by the infatuated Maharaja, who passed his time in drinking-bouts and every debauchery.

CHAPTER XIV.

"HORROR ON HORROR'S HEAD."

THE KABUL DISASTER—GARDNER ACCOMPANIES THE DOGRA TROOPS TO PESHAWAR — BRIGADIER-GENERAL WILD DELAYED BY GULAB SINGH—SIR HENRY LAWRENCE—BAD NEWS—MURDERS OF MAHARAJA SHER SINGH AND OF DHYAN SINGH—*SATI* OF HIS WIDOW AND THIRTEEN SLAVES — CHARACTER OF HIRA SINGH — RANI JINDAU—DEATH OF SUCHET SINGH—GARDNER DISGUISED AS AN AKALI — DEATHS OF HIRA SINGH AND JAWAHIR SINGH — OUTBREAK OF WAR WITH THE ENGLISH.

THE month of January 1842 was disastrous to the British, for of a large force which was compelled to leave Kabul on the 6th of that month but one single man reached the city of Jalalabad, where a garrison under Sir Robert Sale with difficulty held its own. The few survivors of the Kabul force were prisoners in the hands of Muhammad Akbar Khan, the son of Dost Muhammad.

Shortly before this time Maharaja Sher Singh, who was a staunch supporter of the British, ordered the Dogra force, of some 10,000 men, to proceed to Peshawar, and appointed Raja Gulab Singh governor of that province in the room of General Avitabile, who shared in the unpopularity of Ranjit Singh's old foreign officers. I accompanied the Dogra troops in my capacity of commandant of artillery.

It is recorded in history that General Wild, who commanded the first body of troops, hurried up through the Panjab on the news of the disasters of Kabul, was delayed at Peshawar, and rendered unable to advance through the Khaibar Pass to reinforce Sale's beleaguered garrison of Jalalabad; but it is perhaps reserved for me to explain clearly how this was brought about.

It was on this occasion that I was first brought in contact with Sir Henry Lawrence, then a young "political" officer.[1] I have often since expressed my admiration of that great and good man, and of the tact and ability he brought to bear on his political duties.

The Dogra force was encamped on the west bank of the Indus, and Gulab Singh obviously had no wish to go to Peshawar in accordance with his orders. Under the pretext that his rear was

[1] Sir Henry Lawrence was born in 1806, and was consequently thirty-five at this time. Gardner was, of course, twenty or twenty-one years older.

threatened, he sent frequent messages by myself and others to Peshawar to say that he was unable to advance thither. Meanwhile I was aware that he was receiving daily letters from Kabul. He was, indeed, in constant communication with Muhammad Akbar Khan. These messages were brought by men whom Gulab Singh used to represent as paupers and refugees.

One day an English doctor in the disguise of a Pathan came into camp, requesting aid, in the shape of boats, from Gulab Singh. This assistance was promised, and the doctor departed to Brigadier Wild's camp. Directly he had gone Gulab Singh sent me and another commandant in his confidence (who, like myself, was intimately acquainted with the Yusufzai country and people), and directed us to go all along the Indus and conceal every boat we could lay hands on. He pretended that these boats were required for his own force, and for great British reinforcements coming up in rear. Thus the army of succour of the unfortunate Wild, who was making every effort to get on, was delayed for ten days at Attock instead of two, and in that period the destruction of the army at Kabul was consummated. At last Wild got across, and Gulab Singh then took charge of the ferry at Attock.

Daily rumours of disasters at Kabul arrived, and news now came, to add to the confusion, that the whole Sikh garrison of Peshawar was in open rebellion.

Over and over again did Lawrence write to Gulab Singh, who returned him no answer. The road from Peshawar to Attock, moreover, was beleaguered by mutinous troops.

One day I heard that a sahib had come into camp, and seeing one or two persons under a tree, I went forward and found Lawrence dressed, not very successfully, as a Pathan. He had had the courage to travel right through the Yusufzai country, had crossed the river at a dangerous place (Bazar-ka-patan), and here he was in the midst of the camp asking for Gulab Singh. That astute chief at once ordered large tents to be prepared for the British official, gave him a warm reception, and declared that he had written at least five times a-day, and that his notes must have been intercepted. Lawrence was then closeted two hours with Gulab Singh, and I could see at once on the close of the interview that the wonderful tact of the rising "political" had prevailed, and that he was master of the situation.

It was amusing to listen to the verbal fence of

the two when I was admitted into the audience-tent. Lawrence had got some valuable news from down country, and he was well aware that Gulab Singh's direct news from Kabul would be of the greatest interest to the British. He jocularly offered to swap news. Gulab Singh laughed and agreed. "Give and take," said he; "let it be fair barter: you tell the truth, and so will I."

The bargain was struck, and Lawrence led off by telling Gulab Singh that his expedition to Thibet had utterly failed, and that his agent, Wazir Zorawar Singh, with 9000 soldiers, had been cut off nearly to a man.

"I also have some news," said Gulab Singh in his turn, and then told Lawrence the horrid truth that all was over with the British at Kabul, and that Akbar Khan was pressing Jalalabad with terrific vigour. Lawrence, shocked at the intelligence, demanded proofs, when the two retired once more to a private conference, and Gulab Singh showed him the letter he had received.[1]

[1] The conversation between Sir Henry Lawrence and Gulab Singh, as related by Gardner, agrees sufficiently closely with the account in the Life of Sir Henry written by Sir Herbert Edwardes. The fact that information was given to Lawrence by Gardner is also mentioned, with the explanation that Gardner was exceptionally well-informed in Sikh affairs, because "he had married a native wife, given to him by Rajah Dhyan Singh out of his own house; and

The story of General Pollock's advance to Kabul, and of the subsequent withdrawal of the English army from Afghanistan, need not here be related: suffice it to say that, thanks in a great measure to Sir Henry Lawrence, the Sikh troops of Maharaja Sher Singh took a fair share in the operations. At the conclusion of the war a grand review of the British and Sikh armies took place at Ferozepur, and it was on this occasion that Prince Partab Singh, the heir-apparent, won so much favour with Lord Ellenborough and the English officers.

In February 1843 Dost Muhammad Khan, having been released from his captivity in India, returned to Kabul by way of Lahore, where he contracted a treaty of alliance with the durbar. Soon after this the intrigues and jealousies between the Sindhanwalias and Raja Dhyan Singh recommenced, and eventually cost all of them, and Maharaja Sher Singh, their lives.

The principal Sindhanwalia *sardars* were named Attar Singh and Lehna Singh (who were brothers), and Ajit Singh, who was nephew to both of them.

through her, and living always among the natives, he was behind the scenes, and heard a good deal of the intrigues that were on foot. He had wild moods of talking, letting the corners of dark things peep out, and then shutting them up again with a look behind him, as if life at Jammu was both strange and fearful."

These *sardars* were very powerful, and had exceptional influence on account of their relationship to Maharaja Ranjit Singh. They had left the Panjab for a time after Sher Singh's accession to the throne, but now returned, and were apparently on friendly terms with the Maharaja. Attar Singh, however, distrusted both Sher Singh and Dhyan Singh, and retired to his estates, leaving his brother and nephew to carry on the war.

For a time there was great familiarity between Lehna Singh, Ajit Singh, and the Maharajah, and the three frequently caroused together. Maharaja Sher Singh passed most of his time at his favourite house, known as Shah Bilawal, and here on September 15, 1843, the tragedy occurred.

An inspection of certain soldiers, for whom the Sindhanwalias desired to receive a *jagir*, was fixed to take place on this day, and in the morning the soldiers were marshalled in brilliant array. The Maharaja, however, did not inspect them at the appointed time, and Lehna Singh and Ajit Singh consequently went to him and reproached him in a jocular manner for keeping them waiting. They were each armed with a magnificent new double-barrelled gun. Seating themselves opposite Maharaja Sher Singh, they asked for a *jagir*. He replied, "By-and-bye," and stretched out his hand for Ajit Singh's gun, which he wished to look at. Ajit Singh affected to hand it to him, but brought the muzzle to bear on his breast, pulled the triggers, and lodged the contents in his body. Two cuts of a sword finally ended the career of Maharaja Sher Singh.

Not content with this murder, Ajit Singh went into the inner apartments and cut down Partab Singh, the pretty little son of Sher Singh. Partab Singh ran up to Ajit Singh and knelt before him, calling him "uncle."[1] The brutal Ajit Singh, hot with the blood which already dyed his hand, then penetrated into the harem of Sher Singh, and murdered all the Maharaja's women—one under circumstances of peculiar atrocity, for she was on the eve of giving birth to an infant.

. . . .

With that strange foreboding which seems to attend the coming of terrible events, there was a general uneasiness in the air. I for one was on the alert directly I heard the shots fired, and went at once to find Dhyan Singh, who had already gone to see Maharaja Sher Singh in consequence

[1] Sir Lepel Griffin states that Prince Partab Singh was murdered by Lehna Singh.

of some dark rumours which had reached him. He found Ajit Singh fresh from his deeds of blood and half-way on his return journey to Lahore. Dhyan Singh turned and accompanied Ajit Singh, and the Sindhanwalias said to him, "What is done cannot be undone. Dhulip Singh must now be Maharaja." This was in accordance with Dhyan Singh's views, and all seemed quiet for a few minutes, though he was uneasy at finding himself surrounded by Ajit Singh's followers. On arriving at the outer gate of the fortress they entered together, but at the inner gate all but a very few of the Minister's attendants were excluded.

Presently Ajit Singh drew Raja Dhyan Singh's attention to some men on the parapet of the fort, shot him in the back, and despatched him with a sword. Thus perished the wise and brave Dhyan Singh, whose fall was deplored by the whole army: but it was avenged, and that quickly.

Grief and fury seized the troops. The Sindhanwalias endeavoured to come to terms with Hira Singh and Suchet Singh, the son and brother of the murdered Minister, but they knew better than to trust them. Hira Singh enflamed the rage of the army by fervent appeals, and excited their cupidity by lavish promises of money. The excitement was wound up to frenzy by the conduct of the young and exquisitely lovely wife of Dhyan Singh, the daughter of the Rajput chief of Pathankot. This lady vowed that she would not become *sati* until she had the heads of Lehna Singh and Ajit Singh. I myself laid their heads at the feet of Dhyan Singh's corpse that evening.

The Sindhanwalias attempted to defend the fort, but in a feeble manner at first. Forty thousand men attacked them, and they saw that all was lost. When, however, the wall was breached, and death became imminent, they fought with desperation and inflicted heavy loss on the army. Ajit Singh and Lehna Singh were killed with no more mercy than they had shown, and Raja Dhyan Singh was avenged.

The *sati* of his widow then took place, and seldom, if ever, have I been so powerfully affected as at the self-immolation of the gentle and lovely girl, whose love for her husband passed all bounds. During the day, while inciting the army to avenge her husband's murder, she had appeared in public before the soldiers, discarding the seclusion of a lifetime. When his murderers had been slain she gave directions as to the disposition of his property with a stoicism and self-possession to which no one beside her could lay claim: she thanked her brave avengers, and declared that she would tell of their good deeds to her husband when in heaven. There was nothing left for her, she said, but to join him.

Great efforts were made among the assembly to prevent the sacrifice of a sweet little maiden of nine or ten years of age who had been passionately attached to the murdered Raja. When not allowed to get upon the pyre, she vowed she would not live, slipped from the hands of those who would hold her, rushed to the battlements of the city, and threw herself from them. We picked her up more dead than alive, and the beautiful devotee seated on the pyre at last consented to take the child in her lap to share her doom.

They placed her husband's diamond *kalgi* (aigrette) in her turban, and she then fastened it with her own hands in the turban of her stepson, Hira Singh. Then, smiling on those around, she lit the pyre, the flames of which glistened on the arms and accoutrements, and even, it seemed to me, on the swimming eyes of the soldiery. So perished the widow of Dhyan Singh, with thirteen of her female slaves.

As for Maharaja Sher Singh, no one thought of

avenging his death, and not a thought was bestowed on the sepulture of his remains.

. . . .

The tragic events described above were followed by the succession of the boy Dhulip Singh to the throne, with Hira Singh as *wazir*. The latter now appeared to be all-powerful; but he had powerful enemies, and, moreover, a master in the person of one Pandit Julla, a man of the most repulsive cast of countenance, and of a most tyrannical and ambitious spirit. He had been tutor to Hira Singh in his youth, and the latter, being still quite a young man, was entirely in his hands.

Hira Singh was indeed but a poor copy of his father, whom he in vain attempted to resemble. His character was compounded of many conflicting qualities. Crouching and mean to his superiors; silent and suspicious with his equals; proud, supercilious, and arrogant to his inferiors; subtle and deceitful to all. Too much puffed up to return, or even notice, the salutations of better men than himself; reared as the lapdog of Ranjit Singh and his dissolute companions; with a smattering of English, Persian, and Sanscrit, and pretending to a perfect knowledge of all three languages. Clean, neat, and showy in person, like his father; but too effeminate to resemble him truly; unstable, and, as it seemed, not daring to walk, stir, sit, rise, eat, drink, sleep, or speak without—what? A trifling sign, a careless nod, or some such sufficient guiding token from his mysterious jailor, his familiar spirit, his preceptor, master, father and brother, inferior and superior, Pandit Julla.

No sooner was Hira Singh in power than his actions, under the guidance of the Pandit, caused the greatest dissatisfaction in the army, and intrigues were speedily afoot, having for their object Pandit Julla's downfall and death. The leading spirit in this movement was Sardar Jawahir Singh, brother of the Rani Jindan, and consequently uncle of the young Maharaja Dhulip Singh. Rani Jindan and Jawahir Singh were the children of one Manna, the dog-keeper of Ranjit Singh. Rani Jindan was endowed with extraordinary beauty and great talent. Her father, Manna, was a man of much humour and fun, who used to take great liberties with the old Lion of the Panjab, often rallying him jocularly on the state of his harem, and jocosely asking him to make a queen of his little daughter. Manna used to perch the pretty child on his shoulder, and run with her alongside of the Maharaja's palki when he made his entrances into Lahore, declaring the girl was getting burdensome and heavy. At last the monarch was persuaded, and said, "Very well, bring her." (He did this as Manna used to banter him about his age, and the Maharaja was very sensitive as to his personal decay.)

In the harem the little beauty used to gambol and frolic and tease Ranjit Singh, and managed to captivate him in a way that smote the real wives with jealousy—so much so that Ranjit Singh sent her when thirteen years of age to Amritsar, and gave her an allowance of 5000 rupees per month. Raja Dhyan Singh had charge of her, and this contributed to that able courtier's influence. He took her back to Lahore, treated her with great dignity, and ultimately effected the celebration of the *karewa*, tantamount to the *chadar dalna*,[1] marriage ceremony, between her and Ranjit Singh. Her ascendancy over the Maharaja was soon gained, and never lost.

Now, to increase his influence over the new Minister, Hira Singh, Pandit Julla intrigued so as to produce, if possible, a deadly feud between

[1] The offspring of this form of union was considered legitimate, and had the right of inheritance. *Chadar dalna* means "throwing the sheet."

him and his two uncles, Gulab Singh and Suchet Singh, the remaining Dogra brothers.

Suchet Singh was a splendid swordsman, and the very pink of chivalry. He knew that the Pandit was at the bottom of the estrangement between himself and his nephew, but matters had gone too far to be put straight. Early in December 1844 Suchet Singh received an invitation from the Rani Jindan and her brother Jawahir Singh to come to Lahore, and was assured by them that the army would go over from Hira Singh to him. In an evil moment for himself the gallant Suchet Singh started with only fifty men, and having arrived at Lahore, took up quarters in a small mosque near the Shalimar Gardens.

Pandit Julla knew that the success of Suchet Singh would be death to himself, and took his measures accordingly, distributing to each man in the army a pair of bracelets worth 30 rupees. This reward had been promised by Hira Singh to the army as a reward for the loyalty to his house they had shown in avenging on the Sindhanwalia family the murder of his father, Raja Dhyan Singh. The time for disbursing the reward was well chosen.

On Suchet Singh sending word that he had

arrived, Hira Singh, who loved him in his heart, wanted to go at once and embrace his uncle; but his evil genius the Pandit persuaded him that he would be murdered, and produced a *pothi* or horoscope in which it was written that Suchet Singh or Hira Singh would fall the next day. The Pandit then ordered the army to attack the mosque; but they too loved Suchet Singh, and at first refused to obey. At last they attacked, and under the fire of eighty pieces of artillery the roof of the mosque soon began to fall on the heads of the devoted little band within.

Suchet Singh read his *Granth* calmly, prepared himself for death, and calling his followers around him, told any of them who were not ready to die to go in peace. None would, however, leave him. He then charged the army with his fifty followers, and after performing prodigies of valour they all perished. The troops who attacked them lost 160 killed and wounded. Hira Singh threw himself in great grief upon the dead body of his uncle.

At the time of Suchet Singh's death I had just returned to Jammu from Sialkote, which I had captured from Kashmira and Peshora Singh, adopted sons of Ranjit Singh. I informed Gulab

Singh of his brother's rash journey, and the Raja burst into tears and said, "He will be killed to a certainty! Take your force from Sialkote" (where I had left it), "hasten to Lahore, and defend him."

Gulab Singh would not delay to give me a written order, but took off a small gold ring, which I was to show as a proof that I represented him. I immediately started, picked up my troops at Sialkote, arrived on the third day at Lahore, and fired a salute to let Suchet Singh (as I hoped), and the army also, know of my arrival. I was one day too late.

The hatred towards Pandit Julla rapidly increased, and soon the whole army was won to the side of Gulab Singh. Loud demands were addressed to Hira Singh to give up the Pandit, but Hira Singh refused to comply, and so turned the vengeance of the army against himself. Eventually Hira Singh and the Pandit were compelled to take refuge in the late Raja Dhyan Singh's house at Lahore, known as the "Hira Mandi," but subsequently fled with 1200 men to Shahdera. The army then entered the city of Lahore and commenced killing all the Dogras.

My life, being, as I was, in command of the

troops of that race, was imperilled; but some Akalis, who knew that I was an old officer of Ranjit Singh, took me under their protection, and from motives of personal safety I became a complete Akali in costume and habits.

On the 21st December 1844 the army crossed to Shahdera and yelled to Hira Singh to give himself up to them and let the Pandit meet his fate. Hira Singh, however, fled with the Pandit, and with them Sohan Singh, a son of Gulab Singh. After a running fight of nine miles they were all caught and slain: their heads were cut off and paraded through Lahore city. I myself, dressed as an Akali, carried the Pandit's head in my hands. The whole army was responsible for his death, but Hira Singh's death was caused by his mistaken loyalty to his tutor.

. . . .

After the Akalis had triumphantly carried about the heads of the dead princes for more than a fortnight, I managed with great difficulty to secure the heads and to send them to Jammu to Gulab Singh. The heads were then cremated.

Raja Gulab Singh now thirsted for vengeance on the Sikh nation, which had killed so many members of his family. He determined to make terms for himself with the British, and to leave the Sikhs to their doom. Jawahir Singh especially incurred his wrath for the death of Hira Singh and Sohan Singh.

Jawahir Singh was completely intoxicated by his sudden rise to power, and in the exuberance of his heart began to ill-treat Kashmira Singh and Peshora Singh, two adopted sons of Maharaja Ranjit Singh. This was enough to cause the army to feel furious indignation—any favourite of the old Maharaja was sacred to them. Kashmira Singh and Peshora Singh were shortly afterwards killed, the latter under atrocious circumstances of cold-blooded treachery. One circumstance connected with his murder incensed the army to the last degree. The boy had implored his murderer to give him arms and let him die fighting like a Sikh and a man, and the story reached the army of Lahore. Their first resolution was to march to Attock and avenge the murder, which had taken place there; but the Sikhs are proverbially fickle, and the immediate death of Jawahir Singh was decided on as a preliminary.

The Council of the army deliberated for fifteen or twenty days. Jawahir Singh was in the fort, and dared not show his head: menacing news reached him daily. I had one interview with him, and could hold out no hope, but told him to behave like a man and face the peril. The Council at last closed their deliberations and decided that Jawahir Singh should be slain, and that then the army should march down and attack Delhi.

On September 21, 1845, Jawahir Singh was summoned before the army. He came out on an elephant, holding in his arms his nephew, the young Maharaja Dhulip Singh, the last survivor of the line of Ranjit Singh. The Maharani Jindan accompanied him on another elephant. Jawahir Singh had an escort of 400 horsemen, and two elephant-loads of rupees with which to tempt the army. As soon as the cavalcade left the fort an ominous salute ran along the immense line of the army—180 guns were fired. A roll-call was beat, and not a man of that great host was absent. So terribly stern was their discipline that, after the salute had died away, not a sound was to be heard but the trampling of the feet of the royal cavalcade.

Dhulip Singh was received with royal honours: his mother, the Maharani Jindan, in miserable terror for her brother, was seated on her golden *hauda*, dressed in white Sikh clothes and closely veiled. As soon as the procession reached the middle of the line one man came forward and cried out, "Stop," and at his single voice the whole procession paused. A tremor ran through the host: many expected a rescue on the part of the French brigade; but not a man stirred. The great *Panch* (Military Council) was still sitting on the right of the line. Four battalions were now ordered to the front, and removed Jawahir Singh's escort to a distance. Then another battalion marched up and surrounded the elephants of the royal personages. Ten of the Council then came forward; the Rani's elephant was ordered to kneel down, and she herself was escorted to a small but beautiful tent prepared for her close by.

Then a terrible scene took place. The Rani was dragged away, shrieking to the army to spare her brother. Jawahir Singh was next ordered to descend from his elephant. He lost his head, attempted to parley, and a tall Sikh slapped his face and took the boy Dhulip Singh from his arms, asking him how he dared to disobey the Khalsa. Dhulip Singh was placed in his mother's arms, and she, hiding herself behind the walls of her tent, held the child up above them in view of the army, crying for mercy for her brother in the name of her son. Suddenly, hearing a yell of agony from a well-known voice, she flung the child away in an agony of grief and rage. Fortunately he was caught by a soldier, or the consequences might have been fatal.

Meanwhile the bloody work had been done on the hated Minister. A soldier, who had presumably received his orders, had gone up the ladder placed by Jawahir Singh's elephant, stabbed him with his bayonet, and flung him upon the ground, where he was despatched in a moment with fifty wounds.

Thus did the Sikh army avenge the death of Kashmira Singh and Peshora Singh.

Maharani Jindan now became regent, and with her lover Lal Singh, who was appointed her adviser, decided on a policy of aggression. That policy was indicated by the old Sikh motto, "Throw the snake into your enemy's bosom," which is even more forcible than the English, "Kill two birds with one stone." The snake was the evilly disposed, violent, yet powerful and splendid Sikh army. It was to be flung upon the British, and so destroyed. Thus did the Rani Jindan in her turn plan to avenge herself on the murderers of her brother Jawahir Singh.

The army entered on the war with enthusiasm, and every man took with him a spade from his own home for engineering purposes. The skill with which they used them, and the valiant stand which they made against the British, is a matter of history.

The Sikh army crossed the Sutlej on the 8th December 1845.

CHAPTER XV.

THE FIRST SIKH WAR.

THE SIKH GENERALS—DEPARTURE OF VENTURA AND AVITABILE—THE APEX OF THE ARMY—COLONEL HURBON—GULAB SINGH'S DIPLOMACY—RANI JINDAN AND THE DEPUTATION—OCCUPATION OF LAHORE—TERMS OF PEACE.

AFTER the murder of Wazir Jawahir Singh his sister, the Rani Jindan, was declared regent. Her principal advisers were Diwan Dina Nath, Bhai Ram Singh, and Misr Lal Singh, the first named of whom was a man of remarkable talent, known as "the Talleyrand of the Panjab." When war was declared against the British, and the Sikhs crossed the Sutlej, I was acting as Raja Gulab's agent and factotum at Lahore, and in consequence had great power and influence.

Two more contemptible poltroons than the two generals of the Khalsa army—Lal Singh and Tej Singh, both Brahmans—never breathed. Lal Singh ran away and hid himself for twenty days in an oven at Ludiana, in which the Sikhs would have baked him if they had caught him. Tej Singh always kept at the apex of the army (in the rear), pretending that he could thus have an eye to both divisions, and that it was not his duty to go in front. Tej Singh was never trusted by any one. After the start of the Sikh army for the front Lal Singh and Dina Nath used to receive visitors, and a succession of picnics used to take place at Shalimar Gardens. The Rani's policy was to affect enormous anxiety for the success of the Sikhs, but to afford them no substantial aid. If Delhi was taken, then so much the more glory and loot; if the British were victorious, the Rani, who was corresponding with them, could trust to their protection.

The pusillanimous and ignominious departure of Avitabile and Ventura at this critical juncture much disgusted the army, who wanted efficient and civilised control. There was no necessity to leave that I saw. I was always treated with honour and respect.

The state of the army was such that proscription rolls were made out of all individuals obnoxious to them, and they had to be given up. I started originally with the army, but was recalled by the

Rani to Lahore, and she specially insisted that I was wanted to hold Lahore against the Khalsa. I was privately told to bring back no Sikhs, but as many Mussulmans as I had with me. These Mussulmans were the very brigade which mutinied at Peshawar in 1841, at the time Sir Henry Lawrence was deputed there. The Muhammadans, hating the Sikhs, were enchanted at the recall, and on our return I was, as it were, governor of Lahore. My orders were simple: "No Sikhs are to return; manage that, and the rest shall be as you like." Much more fear was entertained of personal maltreatment by the Sikhs than of the British Government.

Twenty-five of Lord Hardinge's body-guard, thinking matters rather doubtful, deserted and put themselves under my orders at Lahore—fine tall men, swaggering about the city, very different from the slight and active "Manjha" Sikhs. One of them asked for a regiment of cavalry to lead against the British. The resolve of their ruler to destroy the army, anyhow and by whatever means, was known even by the Sikh army itself; but such had been the stern discipline of the *Panch*, such were the hopes of loot from Delhi, such the real belief that the intentions of the

British were aggressive, such the domestic incitements of their families to plunder, and such their devotion to their mystic faith, that one single dogged determination filled the bosom of each soldier. The word went round, "We will go to the sacrifice." One miserable deserter was nearly beaten to death by his Panjabi countrywomen.

"Let us not survive," said some, "the invasion of Ranjit Singh's boundaries." For to their minds the occupation of the protected Sikh States by British troops was tantamount to an invasion.

After the battle of Ferozeshah, which took place on the 22nd December 1845, it was reported at Lahore that the British army had been defeated, and the Maharani and her council, though knowing the truth, were yet afraid that their own army might in the end be successful. They well knew that in that case it would return to Lahore, and that anarchy and bloodshed would once again be the order of the day. They therefore sent congratulatory messages to the troops, and counselled an immediate advance southwards by way of Bhawulpur. By this means, they said, the British army could be taken in flank, and Delhi captured.

The only duty imposed on me was to protect

Maharani Jindan and her child, and to get the dread Khalsa army destroyed somehow.

"Don't come back, gallant men of the 'Guruji,'" said we, "without at all events seeing Delhi." The Fakir Azizuddin foresaw, as well as most of us who were not infatuated by religion or intoxicated with drink, that the British must in the end win, from the elements of real unity which guided their councils, notwithstanding the doubtful state of their native troops.

Lal Singh ran away at Mudki: he preferred the embraces of Venus at Lahore to the triumphs of Mars; and was, as all Brahmans are, held in the highest contempt by the Sikhs. He fled, hid himself in a hayrick, and skulked off from the army. Swapping his handsome horse for a "tattoo," and smearing over his face with ashes like a poor fakir, he hid himself in an oven belonging to an old bakeress at Ludiana. The Rani Jindan led him a dreadful life at first, when he returned to Lahore after twenty days' absence, jeering at him for his cautious behaviour; but he being her favourite, orders were given to stop any further hilarity. Even to Tej Singh the army cried, "Do not betray us!" such was his character for treachery. When he arrived at Ferozeshah he said he was off to bring up the reserve." He never once went to the front. There was another general who actually ran away, and was jeered at by the army as a *lounda kutta* (dog with his tail cut). Tej Singh, keeping in his favourite position, the apex (as he called it) of the army, actually built a bomb-proof mud hut, like a small tent, for himself, inside which he sat doing *puja* (*i.e.*, "saying his prayers"), his Brahman astrologers being instructed to give out that everything depended on the safety of the holy man. When he disappeared after the battle of Ferozeshah he gave out that he was outflanked by the British, and was turning to meet his new enemy in the rear. He declared that he was panting for the war, but that his Brahmans would not let him out of his hut.

Hurbon was a fine soldier: he was a Spaniard, and had come out to the Sikh service on hearing the accounts of the large emoluments received by Ventura and Avitabile. He was told to show his mettle in the campaign, which he did, and bravely, being the engineer, moreover, who did all the castrametation which so surprised the British army.

All this time Gulab Singh, who could have

brought 40,000 men by a sign of his finger, was being implored by the Sikhs to aid them. At that moment he had a difficult and critical game to play. The army offered to make him (Dogra though he was) Maharaja, and to kill the traitors Lal Singh and Tej Singh. Fortunately for the British, their prestige had its influence on his mind, and his memory recounted the treacheries of the Sikhs to himself and his countrymen, and he decided otherwise. He remained firstly at Jammu, the Rani Jindan telling him not to stir unless she required him. Meanwhile Gulab Singh cajoled the whole of the leading *panchayets* of the Sikh army, affecting to see every visitor from the battles at any moment, whether he was bathing or eating, as if his whole heart was with the Sikhs. He got all the wheat-carriers in the country, loaded them with immense display with about one-fourth of what they could carry, put placards in "Gurmukhi" on their necks to the effect that they were carrying supplies from Gulab Singh, and told them, under pain of mutilation, not to go two abreast, in order that the army and the country might imagine that incessant and enormous supplies were being forwarded to the stalwart and devoted Khalsa by their loyal and affectionate friend. "I'm not going empty-handed to the great campaign that is to end at Calcutta," gave out Gulab Singh. "When all is ready for campaigning, off I start. This will be a long war," said he. "It's a race to the capital, and devil catch the hindmost." Thus he temporised. But he held the power, and would have used it (if Dhyan Singh had been alive, or if he himself had been a Sikh) to create an insurrection which would have shaken the British power more even than the mutiny of 1857. All the protected Sikh States in the Malwa—Nabha, Jhind, and Patiala—were ready to envelop the British army in case of a reverse.

When at last, after the defeat at Sobraon on February 10, 1846, the remains of the Sikh army passed Hari-ka Ghat, Gulab Singh moved from Jammu. I went to meet him. "How is her Majesty?" said he, the first words. I went with him to meet Major Lawrence. I had about 500 men, Gulab Singh some 2000, and 20,000 or 30,000 men within hail. Now here were the Sikhs crossing at Hari-ka Ghat, and the British at Kussur, who were therefore in a most critical position, as they were between the Sikh and

Dogra armies. Of course Gulab Singh had a double move; and Lawrence seemed to be anxious at the military mistake of moving the British army between one strong, though beaten, force, and another fresh in body and of a doubtful course of policy. Though Sir Henry tried to pump me, I only said, and could say, as an honest paid servant of my masters, "Keep up a bold face, and look to your right: the Dogra force may be secured to act as light infantry in case of any further trouble."

A very dramatic and characteristic scene occurred between the battles of Ferozeshah and Sobraon. The unfortunate Sikhs were hurried on to their fate, and were literally starved for want of rations. They sent a deputation of 500 picked Sikhs to Lahore to urge the dire necessities of the army—for three days they had lived upon grain and raw carrots. The Rani at first would not allow the deputation to enter Lahore. She feared justly for her personal safety at the hands of these desperate men. I therefore placed four battalions of infantry in guard over the queen, and she at last consented to hold a durbar and receive the deputation. They were told to come armed with swords only. Under the pretence of this being a State occasion, I turned out a very large personal guard for the queen, who waited behind a screen the arrival of the envoys. I was standing close to the Rani, and could see the gesticulations and movements of the deputation. In answer to the urgent and loud complaints of the sacrifice to which the army was exposed, she said that Gulab Singh had forwarded vast supplies. "No, he has not," roared the deputation; "we know the old fox: he has not sent breakfast for a bird (*chiria-ki-haziri*)." Further parley ensued, the tempers of both parties waxing wroth. At last the deputation said, "Give us powder and shot." At this I saw some movement behind the *purdah* (the little Dhulip was seated in front of it). I could detect that the Rani was shifting her petticoat; I could see that she stepped out of it, and then rolling it up rapidly into a ball, flung it over the screen at the heads of the angry envoys, crying out, "Wear that, you cowards! I'll go in trousers and fight myself!"[1] The effect was electric.

[1] Colonel Gardner has Anglicised this well-known story.

After a moment's pause, during which the deputation seemed stunned, a unanimous shout arose, "Dhulip Singh Maharaja, we will go and die for his kingdom and the Khalsaji!" and breaking up tumultuously and highly excited, this dangerous deputation dispersed, and rejoined the army. The courage and intuition displayed by this extraordinary woman under such critical circumstances filled us all with as much amazement as admiration.

The Rani Jindan was very vain of her attractions, and when I was showing Sir Henry Lawrence and Sir Robert (then Captain) Napier round the Palace of Lahore, immediately upon the occupation after the termination of the first Sikh campaign, the latter officer asked me if I could manage to procure him a sight of her. Knowing that Rani Jindan possessed rather more than ordinary female curiosity, I offered to gratify her with a sight of the victorious English, and thus it was that her beautiful head and neck appeared once or twice over a wall, to the gratification of the officers.

The Rani used to wonder why a matrimonial alliance was not at once formed for her with some officer of rank, who would then manage State affairs with her.

She used to send for portraits of all the officers, and in one especially she took great interest, and said that he must be a lord. This fortunate individual's name has not transpired, and, much to the Maharani's mortification, the affair went no further. She considered that such a marriage would have secured the future of herself and her son.

. . . .

The British army had reached Lahore on the 20th February 1846, and on the 8th of the following month a treaty of peace was ratified between the British Government and the Lahore durbar. Maharaja Dhulip Singh renounced all claim to the territories south of the river Sutlej, and recognised the independence of Gulab Singh as Raja of Jammu and such other hill territories as might be assigned to him. Colonel Sir Henry Lawrence was appointed Resident at Lahore, where furthermore a large British force was to remain till the end of the year.

On the 15th March the Governor-General, Sir Henry Hardinge, invested Gulab Singh with the title of Maharaja of Kashmir and Jammu, and Gulab Singh acknowledged the supremacy of the British Government.

Thus, after a campaign of but sixty days, the proud and fierce Khalsa army was effectually defeated, though by no means disgraced, and the kingdom of Ranjit Singh reduced to a position of dependency and subjection.

CHAPTER XVI.

"PORT AFTER STORMY SEAS."

GARDNER EXILED FROM THE PANJAB—'HISTORY OF THE REIGNING FAMILY OF LAHORE'—GARDNER ENTERS GULAB SINGH'S SERVICE—SETTLES FOR LIFE IN KASHMIR—BIRTH OF HIS DAUGHTER—IMPRESSION OF GARDNER—MR ANDREW WILSON—CAPTAIN SEGRAVE—THE RUSSIAN ADVANCE TOWARDS INDIA—GARDNER'S ADVICE TO JOHN BULL—DEATH OF THE TRAVELLER—THE SUGGESTION OF HIS CAREER.

COLONEL GARDNER, as has been explained, was not called upon to take an active part in either of the wars between the Sikhs and the British. He took the field on the outbreak of the first war, but was almost immediately recalled to Lahore by the Rani Jindan, mother of the young Maharaja, who desired him to take command of her own guards. On the conclusion of peace a council of regency was appointed to administer the government of the Panjab, and one of the leading members of this council was Raja Tej Singh, who was Gardner's personal enemy.

Tej Singh lost no time in taking advantage of his position, and Gardner presently received an order from the council to leave Lahore within twenty-four hours. There was no disputing the order, and Gardner was compelled to seek an asylum on British soil. He went to the frontier station of Ludhiana, where he had friends, and during his brief residence there occupied his leisure by giving to Colonel Carmichael-Smyth of the 3rd Bengal Light Cavalry the information which the latter embodied in a work entitled 'The History of the Reigning Family of Lahore.' Those who have read that curious and little-known work will recognise some of the incidents contained in the foregoing pages.

Gardner's period of exile was very short: he was soon afterwards permitted to enter the service of Gulab Singh, now created an independent sovereign as Maharaja of Jammu and Kashmir.

The latter province was ceded to the Maharaja for reasons which need not here be discussed, but they did not commend themselves to Sheikh Imam-ud-din, the governor of Kashmir under the Sikh Government. Imam-ud-din declined to surrender Kashmir to the new Maharaja, who was therefore compelled to obtain possession of his kingdom by force of arms. Gardner accompanied Gulab Singh in the operations which ensued, and when Imam-ud-din had been overthrown and the new sovereign "had his own," Gardner received the reward of his long and faithful services to the Maharaja and his family. He received command of the "Ranbir" regiment of infantry, and of all the Kashmir artillery, with a salary of 500 rupees per mensem. This income, with the revenues of some villages bestowed upon him by the Maharaja, gave Gardner a comfortable income for the remaining thirty years of his long life. He lived in good style, after the native fashion, being from long habit a complete Oriental, and retained his activity of mind and body to the very last.

Gardner was held in high respect by his native neighbours, and more especially by the old soldiers of the Khalsa who had settled in Jammu or Kashmir. These veterans loved to meet one who had enjoyed the confidence of Ranjit Singh; and those of them who live still, though now extremely old, are full of recollections of "Gordana Sahib."

Colonel Gardner's last years were rendered interesting to him by the birth of a daughter, who received the name of Helena: there is pleasing evidence in his letters that the wellbeing of this child of his old age occupied many of his thoughts. This daughter, now Mrs Botha, has inherited much of her father's adventurous and roving spirit, and recently visited her birthplace. Many ancient Sikh soldiers came from all directions to see her, and to tell her of their attachment to her father. One fact about Gardner they never failed to mention, which was the curious habit that he had of clutching his neck with an iron pincer when about to drink. This operation was rendered necessary by the severe wound in his neck, which has been mentioned elsewhere. His Highness, the reigning Maharaja of Kashmir, also told Mrs Botha of this peculiarity of her father, he having been greatly impressed by it when a boy. Colonel Gardner's daughter has two children, a son and a daughter, on the former of whom she has bestowed the name of Alexander, in memory of his grandfather.

It will be readily imagined that English visitors to the vale of Kashmir lost no opportunity of calling on the old adventurer, and of hearing the strange story of bygone days which he was so ready to tell. Some of those who delighted thus to hear of ancient wars were famous soldiers, among whom may be mentioned Lord Strathnairn, "a first-class fighting-man," and Sir Henry Durand, the hero of the Gate of Ghuzni.

Many of these English visitors have left on record their impressions of Gardner, and the description of him by Mr Andrew Wilson in his charming book, 'The Abode of Snow,' merits quotation. "Colonel Gardner," he writes, "a soldier of fortune, ninety years of age, was born on the shores of Lake Superior, and had wandered into Central Asia at an early period. It was something almost appalling to hear this ancient warrior discourse of what have now become almost prehistoric times, and relate his experiences in the service of Ranjit Singh and other kings and chiefs less known to fame. If (as I have no reason to believe) he occasionally confused hearsay with his own experiences, it could scarcely be wondered at considering his years, and there is no doubt as to the general facts of his career. Listening to his graphic narrations, Central Asia vividly appeared as it was more than half a century ago, when Englishmen could traverse it, not only with tolerable safety, but usually as honoured guests."

Captain Segrave supplies a vivid portrait of Colonel Gardner in his old age, which may explain the costume in which he appears in the frontispiece. In writing of his first meeting with Gardner, Captain Segrave says: "I can perfectly recollect my first interview with him. He walked into Cooper's reception-room one morning, a most peculiar and striking appearance, clothed from head to foot in the 79th tartan, but fashioned by a native tailor. Even his *pagri* was of tartan, and it was adorned with the egret's plume, only allowed to persons of high rank. I imagine he lived entirely in native fashion: he was said to be wealthy, and the owner of many villages."

Gardner took a keen interest in public affairs, and wrote voluminously on the subject of the Russian advance towards India. He was an advocate of the "forward policy," and perhaps showed some want of tact in impressing his views on this subject on Lord Lawrence during the latter's viceroyalty.

Other opinions of Gardner's might have found more favour with Lord Lawrence, and to those interested in the future destiny of our Indian empire there may appear to be something of value in the following letter, which is obviously modelled on the well-known "Brahminee-Bull" letters. It shows, at any rate, the impressions of a white resident in India who had had peculiar opportunities of ascertaining native opinions, and whose sympathies were rather with the natives than with their English conquerors. It may be deemed worthy of note also in consideration of the great age (ninety-one) of its writer.

"A few plain, simple, and brotherly words from John Bull of India to his much beloved Aryan brother, the Right Honourable Sir John Bull of England.

"MY DEAR JOHN,—There is no occasion here to call upon the great and erudite professor, Max Müller, or any other Max, to rise from his chair to prove our relationship, as it has been so long acknowledged both by ourselves and by all the literati, antiquarians, and historians of Europe and the East. Therefore, my dear John, let it suffice, I say, that I and nearly all my brethren and kindred here really and seriously believe that the time has arrived when a true and sincere community of feeling, thought, word, and deed should exist between us for our mutual and common interests; and should by all possible means be promoted for the future welfare and happiness of the great Aryan family. But to carry this design to its legitimate end, it is of the greatest importance that all future correspondence between us, as brothers, should be conducted in a plain, open, and candid manner; that is, we must use plain, common English, without any parliamentary beating around the bush, or unmeaning and ambiguous phrases. This is really so much a necessity, that I cannot believe but that it has already been settled and agreed between us. Therefore, to commence, I will first make the simple remark that it is of little use to remind you of the manner in which you originally, about 250 or 300 years ago, became acquainted with us; nor to ask you whether you then entered our house by the front door, the back door, or the skylight.

"But, dear John, when you did enter, you very soon succeeded by your wisdom and discretion in making yourself completely and comfortably at home, inducing us to believe that you had come on a brotherly visit; consequently we received you as brothers should, and we respected you both as a brother and a friend, although we had previously neither seen you nor heard much of you for five or six thousand years.

"But, dear John, you cannot but remember that

when you had become a guest or lodger in our house it was not long before you began to lay claims on all our goods and chattels; in fact you seemed inclined (of course in a friendly and brotherly way) to make everything your own; and you next, very wisely, began to make laws of your own by which you aptly and adroitly made it appear that everything you had done was right and inevitable, according to your laws, will, and pleasure. At the same time, by the magic aid of your Western talent and wisdom, the various family feuds and internal broils, which unfortunately always exist among us, afforded you a fair opportunity of assisting one party against another; and thus it came about that while confusion and warfare stalked through the land, peace seemed to be your will and your gift. So matters continued until the great Lord Clive, Sahib Bahadur, appeared upon the stage, and played so distinguished and conspicuous a part in the Indian drama; and although he came to India with merely a humble *kalamdan*[1] in his pocket, such was his genius that he laid the sure foundations of that glorious fabric, the British empire in the East.

[1] Inkstand.

"Aided as you were by the genius of Lord Clive and his successors, is it not true, dear John, that it was our folly and disunion that permitted—or, to speak more politely, compelled—you to advance from the Bay of Bengal to Peshawar, and from Cape Comorin to the Himalayas.

"This, however, dear John, is ancient history, and we might be content to forget it, but that it is all written with our own records, and must therefore at times come to our memory. Another fact, too, is recorded, with which you, dear John, must be familiar—namely, that India was famed in ancient times as one of the richest countries of the earth, the land of jewels and gold. Now all this wealth has vanished, and India to-day is actually impoverished, perhaps one of the poorest of all countries.

"Now, my dear John, I shall ask you a plain and simple question—*Where has all this wealth gone to?* You surely do not consider us profligates or spendthrifts, who have squandered all our national belongings in frivolity and vanity? That, dear John, is not our traditional character. We are well known throughout the world as a thrifty and prudent race. You will hardly assert that we have been so mad as to throw our wealth into the sea; nor have we sent it to the Emperor of China, nor thrown it away on the dogs and bears of the North Pole; any more than we have made a present of it to the woolly-headed "Habshis" of Africa. Then, dear John, to what quarter of the globe do you think it can have gone but to the West? In fact, some of our star-gazers and astrologers assert (though I can hardly believe them) that you have been adroitly milking the poor Indian milch cow to your heart's content from the day you first entered the country to the present time. If this be true, dear John, all we can say is, that although you have always loved us well, you seem to love the poor old milch cow better; and there is no doubt whatever that she has now become so lean on it that she is now only fit to be laid up in some humane and charitable hospital for worn-out animals. It is indeed a fact, too, that while India has become one of the poorest, England has become one of the richest, countries on the earth.

"A few days since one of our promising youths (I believe they call him "Young Bengal") declared at a debating club that it was a positive and historical fact that, when you first entered our house, you appeared so amiable that, in our usual polite way, we frankly asked you to consider the house your own, and you certainly lost no time in taking us at our word; for, very shortly, you not only were quite at home in our house, but actually took upon yourself the heavy responsibilities of paterfamilias. In this capacity, he added, you went to great expense in dressing us out in red coats, of which we were so proud that we strutted about in them like peacocks on a green. Seeing this, you kindly made cheap "Charlies" of us, to watch the house and cry aloud, the livelong night, "All's well"; and so well did we do our duty that *no robbers came to rob the robber!*

"Dear John, from the happy days of our revered Shri Ram Chandra to the present time we never heard of such a thing as a National Debt, but now you have in some way placed upon our weak and emaciated shoulders the Atlas-like burden of a hundred and fifty millions of money; but as you say you have done it for our benefit, we must so accept it. For the kind exertions you are making for our education, thus placing us on the highroad to enlightenment and civilisation, we beg to offer you our sincere thanks; for we are conscious that knowledge is power, and that this is the only path by which we can in time attain to national greatness. But we must ask more immediate help. You well know, dear John, the numerous occasions on which ere now we have proved our loyalty to the throne,—how often we have fought, and freely spilt our best blood, in your cause, not only in India, but in Egypt, in China, in Persia, in Burma, and other lands; and in return you surely will not think it too much if we ask you to bestow on us three small favours. The first of these is the full development of the natural resources of India, both mineral and vegetable. They are rich and varied, and can only be fully developed by means of a hearty and full measure of the necessary legislative initiation and encouragement: there is no doubt that you would soon be proud to see the happy results of such action on your part in an improved and modernised system of agriculture, horticulture, husbandry in general, and irrigation; and I further undertake that soon we should boast of our Manchesters, Leeds, Sheffields, and Newcastles. Secondly, we earnestly request you to open for our preferment the door so long closed, and to give us access to the higher grades in the civil and military services. My dear John, it is mere folly, an unwise and unworthy subterfuge, to say, or affect to believe, that we have not clever and trustworthy gentlemen of high rank and proved respectability, fully capable of acting as Deputy Commissioners, Political Agents, Residents, or even Lieutenant-Governors; as well as Captains, Majors, Colonels, and Generals in the army. I can assure you that we have many scions of noble and princely birth, who, with a fair meed of encouragement, would soon qualify themselves for, and would prove a credit to, your civil or military service.

"Our third and chief request is that, for the future benefit of both India and England, we should be allowed to have representatives both in the House of Commons and the House of Lords, as well as in the Indian Councils of London and Calcutta.

"My dear John, you often say that you have won India by the sword; but I beg to assure you that if you grant us these three requests you will fairly and completely win the hearts of your three hundred million, more or less, of Indian subjects.

"As to the native army, I beg to assure you that you possess as good material as can be found in any part of the world; but I would suggest that clan corps, or clan divisions, would be the best system that you could adopt. For instance, a Rajput, a Goorkha, an Oude, an Afghan, or a Sikh division, of well-chosen men, organised to suit their own national ideas (not yours), and commanded by officers of their own clan or race, would prove not only loyal to you, but of the highest value in every respect. I assure you that such officers, chosen from the chiefs and nobles of the land, would not only be held to loyalty by their high birth, high caste, rank, and family pride, but would by them be stimulated to a noble ardour and desire to distinguish themselves in the field as brave soldiers.

"As to the reigning princes of India, you have only to treat them honourably, justly, and candidly, and they will assuredly prove the strongest and truest pillars of the State, and the best supporters of your empire in the East.—With kind regards and best wishes, I beg to remain, dear John, your affectionate Aryan brother,

"JOHN BULL of India.

"*22nd July* 1876."

The story has been told. The long and eventful life came at last to a peaceful close, and Alexander Gardner, one of the last of the Indian adventurers, died in his bed at Jammu on the 22nd day of January 1877, being then in the ninety-second year of his age. At the end Gardner wished to lie among Christian men, and he was accordingly buried in the military cemetery at Sialkot, the nearest English cantonment.

In that quiet nook he, who had seen men and nature under such strange and varied circumstances, rests from his labours. The field of adventure which attracted him has ceased to offer inducements to the bold spirit of the wanderers, but there are yet dark places on the earth where they may do good work. To those who have in them the divine spark of enterprise these pages may not be without a suggestion and a lesson.

APPENDIX

CONTAINING

SOME ACCOUNT OF MAHARAJA RANJIT SINGH AND HIS WHITE OFFICERS

By Major HUGH PEARSE

COLONEL GARDNER'S LIST OF RANJIT SINGH'S OFFICERS.

1.	General Ventura	Italian	Infantry.
2.	" Allard	French	Cavalry.
3.	" Avitabile	Italian	Infantry.
4.	" Court	French	Artillery.
5.	" Harlan	American	Infantry.
6.	" Van Cortlandt.	English	"
7.	Colonel Ford	"	"
8.	" Foulkes	"	Cavalry.
9.	Captain Argoud	French	Infantry.
10.	Colonel Canora	American	Artillery.
11.	" Thomas	Anglo-Indian	Infantry.
12.	Lieut.-Col. Leslie, *alias* Rattray	"	"
13.	Colonel Mouton	French	Cavalry.
14.	" Hurbon	Spanish	Engineer.
15.	" Steinbach	English (?)	Infantry.
16.	Captain de la Font	French	"
17.	" M'Pherson	English	"
18.	Mr Campbell	Anglo-Indian (?)	"
19.	Mr Garron (Carron ?)	French	Cavalry.
20.	Gordon	Anglo-Indian.	"
21. 22.	De Fasheye (father and son)	French.	"
23.	Alvarine	Italian	Infantry.
24.	Hommus	Spaniard	"
25.	Amise	French	"
26.	Hest	Greek	"
27.	De la Roche	French	"
28.	Dubuignon	"	"

29. John Holmes	Anglo-Indian	Infantry.
30. Vochus	Russian	"
31. De l'Ust	French	"
32. Hureleek	Greek	"
33. Fitzroy		"
34. Barlow		"
35. Martindale	Anglo-Indian	"
36. Jervais	French	"
37. Mœvius	Russian	"
38. Bianchi	Italian	"
39. Dottenweiss	German	Engineer.

MEDICAL OFFICERS.

1. Dr Harvey	English.	
2. Dr Benét	French	Drew 500 rupees per mensem in 1838.
3. Dr Martin Honigberger	Austrian	Drew 900 rupees per mensem same year. A clever doctor, an enterprising traveller, and an amiable man; author of an interesting work, 'Thirty-five Years in the East.'

GENERAL ALLARD,

ORGANISER OF THE SIKH CAVALRY.

RANJIT SINGH AND HIS WHITE OFFICERS.

THE Sikhs, who became eventually the most powerful nation encountered by us during the conquest and consolidation of the Indian Empire, were in the beginning no more than a weak and persecuted religious community.

Nanak, the founder of their religion, was born in the year 1469, and the name "Sikhs"—literally, learners or disciples—given by him to his followers, became in time the descriptive title of the whole people.

Nanak was succeeded by nine other prophets, the last of whom, Govind Singh, was assassinated in 1708. At the time of Govind Singh's death the Sikhs had become a warlike and powerful people, but they had yet to await the coming of the man who was to weld them into a nation and bestow on them the gift of discipline.

At length, in the year 1780, Ranjit Singh, destined to become a great leader of men, was born at Gujrat, the son of Mahan Singh, chief of one of the least important of the twelve confederacies into which the Sikhs were at that time formed.

Mahan Singh died in 1791, and the young Ranjit Singh, only eleven years of age, would hardly have been permitted to arrive at manhood but for the protection given him by two remarkable women. These were his mother, Raj Kour, daughter of Raja Gajpat Singh of Jind; and his mother-in-law, Sada Kour,[1] who had succeeded, as widow and heiress of her husband, to the chiefship of the powerful Kanheya confederacy. This confederacy ranked fourth in importance among the twelve, and Ranjit Singh, having grown up under the protection of its chieftainess, took no rest until he had dispossessed Sada Kour from authority. She died in the year 1827 in the prison to which her ungrateful *protégé* had consigned her.

Ranjit Singh's treatment of the other cherisher of his youth was yet more ungrateful, for, unless rumour foully belies him, he killed his mother, Raj Kour, with his own hands—following in this action the example left him by his father and grandfather.

It would be wearisome to the reader to trace minutely the measures, alternately violent and treacherous, by which Ranjit Singh gradually brought confederacy after confederacy under his rule, but some notice must be taken of an eventful period in which the young chief seized the golden opportunity of his lifetime.

The city of Lahore, the ancient capital of the Panjab, had been occupied in the years 1797 and 1798 by Shah Zaman, the Afghan invader of Northern India; but in the latter year domestic troubles recalled him somewhat suddenly to his own dominions, and while crossing the river Jhelam in flood he lost twelve pieces of artillery which were imbedded in quicksands. Not being able to

[1] Ranjit Singh had married, after the oriental fashion, at the age of six years, Mahtab Kour, daughter of Sada Kour. The title "Kour" means princess.

tarry until the guns had been extricated, Shah Zaman promised Ranjit Singh, whose inherited territory lay near Lahore, authority to take possession of that city and district from its then rulers, if he would save the imperilled guns (whose possession was at that period a matter of importance) and send them to Afghanistan. Having extricated the guns, Ranjit Singh made short work of capturing Lahore, whereupon he assumed the title of Maharaja, by which he is known in history: moreover, he soon afterwards annexed Amritsar, the religious capital of the Sikhs.

It will be understood that this rapid rise to power of a competent and ambitious ruler, and the consequent consolidation of the Sikhs, could not escape the notice of the English Government; and resulted, in fact, inevitably in the development of political relations between the two Powers, now become neighbours.

In 1809 a mission under Mr (afterwards Lord) Metcalfe effected an alliance between the British and Ranjit Singh, to which the latter honourably adhered during the remainder of his life.

An incident occurred during the visit of Mr Metcalfe's mission which brought home to Ranjit Singh's mind a sense of the true value of discipline, and determined him to form an army on the European system. Among the Sikh troops of 1809 were a turbulent and fanatical set of men known as the Akalis, or Immortals, whose headlong valour had often served Ranjit Singh and turned the fortunes of a doubtful battle. The Akalis, infuriated by the sight of the religious observances of Mr Metcalfe's Hindu escort, suddenly and without the slightest warning made an attack in overwhelming numbers on the camp of the British mission, which was defended only by two companies of native infantry. Though taken by surprise, the escort quickly rallied and repelled the attack of the Akalis, who incurred the wrath of Ranjit Singh even more for their ignominious defeat than for the inconvenience caused by their misconduct in making the attack. Profiting by this experience, and with the object of raising his own troops to a state of discipline similar to that of the British-Indian army, the Maharaja gave employment to certain deserters from our service, with whose assistance considerable progress was made.

Finally, the absorption, in the year 1820, of the great Kanheya confederacy, removed the last remaining faction of any strength, and left Ranjit Singh free to devote his attention in earnest to the formation of a disciplined army for the now united Sikh nation. With a natural prejudice against Englishmen, the Maharaja proceeded with great caution in the selection of officers to assist him in his task, and it was not until the spring of the year 1822 that the two pioneers of the band of adventurers in the Panjab appeared on the scene. These were the Chevalier Ventura and the Chevalier Allard, officers of the great Napoleon's army, who had served the Emperor with honour and credit, and who, after the fatal day of Waterloo, had wandered to Egypt, and thence successively to Persia, Afghanistan, and the Panjab, in search of fortune.

The arrival at Lahore of Ventura and Allard did not put an immediate end to the difficulties which had attended their journey; for Ranjit Singh was of an extremely suspicious turn of mind, and took some time to assure himself that the two foreigners (who were in a state of extreme poverty) were really what they declared themselves to be, and not secret emissaries of the dreaded and suspected British Government.

Before describing the careers of Ventura and his companions in arms, a brief description must be given of the old Sikh army—the "Dál Khálsa," or army of God, as it was called—and of the Maharaja, its creator.

The army consisted for the most part of cavalry, raised and paid under a feudal system. Each chief furnished his followers with arms and horses, and the mounted soldier alone was held in respect. The exceptional estimation in which the Akalis (the fanatics already mentioned) were held, was partly due to their religious character and partly to the desperate courage which they showed in action. They usually fought on foot, but all other Sikhs mounted themselves before going on active service if possible, or at any rate on the first opportunity that offered itself.

The Sikh weapon was the sword, which, when mounted, they used with great skill. Bows and arrows were used by the infantry, and a few matchlocks; but in the early days of Ranjit Singh's career the Sikhs disliked firearms and artillery of all descriptions, and possessed little or no skill in their use.

The picture of a Sikh soldier of the unreformed army, drawn for Bellasis by Chand Khan,[1] is probably as accurate as it is spirited, due allowance being made for the supposed bias of the speaker: "Go to the bazaar, take any dirty, naked scoundrel, twist up his hair, give him a lofty turban and a clean vest; comb out and lengthen his beard, and gird his loins with a yellow cummerbund; put

[1] In 'Adventures of an Officer in the Panjab,' by Sir Henry Lawrence.

a clumsy sword by his side and a long spear in his cowardly hand; set him on a strong bony two-year-old horse, and you have a passable Sikh." Omitting the adjective "cowardly," the above description may be accepted; but such men as those so unflatteringly described had done great things for Ranjit Singh. The swords may have been clumsy, but they were wielded by no cowardly hands when Multan was captured by the Khalsa from its gallant Afghan defenders.

With the arrival of Ventura and Allard came the day when the Maharaja could put into execution his long-cherished design, and commence to form his undisciplined hordes of horsemen into that Sikh army which in the end faced, and for a time faced successfully, the conquerors of Napoleon and his legions.

At the death of Ranjit Singh (1839) the strength of the regular army of the Panjab is stated by Sir Lepel Griffin to have been 29,000 men, with 192 guns. The monthly cost was Rs. 3,82,088, or say £500,000 per annum.

The irregular levies were estimated at about the same strength, and, says Sir Lepel Griffin, "were the picturesque elements in the Maharaja's reviews. Many of the men were well-to-do country gentlemen, the sons, relations, or clansmen of the chiefs who placed them in the field and maintained them there, and whose personal credit was concerned in their splendid appearance. There was no uniformity in their dress. Some wore a shirt of mail, with a helmet inlaid with gold and a *kalji* or heron's plume; others were gay with the many-coloured splendour of velvet and silk, with pink or yellow muslin turbans, and gold-embroidered belts carrying their sword and powder-horn. All wore, at the back, the small, round shield of tough buffalo-hide. These magnificent horsemen were armed some with bows and arrows, but the majority with match-locks, with which they made excellent practice."

And what manner of man was the great Maharaja who had welded together this valiant, powerful, and picturesque army?

Of the many descriptions of him that have been handed down to us, none is more vivid than that written by the traveller, Baron von Hügel: "In person he is short and mean-looking, and had he not distinguished himself by his great talents, he would be passed by without being thought worthy of observation. Without exaggeration I must call him the most ugly and unprepossessing man I saw throughout the Panjab. His left eye, which is quite closed, disfigures him less than the other, which is always rolling about wide open, and is much distorted by disease. The scars of the smallpox on his face do not run into one another, but form so many dark pits in his greyish-brown skin; his short straight nose is swollen at the tip; the skinny lips are stretched tight over his teeth, which are still good; his grizzled beard, very thin on the cheeks and upper lip, meets under the chin in matted confusion; and his head, which is sunk very much on his broad shoulders, is too large for his height, and does not seem to move easily."

It must be remembered that this striking picture was drawn late in the Maharaja's life, and Sir Lepel Griffin tells us that in earlier days Ranjit Singh, though short of stature and cruelly disfigured by smallpox, was the *beau idéal* of a soldier, strong, spare, active, courageous, and enduring. An excellent horseman, he would remain in the saddle the whole day without showing any sign of fatigue. His love of horses amounted to a passion; he was a keen sportsman and an accomplished swordsman. His dress was scrupulously simple, contrasting strongly with the gorgeous costumes of the Sikh *sardars.*

That Ranjit Singh was indeed a great man, a king of men, cannot for a moment be doubted. He was a born ruler, with the natural genius of command. Men obeyed him by instinct and because they had no power to disobey. Yet his moral character was extremely low—selfish, false, avaricious, grossly superstitious, shamelessly and openly drunken and debauched. That a man with these characteristics exercised an absolute control, even when paralysed and indeed half dead, over the turbulent Sikh people, testifies to his greatness.

Without attempting to present a complete picture of so complex a character as that of Ranjit Singh, two points call for our special attention when considering the Maharaja as a ruler and as the creator of an army: the first, his appreciation of the value of European discipline; and the second, his discrimination in the choice of agents.

The sketches of the Maharaja's chief officers, which follow, show how wisely they were chosen and how judiciously they were employed. From these pages and from the record of Colonel Gardner, some idea may be derived of the Dál Khálsa, or Sikh army.

I. GENERAL VENTURA.

For several reasons the name of General Ventura deserves to stand first in the roll of Ranjit Singh's white officers. He stood second to none in the estimation of his royal master, and was held in like respect by those British officials, both civil and military, with whom he came in contact. He was, moreover, with Allard, the first to enter Ranjit Singh's service, and he remained in it faithfully until and after the end of the Maharaja's life.

The fact, however, which influences me most strongly in according the place of honour to Ventura is his selection by Ranjit Singh to command the "Fouj Khas," or model brigade—the first in rank, discipline, and equipment in the reformed army. The four infantry battalions of this brigade were the models on which the remainder of the army was formed, and it was by the conversion of his main strength from indifferent irregular cavalry to infantry of a very high class that Ranjit Singh effected the marvellous results which establish his claim to be considered a great military organiser. In this conversion Ventura was his right-hand man, and the only thing to be regretted is that the account of his career, that of an honourable and brave soldier of fortune, is perhaps less entertaining than those of some of his less reputable colleagues.

Of the early life of Ventura I have been able to ascertain but little. It is usually stated (on the authority of Henry Prinsep) that Ventura, an Italian by birth, had held the rank of colonel of infantry in the army of the Napoleonic Empire; and there is no reason to doubt the fact. There is, unfortunately, no record in the French War Office of the services of individual members of the Italian contingent of the army of the First Empire, nor can information on the subject be obtained from the War Office of the present Italian army.

Joseph Wolff, the heroic missionary-traveller, states that Ventura was a Jew by birth, and that his name was

Reuben Ben-Toora. Be this as it may, Maharaja Ranjit Singh, when his first distrust had worn off, rapidly took Ventura into favour, gave him at first the command of two battalions, and very shortly afterwards that of a brigade. For a dwelling the Maharaja assigned to Ventura the remarkable building close to Lahore known as the tomb of Anarkali. This building had previously been occupied by Prince Karak Singh, the heir-apparent—a fact which shows the high social position accorded to Ventura.

The Maharaja desired his officers to engage not to eat beef, not to shave their beards, and not to smoke tobacco; but on Ventura and Allard agreeing to the first two conditions, the third was dispensed with.

General Ventura had not long to wait before an opportunity offered itself to him to show the Maharaja and the Sikh army the merits of his system of discipline, and also to illustrate his skill as a tactician. In March 1823, only a year after Ventura's arrival at Lahore, the Sikh army was engaged against the Afghans in the battle of Nowshera or Theri. The Afghans were in great strength—their regular troops holding a position on the right bank of the Kabul river, while 20,000 mountaineers of the Khatak and Yusufzai tribes occupied a strong position on the left bank.

Maharaja Ranjit Singh now showed his confidence in Generals Ventura and Allard by sending them with a small force of eight battalions and two batteries to keep the regular Afghan troops in check, while he with his main strength fell upon the Ghazis. The battle was severely contested, but, thanks to the superior generalship of Ranjit Singh, resulted in a complete victory for the Sikhs. The loss of the victors was estimated by Captain (afterwards Sir Claude) Wade[1] at 2000 men out of a total force present of 24,000.

The Afghan tribesmen had more than 3000 men killed, but gallantly rallied on the day following the battle and were ready to renew the fight. Muhammad Azim Khan, however, who commanded the Afghan regular troops, fearing lest his treasure and harem might fall into the hands of the Sikhs, broke up his camp, and, crossing the Momand hills with undignified haste, regained the valley of Jalalabad. He was pursued for a considerable distance by Ventura and Allard, whose force had been increased by a contingent under Prince Sher Singh — one of the Maharaja's sons, and a brave soldier.

In consequence of this victory Ranjit Singh occupied the city of Peshawar, and his troops plundered the whole district up to the Khaibar Pass.

General Ventura was highly favoured by the Maharaja in consequence of his services on this and subsequent occasions, and was granted pay at the rate of 2500 rupees a-month. He also was at various times given large *jagirs*, or feudal grants of land, by his royal master; and towards the end of the Maharaja's life Ventura received two villages as a special gift for his young daughter Victorine.

In spite of this large income the General was not so rich a man as might have been expected. He was too honourable to add to his fortune by illicit means, and his salary was usually in arrears to a very considerable extent. For years the debt amounted to no less than

[1] Sir Claude Wade held charge for many years of our political relations with Ranjit Singh, and was on most intimate terms with the Maharaja.

150,000 rupees, or five years' income; and whenever Ventura asked for the money due to him the Maharaja would say, "What do you require it for? Is not all I have yours?"

In 1825 General Ventura was married to a European lady at Ludhiana, and in honour of the event a ceremonial took place at Lahore, when the bridegroom received gifts of 10,000 rupees from the Maharaja and 30,000 from the courtiers.

The first campaign in the year 1826 was directed again Kotler, the chief command being intrusted to Jamadar Khushal Singh, a favourite officer of the Maharaja. In this campaign a number of Sikh *sardars* or chiefs, and soldiers, refused to serve under Ventura and Allard, and threatened to resist their authority by main force. The two generals complained to the Maharaja, who at once proceeded to the army, degraded the mutinous officers, and severely punished the ringleaders of inferior rank.

Later in the year General Ventura accompanied Sardar Hari Singh Nalwa, one of the bravest and best educated of the Sikh chieftains, in various small expeditions. A rising at Gandgarh was quelled after a smart action, the hill fortress of Srikot was captured; and finally Ventura took part in a demonstration under Prince Sher Singh, the object of which was to exact payment of the annual tribute from Yar Muhammad Khan, at that time ruler of Peshawar. The tribute was paid without fighting, and so ended a year of great military activity.

In the year 1827 occurred the curious incident of the horse Laili, which has been so often dilated on by writers of Sikh history. This horse was believed to be of surpassing beauty and excellence, and it is said that Fatteh Ali Shah, of Persia, offered 75,000 rupees for the animal. Maharaja Ranjit Singh also set his heart on becoming the owner of Laili. Yar Muhammad Khan of Peshawar, the owner of the coveted horse, had it noised abroad that Laili was dead; but this having been disproved, the Maharaja sent an expeditionary force under the command of his son, Prince Sher Singh, and General Ventura, and at length obtained possession of Laili. The presence of General Ventura, and subsequently of General Allard, at Peshawar, in connection with this affair, proved to be of material service to the Maharaja, as he was thereby enabled to rescue that city and district from the fanatical followers of Syad Ahmad the Reformer, who had defeated the Afghan troops and slain Yar Muhammad Khan himself. Peshawar was for a time relinquished to the Afghans and the Sikh army withdrawn. The ultimate fate of Syad Ahmad is related by Colonel Gardner in chap. ix. of this work.

To avoid undue repetition, it will suffice to say that, from the time of his entering Ranjit Singh's service, General Ventura took an active part in all the campaigns and expeditions by means of which the Maharaja increased year by year the extent of his dominions and the efficiency of his army.

The confidence shown in Ventura, and the other foreign officers who will next be introduced to the reader, aroused so much jealousy among the Sikh princes and chieftains that, in general, the leadership of those expeditions in which the Maharaja himself did not exercise the command was bestowed on one of the reigning family, or one of the few chiefs who could be trusted in independent employment: thus in the year 1831, that of Colonel Gardner's arrival in the Panjab, General Ventura shared with Shahzada Sher Singh the command of the force sent out from Peshawar against the reformer Syad Ahmad. As is related in Gardner's narrative, this force completely defeated Syad Ahmad's followers, and the prophet himself was slain, at a place called Balakot. Gardner was just too late to take part in the action; but it is probable that Ventura became aware that Gardner had intended to assist the insurgents, and that this fact, coupled with Gardner's adherence to the Dogra faction, caused the ill-will which is shown by Gardner's language to have existed between them. The French and Italian officers in Ranjit Singh's service held much aloof from those of other nationalities, and this also must have contributed to the unfriendliness.

Later in the year 1831 General Ventura was sent to Multan, in command of a force of 10,000 troops and thirty pieces of artillery, for the purpose of collecting the tribute of that province.

Space does not permit me to detail Ventura's military achievements in the service of Maharaja Ranjit Singh: suffice it to say that he served that exacting master faithfully to the end of his life, and after the Maharaja's death he in like manner served his successors.

In addition to the rank of general, conferred on Ventura soon after he entered the Sikh service, Ranjit Singh created him *kazi* and governor of Lahore, which appointment gave him the third seat in durbar.

During the early years of his service in the Panjab General Ventura had lived with General Allard in a large mosque near the Lahore cantonments. It is related that when Ventura was absent in France for two years (1838-1840), his family, together with forty or fifty female slaves, lived during the whole period in this mosque without once moving out of doors.

General Ventura was a high-minded and honourable soldier, much respected by the Sikhs, and also by all the English officers with whom he was brought in contact. He eventually retired from the Panjab in 1843, possessed of an ample fortune, and passed the remainder of his life at Paris, where he lived in very good style.

II. GENERAL ALLARD.

The second of Maharaja Ranjit Singh's foreign generals was Jean François Allard, born at Saint Tropez, a small seaport on the Mediterranean coast of France, on March 8, 1785. Allard joined the French army on December 6, 1803, his first regiment being the 23rd Dragoons, in which he passed through the various grades to the rank of squadron quartermaster-sergeant.

Allard served in Italy during the years 1804 to 1806, and was transferred in the latter year to the royal guard of the army of the kingdom of Naples. In February 1807 he became quartermaster of the Neapolitan regiment of light cavalry, and towards the end of the following year accompanied that corps to the theatre of war in Spain.

Allard became sub-lieutenant on the 15th June 1809, and lieutenant on the 10th July 1810. On the 31st July 1813 he received two sword-cuts in the skirmish of Aleazar, near Alcala, and a year later was transferred to the 2nd regiment of dragoons of the Imperial Guard of France. In July 1814 he was again transferred to the 2nd Hussars, and on 28th April 1815 he was promoted captain in the 7th Hussars.

His services had been rewarded with the crosses of the Royal Spanish Order and of the Legion of Honour, and he held the appointment of aide-de-camp to Maréchal Brune. Fortune appeared, therefore, to smile on the young soldier, and a successful career in the military service of France seemed fairly within his reach. The fatal day of Waterloo, and the murder of his patron, Maréchal Brune, dashed his hopes to the earth, and after four years of hesitation and of half-hearted attempts to make a fresh start in the royal army, Allard decided to seek his fortune abroad. His first intention was to visit the United States, but a communication from his friend Colonel Ventura caused him to change his plans and accompany the latter to Persia, where they entered the service of Abbas Mirza, the heir-apparent. Here the friends were treated with kindness and respect, but their aspirations in the matter of salary were very far from satisfied; so in the fulness of time they took leave of Abbas Mirza and passed through Afghanistan into the Panjab.

Their early troubles in this kingdom have been related in the account of Ventura, and on that subject it need only be stated that at the same time that Ventura received command of a body of infantry, Allard was commissioned to raise a corps of dragoons, who were to be armed and disciplined like the cavalry of European armies. Into this task Allard entered with unbounded enthusiasm, and with a considerable amount of success.

Lieutenant William Barr, of the Bengal Horse Artillery, who accompanied Sir Claude Wade in his successful operations in the Khaibar Pass, gives an excellent description of the Sikh cavalry at the time of Allard's death. After an unfavourable review of the artillery (who were, however, much better than they looked), Barr writes:—

"We then reached the cavalry, the dragoons occupying the left. These were well mounted, and form a fine body of men and horses. On their right were two regiments of Allard's cuirassiers, the most noble-looking troops on parade. The men and horses were all picked, and amongst the former are to be seen many stalwart fellows, who appear to advantage under their cuirasses and steel casques. Particular attention seems to have been paid to setting them well up, and their accoutrements are kept in the highest order. Many of the officers wear brass cuirasses, and their commandant is perhaps the finest man of the whole body, and looks extremely well in front of his superb regiment. . . . It used to be poor Allard's pride and amusement to review these men, and their present martial appearance is no doubt owing to that officer's constant care and superintendence."

Barr goes on to say that in marching past, the regularity and order of the cuirassiers could scarcely be exceeded by the Company's cavalry.

Barr and his companions had previously been much struck by the excellent way in which Allard's dragoons were mounted. This was the corps mentioned above as taking the left of the line of cavalry. The dress of these dragoons consisted of a jacket of a dull red with broad facings of buff, crossed in front by a pair of black belts, one of which supported a pouch and the other a bayonet,

—genuine dragoon equipment, in which the Sikh cavalry fought, as the old quip has it, *indifferently* on horseback or on foot. Round the waist the dragoons wore a cummerbund, partially concealed by a sword-belt, from which hung a sabre with a brass hilt and leathern scabbard. The carbine was so attached as to give it the appearance of being slung across the back of the dragoon, but rested, in fact, in a bucket fastened to the saddle. The trousers were of dark-blue cloth with a red stripe, and the turbans of crimson silk, brought somewhat into a peak in front, and ornamented in the centre with a small brass half-moon, from which sprang a glittering sprig about two inches in height.

The officers were attired from top to toe in bright crimson silk, and were armed with a sabre only.

Like General Ventura, Allard took part in all the campaigns of the Sikh army from the date of his arrival in the Panjab. It is related that very soon after Allard had begun to form his regular cavalry Ranjit Singh ordered his Ghorcharas, or irregular cavalry, to cross the Indus. The order was immediately obeyed, but no discipline was observed and no precautions were taken. No less than 500 men are said to have been swept away by the torrent and drowned. Allard then mounted an elephant, and directed his cavalry by trumpet-sounds, and moving them in a suitable formation, succeeded in conveying them across the Indus without loss. Allard was immediately given the rank of general, and received the same pay as Ventura—viz., £3000 per annum.

General Allard, like his friend Ventura, was a man of high character, of polished manners, and of a most amiable disposition. Frequent mention is made of him in the writings of travellers in the Panjab, and, almost without exception, he is spoken of in terms of respect and liking. He showed a princely hospitality to Europeans of all ranks, and a gentleness to the natives of India which earned him the contempt of Avitabile—a fact on which he is surely to be congratulated.

Ranjit Singh seems to have felt a genuine affection for Allard, and it is even said that the Maharaja's death was hastened by the loss of his friend.

General Allard's death occurred at Peshawar on January 23, 1839, and his body was taken to Lahore for burial: the cause of death was heart disease. The Maharaja was in bad health, and his attendants were long afraid to tell him of Allard's death. General Allard was nearly fifty-four years old, and left a wife and large family, to whom he was greatly attached. He was perhaps the most amiable and attractive of soldiers of fortune.

It is worth mentioning that Allard, together with Ventura, Avitabile, and Court, received from King Louis Philippe the rank of general in the French army and the Cross of the Legion of Honour. Allard was also appointed Political Agent of the French Government at the Court of Lahore. In appearance he was said to have been a handsome man, of a benevolent cast of countenance; and Miss Eden amusingly describes the impression made on her by his remarkable beard. "Allard," she writes in a letter from Calcutta dated December 5, 1836, "wears an immensely long beard that he is always stroking and making much of; and I was dead absent all the time he was there because his *wings* are beautiful white hair, and his moustachios and the middle of his beard quite black. He looks like a piebald horse."

III. GENERAL AVITABILE.

In marked contrast to Allard was Avitabile, the third of Ranjit Singh's white generals, who is even better known to us than are Ventura and Allard, as it fell to his lot to occupy a position for many years in which he was able to render signal services to the British Indian Government. This position was that of governor of Peshawar, which city and province were ruled by Avitabile with remorseless cruelty, shameless rapacity, and signal skill and success.

Of the early life which fitted a Neapolitan peasant for such a position but little can be ascertained with certainty, but that little discloses a very remarkable personality. "Paolo di Bartolomeo Avitabile—a general in the armies of the Panjab and of France; Chevalier of the Legion of Honour; of the Orders of Merit and of Saint Ferdinand (of the Kingdom of the Two Sicilies); Commander of the Durani Order (of Afghanistan); Grand Commander of the Lion and Sun and of the Two Lions and Crown (of Persia); and of the Star of the Panjab"—was born at Agerolo in the kingdom of Naples on the 25th October 1791, and served in the local levies of his native State during the years 1807 to 1809.

Avitabile then entered the artillery of the army of King Joseph Buonaparte, and served that sovereign and his successor Murat. Avitabile served several campaigns under Murat in the Italian contingent of the imperial army, and rose to the rank of lieutenant, receiving also the command of the 15th Battery.

When the kingdom of Naples was restored to the Bourbons by the fall of Napoleon, Avitabile retained his rank and command, and served under the Austrian General Delaver at the siege of Gaeta. On this occasion he showed distinguished gallantry, and was twice wounded. General Delaver recommended him for promotion to the rank of captain and for a decoration, but for some unexplained reason Avitabile was removed in the same rank of lieutenant to a light infantry regiment. Disgusted by this treatment, Avitabile determined to seek his fortunes abroad, and embarked for Philadelphia: his voyage was, however, disastrous, and ended in a shipwreck near Marseilles. Here Avitabile was kindly treated, and advised to turn his steps eastward rather than westward: he accordingly took ship for Constantinople, where he found an envoy of Futteh Ali Shah of Persia charged with the duty of obtaining European officers for the Persian army.

Avitabile arrived at Teheran in the year 1820, and served the Shah and his heir-apparent for a period of six years, during which he performed signal services, and was rewarded with the rank of "khan" and the grade of colonel. He also received two of the highest Persian decorations.[1] Discontented with his remuneration, and hearing favourable reports from Ventura of his service in the Panjab, Avitabile and Court (a brother-officer of the Napoleonic army who was in Persia with him) set out for India. After an adventurous journey through Afghanistan, they arrived in the Panjab and were quickly given employment. Ranjit Singh soon discovered that Avitabile's talents lay in the direction of civil government,

[1] This statement is derived from an account of General Avitabile in the 'Livre des Célébrités Contemporaines,' published in 1846. It must, however, be mentioned that Sir George Russell Clerk, who knew Avitabile well, mentions in his Diary that the latter held no military rank in Persia, and, in fact, made his living in that country as a pedlar.

and made him governor of the town and province of Wazirabad.

Avitabile showed great ability in this office, and ruled his subjects, Sikhs and Muhammadans alike, with impartial severity. In so doing he undoubtedly pleased Ranjit Singh, who had all the instincts of a great ruler, but gave great dissatisfaction to the Sikhs, who desired and expected to be treated as the ruling race. In addition to his duties as governor, Avitabile exercised military command over the troops at Wazirabad, and succeeded in impressing something of his own stern character on his infantry regiment.

The Rev. Joseph Wolff, on his arrival in the Panjab (in 1832), found Avitabile at Wazirabad, and gives the following interesting account of him:—

"This famous Neapolitan spoke Italian, French, Persian, and Hindustani with equal facility. He had improved the town of Wazirabad to a remarkable extent. He kept the streets of the city clean, and had a fine palace and a beautiful carriage for himself. He was a clever, cheerful man, and full of fun. He told Wolff at once that he would show to him his *angeli custodes*, and then took him to his bedroom, the walls of which were covered with pictures of dancing-girls.

"He and Wolff one day rode out together on elephants, and he said to him, 'Now I will show you the marks of the civilisation which I have introduced into this country.' They rode outside the town, and there Wolff saw before him about six gibbets, upon which a great number of malefactors were hanging. Though Avitabile was full of fun, yet whenever the conversation was directed to important subjects, he became most serious. Though he had amassed in India a fortune of £50,000, he was always panting after a return to his native country, Naples; and he said to Wolff, 'For the love of God, help me to leave this place!'"

Avitabile continued to govern Wazirabad wisely, and on the whole well, until he was removed in the year 1834 to Peshawar. The government of this new conquest of the Maharaja's had proved too arduous a task for the various Sikh princes and *sardars* who had tried their hands at it.

Peshawar is, as has been well said, a fragment of Central Asia that has accidentally become, geographically and politically, part of India. Of all the cities of the plains its inhabitants have been and are the most savage and unruly. The ruthless Avitabile was the first man who ever held Peshawar in subjection. In the opinion of Sir Henry Lawrence, a man who must have held Avitabile's methods in horror, "the most lenient view of him that can be taken is, to consider him as set in authority over savage animals—not as a ruler over reasonable beings—as one appointed to grind down a race, who bear the yoke with about as good a grace as 'a wild bull in a net,' and who, catching the ruler for one moment asleep, would soon cease to be governed. But the ground of complaint alleged against him is that he acts as a savage among savage men, instead of showing them that a Christian can wield the iron sceptre without staining it by needless cruelty,—without following some of the worst fashions of his worst neighbours. Under his rule summary hangings have been added to the native catalogue of punishments, and not a bad one either, when properly used; but the ostentation of adding two or three to the string suspended from the gibbet, on special days and festivals, added to a very evident habitual carelessness of life, lead one to fear that small pains are taken to distinguish between innocence and guilt, and that many a man, ignorant of the alleged crime, pays for it with his blood. . . .

"Still, General Avitabile has many of the attributes of a good ruler: he is bold, active, and intelligent, seeing everything with his own eyes; up early and late. He has, at the expense of his own character for humanity, by the terror of his name, saved much life. It is but just to state that the peaceful and well-disposed inhabitants of Peshawar, both Hindu and Muhammadan, united in praise of his administration, though all with one voice declared that mercy seldom mingled in his decrees. Believed to fear neither man nor devil, Avitabile keeps down by grim fear what nothing else would keep down, the unruly spirits around him, who, if let slip, would riot in carnage: his severity may therefore be extenuated as the least of two evils."

This is not an unfavourable picture, and it is worth studying, for Avitabile was one of the very few Europeans who has governed an Eastern province on oriental principles.

Avitabile was in appearance "a tall stout man, of sensual countenance, with large nose and lips, something of the Jewish type, and well whiskered and bearded. He wore a laced blue jacket, not unlike that of our horse-artillery, capacious crimson trousers of the Turkish fashion, and a rich sword." The blade of this sword had belonged to the Emperor Akbar, and was a superb one: it cost Avitabile 2000 rupees, and the setting cost him another thousand.

The hilt was of gold, studded with very valuable jewels, as was the scabbard, a very small portion of green velvet being visible in the middle of the latter. It would be interesting to know what has become of this costly relic.

The following anecdote, told by a German traveller in the Panjab at the time of Avitabile's governorship of Peshawar, illustrates the General's ready wit and knowledge of native character :—

"A certain Mohammedan woman of Peshawar had a son and a daughter. Both married, and the daughter and daughter-in-law gave birth, at the same time, to two children, one a boy, the other a girl. Some time afterwards a serious dispute arose between the two ladies. The daughter's child was a girl, that of the daughter-in-law a boy, but the former maintained that the boy was hers and had been stolen from her. The daughter-in-law denied the charge, and was supported in her denial by her husband's mother. The strife became serious, and the contending parties brought the affair before the judge. This magistrate, being no Solomon, was unable to elicit the truth, and dismissed the complainants. The latter were not satisfied, and appealed to the High Court, over which General Avitabile presided. The case was brought before him, and public curiosity was strained to the highest pitch, each eagerly asking his neighbour, 'How will the judge decide?' The statements upon both sides having been gone through, General Avitabile ordered two goats to be brought, one having a male, the other a female kid. This being done, he sent for two sheep that had each a lamb, one a male, the other a female. In like manner he commanded two cows to be brought, of which one had a male, the other a female calf. These different quadrupeds being introduced, he ordered that the goats, the sheep, and the cows should be milked, and the milk of each animal placed in a separate vessel, which should be marked. 'Now,' said the General, 'let this milk be examined, and it will be found that that which belongs to the animals that have male young is stronger than the milk which has been taken from the others.' Upon inspection this was found to be correct. 'Now,' said the judge, 'bring me some milk from the mothers of the children.' The milk was brought, and General Avitabile declared that the milk of the daughter-in-law was stronger than that of the daughter, and that consequently she must be the mother of the boy. The wisdom of the judge astonished every one, and his decision was universally admired."

It is also related that on one occasion General Avitabile quelled a mutiny among his troops by releasing and arming a number of prisoners, by which means he took his troops by surprise and reduced them to subjection.

It is an interesting fact that the best account of Avitabile, after that of Sir Henry Lawrence, is contained in the 'History of the War in Afghanistan' of Captain (afterwards Sir) Henry Havelock. Captain Havelock had marched to Kabul in 1839 with the 'army of the Indus,' in the capacity of aide-de-camp to Sir Willoughby Cotton, and in November of that year arrived at Peshawar on his return to India.

Havelock confirms all that is written by others concerning the lavish hospitality shown to all comers by Avitabile, and his description is worth transcribing, giving, as it does, a curious picture of the life of the adventurer in high places :—

"In the 'Serai,' mentioned by Elphinstone as one of the

glories of Peshawar in 1809, the present governor of the city has established his military headquarters, and his civil and fiscal tribunals. It is called the 'Gorkhatra,' and is a vast quadrangle, the length of each side being 250 yards. This has been rendered habitable, first by building a suite of apartments over the gateway nearest to the country, and next by erecting a very handsome dwelling in the Persian fashion, consisting of three storeys and a *rez-de-chaussée*, on the side nearer the city.

"The governor is a man of princely habits. His dress, chargers, and equipages all partake of a splendour well calculated to uphold his authority amongst a people like the Afghans. He particularly, and very justly, piques himself on the excellence of his table, and keeps an establishment of not fewer than eight cooks, who are well versed in all the mysteries of Persian, English, and French gastronomy. He is, moreover, a frank, gay, and good-humoured person, as well as an excellent ruler and skilful officer."

As Captain Havelock passed a complete month in close association with Avitabile, this very favourable picture of the redoubtable Italian possesses much value.

On the occasion of the advance of the British army in 1842, under General Pollock, to avenge the destruction of Elphinstone's army in Afghanistan, Avitabile was again brought in contact with a large number of English officers. From what motives he acted it would perhaps be ungracious to inquire too closely, but it is undeniable that General Avitabile rendered very important services to England at that critical juncture. No stone was left unturned by him to facilitate the movement of our troops through the Peshawar province, and the General also lavished personal kindnesses and hospitality on the English officers.

Among other friendly actions of Avitabile may be mentioned the advance of large sums of money to the British field-treasury. This, however, was at least as convenient to the lender as to the borrower, for Avitabile was thus enabled to transmit to England a considerable portion of his fortune. No less than ten lakhs of rupees were advanced in this manner by the General.

After Avitabile's return to Europe he asked for some mark of the satisfaction of the East Indian Company, and in due course the Court of Directors resolved (27th August 1845) "that the eminent services of General Avitabile, while governor of Peshawar, in co-operation with the British troops during the Afghanistan campaign, fully entitle him to some enduring testimonial of the Court's grateful sense of his conduct." Avitabile was subsequently presented by the Court with a sword worth 300 guineas.

Reference has already been made to Avitabile's kindness to European travellers. Like Generals Ventura and Allard, he ever received such wanderers with princely hospitality, and he behaved generously also to those natives of the Panjab whom he ruled with such iron severity. Sir Richard Burton relates that, when passing through Egypt on his celebrated pilgrimage to Mecca, he was in some way mistaken for Avitabile; and that a party of Indian Muhammadan pilgrims travelled a long distance to see him, relying on the well-known liberality of "Abu-Tabile" for assistance.

Avitabile's government of Peshawar came to an end during the disturbed year of 1843. He was compelled to leave the city and to take refuge at Jalalabad. Eventually he retired to British India, and thence made his way to his native Naples.

General Avitabile received the same rate of pay as General Ventura—viz., £3000 per annum, in addition to a *jagir* worth £2000 per annum, as governor of Peshawar. His further emoluments are supposed to have been very great, more particularly after the death of Maharaja Ranjit Singh, when all business fell into confusion.

After his retirement from the Sikh service General Avitabile built a fine house at Castellamare near Naples, but did not long live to enjoy it. An over-devotion to champagne carried him off, and his large fortune soon found its way into the pockets of the lawyers—so many *soi-disant* relations asserting their claims to a share of the General's goods as to make "Avitabile's cousins" a byword in Italy. Thus for the hundredth time did the pen profit by that which the sword had earned.

IV. GENERAL COURT.

The fourth and last of Ranjit Singh's white generals is less known to history than the three whose record has been briefly sketched.

It appears from the official records of the French War Office that Claude Auguste Court was born on the 26th September 1793, and entered the École Polytechnique of Paris on the 24th April 1812. He was appointed sub-lieutenant in the 151st Regiment of the Line in 1813, and was transferred to the 68th Regiment in the following year. He was permitted to resign his commission in

July 1818; but his service in the French army, though short, had not been undistinguished, for he served the campaign of 1813 in Saxony, of 1814 and of 1815, and was wounded by a musket-shot in the left leg on the 28th March 1813 at the skirmish at Halle.

Court next took service in Persia, when he made the acquaintance of Avitabile, and finally travelled to the Panjab in company with him. This journey to Kabul was performed in the autumn of 1826, and in the spring of 1827 Court and Avitabile entered the service of Maharaja Ranjit Singh. The Maharaja was anxious to improve and increase his artillery, and appointed Court to the command of that arm—a duty for which his very considerable talents and scientific attainments fitted him. The striking improvement in the Sikh artillery which was effected in the twelve remaining years of the Maharaja's life must be largely attributed to Court's exertions, for all accounts of the Sikh army agree in stating that he was an excellent officer, and entirely devoted to his professional duties.

It would probably be wearisome to the readers to give a long description of the artillery of the Khalsa army as perfected by General Court. It may be found by the curious in Barr's 'Journal of a March through the Punjab.' Barr, an officer of the Bengal Horse Artillery, concludes his remarks with the following words: "When it is considered that all we saw was the work of the General's own knowledge, and when we reflect on the difficulties he had to surmount, it is a matter almost of wonder to behold the perfection to which he has brought his artillery." How staunchly this artillery fought against us is well known.

As an instance of Maharaja Ranjit Singh's fitful generosity, it is stated that the first shell constructed by General Court was worth 30,000 rupees to him—probably a record reward to an artillery officer.

In the agreements signed by Court and the other European officers it was stipulated that they should abstain from eating beef, should grow their beards, and should marry native wives. This last clause was not insisted on in the case of Ventura, who married a European lady; but Allard, Avitabile, and Court fell in with their master's wishes. Avitabile, indeed, married with oriental profusion; Allard married a charming lady of Kashmir, by whom he had a large family; and Court twice married natives of India.

In addition to his domestic amenities General Court took much interest in archæology. The results of his researches in the antiquities of the Panjab frequently adorned the pages of the Journal of the Asiatic Society of Bengal, and his cabinet of coins and other treasures is said to have been superb. "He is at all times," says M'Gregor the historian, "ready to exhibit them with a politeness which reflects equal credit on him as a gentleman and a savant."

Barr describes Court as a short, thick-set man, pitted with smallpox, and with the appearance of a rough-and-ready sailor. His uniform consisted of an open horse-artillery jacket, displaying beneath it a red waistcoat profusely ornamented with lace. Like Avitabile, he wore a handsome sabre attached to an embroidered belt; but, unlike him, Court was a man of very simple habits. He was accustomed to live in a small house in the garden of the larger building occupied by his family.

General Court received £2400 a-year in pay, in addition to a *jagir* worth £100 a-year.

During the lifetime of Ranjit Singh the foreign generals were enabled to keep clear of the conflicting factions of the Court, but after the Maharaja's death such conduct was impossible. All who served Karrak Singh and his successors were compelled to form part of one faction or the other. Thus when Prince Sher Singh was about to march to Lahore in January 1841, to assert his claim to the throne, he called General Ventura to his side. Ventura's influence was great, and over none was it stronger than his friend Court. The two Generals therefore accompanied Sher Singh to Lahore, and took part in the siege of the fort of Lahore, in the defence of which Colonel Gardner took so prominent a share.

As has been related by Gardner, the accession of Sher Singh to the throne was followed by an outburst of violence on the part of the Sikh army which threatened to wreck the great fabric which had been created by the genius of Ranjit Singh. A large number of officers who had incurred the enmity of the soldiery were murdered in cold blood; and General Court, for some reason, was among those held to be most obnoxious. Court's house was attacked by his own troops, and the General was compelled to seek refuge in the camp of General Ventura, who had to use his artillery to protect himself and his friend.

General Court subsequently left Lahore and took up his abode on the British side of the Sutlej, where he remained for several months, repeatedly claiming his discharge from the Sikh Government. It was refused. So, disdaining to decamp without leave, he returned to Lahore; but foreseeing the probability of some such *bouleversement* as afterwards took place, the General wisely left his zenana in safe quarters at Ludiana.

General Court eventually returned to France, where his wife was formally christened and remarried to him, according to Catholic ceremonies, by the Archbishop of Marseilles. After General Court's death a *jagir* worth £480 a-year was settled on Madame Court. The General appears to have been an honourable and highly amiable man, and a good soldier.

V. DR HARLAN.

In addition to General Ventura, Allard, Avitabile, and Court, whose claims to the rank of general are indubitable, that position is also claimed by one Josiah Harlan, usually described by historians as Dr Harlan. The doctor himself prefers the rank of general, a fancy in which he is followed by some of his profession at the present day; and although his claim to that title may be doubtful, it is a positive fact that Maharaja Ranjit Singh not only made him governor of an important province, but conferred on him the command of a body of troops.

Those whose good fortune it is to have read that truly delectable book 'The Travels and Adventures of Dr Wolff,' may remember that when Wolff entered the Panjab he arrived "at Attock, when he crossed a suspension bridge on the back of an elephant. According to his custom, whenever he crosses water, Wolff screamed out, which he did on this occasion in crossing the Indus."

Then, journeying on, this most valiant of cowards (for

a right brave man he was, as all who know his history will testify) proceeded to the pleasant city of Gujrat, "a considerable town, which also belonged to Ranjit Singh." He arrived there late at night, and was brought to the palace of the governor, who had expected him; when, "to his great surprise, he heard some one singing "Yankee Doodle," with all the American snuffle. It was his Excellency the Governor himself. He was a fine tall gentleman, dressed in European clothing, and with an Indian hookah in his mouth." Wolff asked how he came to know "Yankee Doodle." He answered, in nasal tones, "I am a free citizen of the United States, from the State of Pennsylvania, city of Philadelphia. I am the son of a Quaker. My name is Josiah Harlan." As this man's history seemed romantic to Wolff, he recorded it (as far as it then went) with sufficient accuracy in the following words:—

"Harlan," he said, "had in his early life studied surgery, but he went out as supercargo in a ship to Canton. He then returned to America, where he had intended to marry a lady to whom he was engaged; but she had played him false. He then went to India, and came to Calcutta, whence Lord Amherst, at that time Governor-General of India, sent him as assistant-surgeon with the British army to the Burmese empire. Afterwards he quitted the British army, and tried to make himself king of Afghanistan; but, although he actually took a fortress, he was defeated at last by a force sent against him by Ranjit Singh, which made him a prisoner. Ranjit Singh, seeing his talents, said to him, 'I will make you governor of Gujrat, and give you 3000 rupees a-month. If you behave well I will increase your salary; if not, I will cut off your nose.' So Wolff found him, and his nose being entire was evidence that he had behaved well."

Such was the story told by Harlan to Wolff, and recorded by the latter with his inimitable simplicity of manner, and it was fairly accurate. It is worth mentioning that Harlan's service in the first Burmese war was in the capacity of assistant-surgeon to the battery of artillery commanded by Major (afterwards Field-Marshal Sir) George Pollock.

Harlan did not distinguish himself in the British service, and soon left it, finding his way eventually to the Panjab frontier. It was not in Afghanistan (as he told Dr Wolff, or as the latter wrongly understood him) that Harlan set up the star-spangled banner, but on the debatable land south of the river Sutlej, over which Ranjit Singh claimed sovereignty and the British Indian Government exercise protection.

Whether or not Harlan crossed the Sutlej is doubtful, but he fell into the hands of Ranjit Singh, who took him into favour and gave him employment. Harlan now entered on the dangerous career of a secret agent—doubly dangerous in his case; for not only did he act as envoy from Ranjit Singh to Dost Muhammad, visiting Afghanistan twice at least in that capacity, but he also was the agent in the Panjab of the exiled Shah Shuja, the legitimate king of Afghanistan.

In 1828 Harlan visited Kabul, travelling in the disguise of a dervish, and while ostensibly employed by Ranjit Singh, secretly intriguing in the interests of Shah Shuja. His mission was, in fact, to revolutionise Afghanistan, and with that object Harlan took up his abode in the house of one of the Amir's brothers.

Harlan evidently feels that some apology for his conduct is required, and exclaimed: "Let no Christian be deceived by the fraternal appellation. Amongst the customs of Orientals we meet with strange perversions of our commonest received principles, and the term 'brother' in a community which springs from a system of polygamy means a natural enemy, a domestic adversary, expectant heir of a capricious parent, contending for mastery in the disturbed arena of family feuds."

Harlan found Dost Muhammad too firmly established in power for his intrigues to meet with success, but his visit to Kabul was by no means wasted. He obtained the confidence of Dost Muhammad, who admitted him to great intimacy. Harlan seems to have understood the greatness of his host's character, and in his 'Memoir' describes the Amir's manner of life in a most interesting way; indeed his sketch of Dost Muhammad's daily round is the most vivid that has been recorded. Harlan's style is turgid, but by no means devoid of power, and in his pages we see described Dost Muhammad's neglected childhood and dissolute youth; his unexpected rise to power; his public renunciation of the follies and crimes which had hitherto marked him; his wisdom, strength, justice, and moderation when in power; and his calm endurance in the day of adversity.

While thus observing and admiring the qualities of a great ruler, Harlan felt that life in the Panjab was more lucrative as well as more congenial than a precarious existence in Afghanistan. He returned, therefore, to Lahore, with a mission to act there as the agent of Dost Muhammad. His life at this time must indeed have been somewhat complicated.

For the next seven years Harlan was governor of Jasrata and Nurpore, and subsequently of Gujrat, gaining the confidence of Maharaja Ranjit Singh, and serving him for a time with zeal and ability; but at the end of this period, it is stated by Sir Henry Lawrence that "any regard that may have obtained between them was converted into hate."

In 1835 Harlan was removed from his governorship. It is stated that Ranjit Singh found that Harlan was coining base money under the pretence of studying alchemy. Be this as it may, the Maharaja considered Harlan an eminently suitable person to act as his ambassador to Dost Muhammad, who was now threatening the town and province of Peshawar, so long in dispute between the Sikhs and Afghans. Harlan was sent with Fakir Azizuddin, the confidential barber and minister (oriental combination) of the Maharaja, with instructions to delay the Afghans until the Maharaja had gained sufficient time to assemble the Sikh army on the northern frontier.

Harlan states, with evident pride, that while ostensibly an ambassador, his real mission was to corrupt the Amir's chiefs, and sow distrust and disloyalty among them. An excuse for Harlan may be found in the conduct of Dost Muhammad, who, with all his merits as a ruler, was a consummate scoundrel if judged by the European standard of honour. He proposed on this occasion to seize Harlan and Azizuddin, the latter being known to be indispensable to the Maharaja (as he alone could prepare the mysteriously compounded cordial which gave the paralysed monarch fictitious strength), and to make use of them to compel Ranjit Singh to abandon Peshawar. This intended treachery towards the sacred persons of ambassadors perhaps justified Harlan's line of conduct: he knew the man he had to deal with.

To escape the odium which, even in the East, would have followed on the seizure of the envoys, the Amir made his brother, Sultan Muhammad Khan, swear many oaths on the Koran to make Harlan and the fakir prisoners. Harlan, however, found means to induce Sultan Muhammad Khan, who was the Afghan governor of the Peshawar province, to come to terms with Ranjit Singh and desert Dost Muhammad; and the prince was the more readily led to that course of conduct by the feeling that the Amir would reap the benefit if the envoys were seized, while the odium would fall on himself, they being his guests.

Sultan Muhammad Khan, therefore, marched his followers, amounting to some 10,000 men, to the vicinity of the Sikh forces (which now confronted the Afghan army), and wrote to the Amir to announce his defection.

Masson, another adventurer, who was with Dost Muhammad at the time, gives a most amusing account of the transaction; and states that Sultan Muhammad's letter to his brother was couched in such abusive terms that when it was read in open durbar before the Amir many of those who heard it were obliged to go out from "the presence" to conceal their mirth. It was a case of "the biter bit"; but it is somewhat humiliating to find that the most successful knave in so choice a collection was the white man. In consequence of this diplomatic success of Harlan, the Afghan army shortly melted away, Dost Muhammad was compelled to return to Kabul, and Peshawar was finally lost to the Afghans.

Harlan, however, had lost Ranjit Singh's favour, and soon left his service, whether by resignation or dismissal is not quite clear. Harlan himself writes: "Monarch as he was, absolute and luxurious, and voluptuous in the possession of treasured wealth and military power, I resolved to avenge myself and cause him to tremble in the midst of his magnificence." With this benevolent intention he left the Panjab and entered Dost Muhammad's service towards the end of the year 1836. He states that the Amir "received him with much the same feeling of exultation that the King of Persia is known to have indulged when his Court was visited by Themistocles."

Dost Muhammad, he states, received him as a brother and addressed him by that title, seated him in durbar at his side, gave him the command of his regular troops, and at his instigation again declared war against the Sikhs, who had recently annoyed him by erecting a fort at Jamrud, which commanded the mouth of the Khaibar Pass.

In the battle which took place before this fort in April 1837 the Sikh general, Hari Singh, was slain, and, as Harlan puts it, "the proud King of Lahore quailed on his threatened throne, as he exclaimed with terror and despair, 'Harlan has avenged himself—this is all his work.'" However, as a matter of history, the Afghans shortly afterwards retreated from the frontier without again giving battle.

In the following year (1838) Harlan was sent in charge of a military expedition, despatched by Dost Muhammad against the Prince of Kunduz. His account of his exploits is too good to lose. "In the execution of this enterprise," he writes, "I surmounted the Indian Caucasus, and there upon the mountain heights unfurled my country's banner to the breeze under a salute of twenty-six guns. On the highest pass of the frosty Caucasus, that of Kharzar, 12,500 feet above the sea, the star-spangled banner gracefully waved amid the icy peaks and soil-less rugged rocks of a sterile region, seemingly sacred to the solitude of an undisturbed eternity. We ascended passes through regions where glaciers and silent dells, and frowning rocks, blackened by ages of weather-beaten fame, preserved the quiet domain of remotest time, shrouded in perennial snow. We struggled on amidst the heights of these alpine ranges—until now supposed inaccessible to the labour of man,—infantry and cavalry, artillery, camp-followers, and beasts of burden"—and so forth. The General was, in fact, a poet as well as a doctor and a soldier.

During this expedition he became also a sovereign prince, the crown of Ghor having been secured to him and his heirs by a voluntary act of the then prince, Muhammad Reffi Bey, although, as he writes, he "looked upon kingdoms and principalities as of frivolous import, when weighed in the balance of the more honourable and estimable title of American citizen."

It is not recorded that the General met with any striking military successes; but there is some interest for us in the personality of a youthful prince, who was intrusted to his care and tuition, and who was the nominal commander of the expedition. This was Akram Khan, son of the Amir "by a Highland lassie, whom he married to strengthen his authority in the Kohistan," or hill country. Akram Khan subsequently commanded the contingent sent by Dost Muhammad to strengthen the Sikhs against us in 1848.

Harlan made his last appearance as a negotiator in August 1839, when Lord Keane's army approached Kabul. The General tells us that Dost Muhammad and his chiefs unanimously decided to depute him to meet Sir Alexander Burnes, with absolute power to make any settlement that he might think advisable. An official was, he says, despatched to Burnes's secretary (the worthy Mohan Lal), conveying an intimation of the appointment of Harlan as plenipotentiary, and by return of the messenger an official response was received, indirectly declining the proposition by deferring the measure to a more convenient opportunity.

Eventually Burnes, or more probably the envoy, Sir William M'Naughton, declined to treat in any way with the Amir, who consequently withdrew from the neighbourhood of Kabul.

Harlan gives a dramatic account of the abandonment of Dost Muhammad by all his principal followers, which, in the words of Kaye, only wants a conviction of its entire truth to be most interesting and valuable.

Harlan's last appearance at Kabul is eminently characteristic. On the arrival of the British army at that city Dost Muhammad fled to the mountain country in the north, and was promptly deserted by Harlan, who is last mentioned as having breakfast with Sir Alexander Burnes on the morning after the latter arrived at the capital.

Of how Harlan found his way to India, and thence to Philadelphia, we are told nothing, yet we cannot but admire the adroitness with which he must have managed his journey through the Panjab. Doubtless the death of Ranjit Singh, who had expired on the 27th June, spared the General an awkward meeting. As to the later days of this strange character history is silent.

VI. GENERAL VAN CORTLANDT.

Henry Charles Van Cortlandt was the son of Lieutenant-Colonel Henry Clinton Van Cortlandt of the 31st Regiment. He was educated in England, and entered the service of Maharaja Ranjit Singh in 1832. He served in the various frontier campaigns that occurred yearly during the lifetime of the Maharaja, and was present at the battle of Jamrud, in which the Sikh general, Hari Singh Nalwa, was killed.

Van Cortlandt, then a colonel, served with the Sikh contingent which shared in Sir George Pollock's operations in the Khaibar Pass, and he was also present (as is mentioned by Colonel Gardner) at the siege of Lahore by Maharaja Sher Singh.

Sher Singh gave Colonel Van Cortlandt charge of his eldest son, Prince Partab Singh; but Van Cortlandt was shortly afterwards sent away from Lahore on military duty, and during his absence the Maharaja and Partab Singh were murdered by the Sindhanwalia *sardars*, as is related by Colonel Gardner.

When the first Sikh war with the British broke out Van Cortlandt was on leave at Mussoorie, and not being allowed to return to Lahore, proceeded to Ferozepur. Finally he was employed with the British army as Political Agent, and in that capacity was present at the battles of Ferozeshah and Sobraon. After the war Van Cortlandt returned to the Sikh service with the rank of general, and was made governor of the province of Dera Ishmail Khan.

On the outbreak at Multan, which was the first symptom of the second Sikh war, General Van Cortlandt loyally supported Lieutenant (afterwards Sir) Herbert Edwardes, and took an honourable part in the gallantly fought actions of Kinari and Sadusam. It deserves mention that Mrs Van Cortlandt showed herself on this, as on other occasions, the fit wife of a soldier—suppressing by her own vigour and courage an incipient mutiny.

On the annexation of the Panjab in 1849 General Van Cortlandt was transferred to the British service, and was employed in a civil capacity; but on the outbreak of the Indian Mutiny the General again drew the sword, raised a field force in the district in which he was employed, and with it rendered valuable service, fighting several successful actions with the rebels. For this service General Van Cortlandt was made a Companion of the Bath.

Particular importance was attached to the conduct of Van Cortlandt's force, as it was then considered doubtful if the Sikhs, so recently conquered, were to be trusted. However, the old soldiers of the two regiments (the Suruj Mukhi and Katur Mukhi) which Van Cortlandt had long commanded in the Panjab remained staunch.

General Van Cortlandt's last civil post was that of Commissioner of Multan, where he remained till his retirement in March 1868.

He survived his retirement twenty years, dying in London on March 15, 1888, at the age of seventy-four.

VII. COLONEL FORD.

Colonel Matthew William Ford, whose melancholy fate will presently be related, entered the English army as ensign in the 8th West India Regiment in the year 1803. He became a lieutenant in the 70th Regiment in the following year, and captain in the same regiment in 1812. He remained eleven years in this rank, serving successively in the 70th, 7th Fusiliers, and 1st Royals, from which regiment he exchanged to the half-pay list of the 24th Light Dragoons.

In 1823 he became paymaster of the 16th Regiment, and leaving the British service in 1837, entered the Sikh army towards the end of that year or early in 1838. He is shown by the Khalsa Durbar Acquittance Rolls to have drawn pay at 800 rupees per mensem, in the latter year.

There are occasional references to Colonel Ford in books and magazines of the period, and it is recorded that the regiment of the Khalsa army which he commanded was one of those which lined the streets of Lahore at the funeral of Maharaja Ranjit Singh.

On the occasion of the mutiny of the Sikh army during the reign of Maharaja Sher Singh, recorded by Gardner, Colonel Matthew Ford was one of the victims. He was plundered by his men of everything that he possessed, even to the ring on his finger, and so maltreated that he died at Peshawar, which place he barely contrived to reach alive. He is said to have been an estimable and very amiable man.

VIII. COLONEL FOULKES.

The fate of this officer was even worse than that of Colonel Ford. I have been able to discover nothing concerning his antecedents, and but a brief statement that he entered the Sikh service in the year 1835. The Khalsa Durbar Acquittance Rolls bear that his pay was 500 rupees per mensem, and he is shown in Gardner's list of the European officers as employed in the infantry branch.

At the time of the mutiny of the Sikh army under Maharaja Sher Singh, Colonel Foulkes was, however (it is stated by Steinbach), stationed at Mandi, in command of a large body of cavalry, where he fell a victim to the ferocity of his men.

Colonel Foulkes, who was universally beloved, was warned of his peril and urged to escape, but, with a spirit worthy of his English birth, he resolved to remain at his post and take the consequences. During the night he was attacked by the Sikh soldiers, who cut him down, and with demoniacal ferocity threw him on a blazing fire before life was extinct.

IX. CAPTAIN ARGOUD.

This officer, who is said to have been the best drill-instructor in the Sikh army, was for a considerable time in the service of Ranjit Singh, but unfortunately quarrelled with both Sikhs and Europeans, and being also of very intemperate habits, was eventually compelled to leave the Panjab and seek employment in Afghanistan.

While travelling thither, by way of Sind, Argoud fell

in with a small party of wayfarers, who afterwards became famous. These were Alexander Burnes and his companions Wood and Lord, who were proceeding from Bombay to Kabul, and had reached Bhawalpur on the 2nd May 1837. Captain Wood, in his delightful 'Journey to the Source of the Oxus,' tells the tale of the encounter so amusingly that I present the narrative precisely as he wrote it:—

"While here, we had an amusing visitor in the person of a Monsieur Argoud. He had quarrelled with Ranjit Singh and his countrymen in the Panjab, and was proceeding to join Dost Muhammad Khan of Kabul.

"We were at dinner when the Frenchman arrived, but no sooner was a European announced than Captain Burnes ran out to bring him in, and before many minutes had elapsed Monsieur Argoud had taken wine with every one at table.

"The poor man's failing was soon apparent, for he proceeded to beat the tattoo with his elbows on the table, and as a tenor accompaniment he made a knife vibrate between its under surface and his thumb. It was really done very cleverly, and the performance being highly applauded, the complaisant Frenchman knew not when to desist. Fatigue, sleep, and wine at length got the mastery, and we saw him safely to bed.

"Next morning at an early hour our guest was astir, roaming up and down the courtyard till he chanced to stumble on Lord, engaged in dissecting and stuffing birds.

"Watching him for some time, he exclaimed, 'Quelle patience!' and with a shrug of the shoulders passed into Captain Burnes's room.

"That officer was not yet dressed, on which Monsieur

Argoud called out, 'Why, sare, the battle of Wagram was fought before this hour, and you are still in *déshabillé*. Vill you take vine vith me?' 'No,' replied Captain Burnes; 'I never take wine before breakfast, but I shall order you some claret, as your countrymen, I am aware, like light wine in the morning.' 'Then, sare,' replied Argoud, 'you insult me, you refuse to take vine vith me, and I demand de satisfaction.'

"He ran out, and soon reappeared armed with a rapier, and asked Captain Burnes to send for his small-sword; but the latter thought that, considering the shortness of their acquaintance, he had already sufficiently humoured this fiery little Frenchman, and Monsieur Argoud was politely requested to continue his journey, which he accordingly did that same evening.

"This unfortunate gentleman had many good points in his character, but they were unknown to us at the time of his first visit. As a soldier and drill-officer he was the first in the Panjab; but his drunken habits and violent temper made him disliked by his brother-officers.

"At Kabul in October following we fell in with him a second time, so that his journey from the Indus had occupied him fully five months. Whilst on the road his dislike to Mussulmans had nearly cost him his life. It was only spared on his repeating the Kulmah or Mahomedan creed.

"Immediately on his arrival being known to us, Captain Burnes sent him a kind note, inquiring if he could be of any service to him; but the good-hearted Frenchman was so ashamed of his conduct at Bhawalpur, and so oppressed by this unexpected return, that he could not be persuaded to visit us, and on his failing to obtain employment from Dost Muhammad Khan, he set out for Peshawar without our having met him.

"We, however, learned that the day previous to his departure he had been employed in moulding leaden bullets, and that he had sworn to be revenged on the Mussulmans for the ill-treatment on his former journey.

"The cause of Monsieur Argoud's failure in obtaining service was his ignorance of the Persian language.

"Dost Muhammad Khan was partial to him, and though regretting his attachment to the bottle, offered him a regiment.

"Unfortunately for the Frenchman, the interpreter took advantage of his ignorance of the language, and in reply to a question on Argoud's qualifications for command, reported as his answer that if the Amir wanted a *drummer*, he could not suit himself better. The Frenchman required but little pressing to beat a tattoo, and the result was that he got his discharge that evening, and next day the interpreter (a brother adventurer) obtained the regiment."

Sir Alexander Burnes adds to the above account that "Benoit Argoud was a red-hot Republican; his father had been killed at the battle of Wagram. He reached Kabul by way of the Bolan Pass and Kandahar—no easy feat."

I can only add to the above the information that Argoud not only found his way back to the Panjab from Afghanistan in 1838, but that he actually returned to Kabul in 1839, as appears from the following letter to

Sir Claude Wade, which has been kindly lent to me by Mr C. F. Wade:—

(*Translation.*)

KABUL, 12*th August* 1839.

TRÈS AIMABLE COLONEL,—A terrible destiny has again brought me to this savage country, and no better off than on the first occasion.

I found myself at Calcutta quite without money, and it was therefore impossible for me to return to France. I returned to Kurnal, where I was deceived by false rumours. I set out for Kandahar, but on arriving there I found that King Shuja-al-Mulk was prevented, by treaty with Great Britain, from employing foreigners. Colonel Burnes truly treated me more like a father than a stranger; he is a most worthy man, and I shall never forget him.

I hope to have the pleasure of seeing you soon.

Agréez, Monsieur le Colonel, l'assurance de la parfaite considération avec laquelle j'ai l'honneur de vous saluer,

ARGOUD.

We may hope that the generosity of Burnes and Wade provided Argoud with a passage to "la belle France,"—at any rate, he appears no more in Afghanistan or the Panjab.

X. COLONEL CANORA.

When Colonel Canora entered the service of Ranjit Singh I do not know, nor is there any record of the early days of his service in the Panjab, nor of his previous life. The story of his death is, however, an honourable one.

In the year 1848 Canora was serving in the province of Hazara, in command of a battery of artillery. The troops in this province were notoriously mutinous, and Sardar Chattar Singh, the governor, shared in their disaffection, and even encouraged it. On the 6th of August Colonel Canora, an American by birth, described to me by General Sir James Abbott as "a rude, uncultured man, but brave and loyal," was ordered by Chattar Singh to bring his guns out of the fort of Harripur, and to encamp on the open ground outside the city. This, Colonel Canora, who suspected the treasonable intentions of Chattar Singh, refused to do, unless with the sanction of Captain Abbott, the British Commissioner in Hazara. Sir James Abbott, in a letter to me, thus relates the sequel:—

"Canora replied that the guns had been posted by me, and begged permission to refer to me previous to altering their position; and immediately despatched a letter to me, asking what he was to do.

"The *sardar* sent a company of infantry to storm his guns. Canora ordered his men to load them with double charges of grape, and to fire. The men, overawed, refused. He seized and applied the port-fire; the guns burnt priming—they had not been loaded. Canora stood at bay, pistol in hand. An armed servant of the *sardar* crept behind him and shot him through the back; then, cutting off his head, carried it to Chattar Singh and received from him a reward of £100.

"The Resident, Sir Frederick Currie, declared that it served him right; but I pronounced it murder, and the Governor-General and his Council backed my verdict.

"I raised a rude monument to Canora's memory, with

an inscription, on the spot where he fell. A small pension was allotted to his family."

So died a brave and determined soldier in the performance of his duty.

The rebellion of Chattar Singh was followed by that of his son Sher Singh, and the results were the second Sikh war and the consequent annexation of the Panjab.

XI. COLONEL THOMAS.

All who love to read romances of real life should know the strange story of George Thomas, the Irish sailor who by sheer courage and enterprise rose to be a reigning sovereign. His story may be found in the work by Mr Herbert Compton, 'The European Military Adventurers of Hindostan.'

Colonel Jacob Thomas, who commanded a *najib*, or foreign (*i.e.*, non-Panjabi) regiment in Ranjit Singh's army, was the son of George Thomas, but a man of a very different character.

Sir Claude Wade and his officers found Jacob Thomas and his regiment at Peshawar in March 1839, and Barr, the historian of the party, describes Thomas as "a dull and heavy man." Thomas was quite unable to exercise authority over his regiment, which mutinied on the 14th April, and turned Thomas and his adjutant out of their camp. As a mark of contempt for Thomas they inverted his chair on the spot where he usually sat. Sir Claude Wade informed the regiment that they could no longer remain with his troops; but how the matter ended is not recorded, nor have I found any further mention of Colonel Thomas.

XII. LESLIE OR RATTRAY.

This individual is mentioned by Gardner as one of Ranjit Singh's officers, but I have found no other mention of him in connection with the Panjab. Sir Alexander Burnes and his companions found him, however, serving under the name of Rattray, as commandant of Fort Ali Masjid in the Khaibar Pass. This was in September 1837, soon after the battle at Jamrud, a few miles distant, in which the Sikhs had been defeated by the Afghans.

Captain Wood describes Rattray as "an ill-conditioned, dissipated-looking Englishman, slipshod, turbaned and robed in a sort of Afghan *déshabillé*—having more the look of a dissipated priest than a military man. His abode was a cave in the mountain, from which he and his hungry followers levied blackmail on the passing *kafilas*.

"The Sikh fortress of Jamrud depended for water on the stream that runs through the Khaibar, and the chief occupation of the young lieutenant-colonel, for so he styled himself, was to stop the supply, and again to permit it to flow on being bribed to do so."

Wood amusingly describes Rattray's attempt to manœuvre his corps, which speedily resulted in a cudgel attack by the lieutenant-colonel on his men. Before the day was over he had modestly requested a loan of £50 to defray the expenses of the march to Kabul, and, by the simple process of dividing his men into guards on the mission, succeeded in inducing Burnes to supply them all with food.

Soon afterwards, during the stay of the mission at Kabul, Colonel Leslie, *alias* Rattray, changed his name for the second time and his religion with it. He declared himself a convert to the Muhammadan faith, and took the name of Fida Muhammad Khan, much against the wish of Dost Muhammad Khan, who thought him a disgrace to any creed, and expressed in strong terms the contempt he felt for men who could change their religion to improve their fortune.

The Khaibar commandant, says Wood, was altogether a singular character, void of all principle, but clever and well informed.

His biography, which he wrote at the request of Sir Alexander Burnes, is said to have afforded another proof of how often the real events of life exceed in interest the wildest conceptions of fiction. I have not been able to discover this biography, if it ever was published, but some of my readers may possibly be able to inform me about it.

XIII. COLONEL MOUTON.

An officer of a very different stamp was Colonel François Henri Mouton, who was born on the 17th August 1804, and entered a French cavalry regiment as a volunteer at the age of eighteen. Four years later Mouton was a "garde de troisième classe," ranking as a sub-lieutenant in the royal body-guard. In October 1838 Mouton was a captain of Spahis of three years' standing, and finding himself unemployed, obtained permission to live in India for three years. This he did at the suggestion of General Ventura, who was about to return to the Panjab from leave of absence. Captain Mouton, who was accompanied by his charming and courageous wife, accompanied General Ventura to India, travelling from Bombay by the most direct road to Lahore, that by Ajmir and Hansi.

Colonel Mouton was employed as a commandant of cavalry, and having entered on a second period of service, he and Madame Mouton narrowly escaped death in the mutiny of the Sikh army during the reign of Maharaja Sher Singh. Nothing deterred, Colonel Mouton, who had visited France in 1844, returned to India in the month of September of that year, and remained in the Panjab until the outbreak of the first Sikh war.

The official record of his services states that Colonel Mouton returned to France in July 1846, and in the April following was restored to full pay.

Colonel Mouton received the decoration of the Legion of Honour in 1848, and was promoted to the grade of "officer" in 1856 for services in the Crimean campaign, for which he received also the Order of the Medjidis of the 4th class. The gallant colonel was finally placed *en retraite* on account of length of service in January 1865, and died in Algiers in November 1876.

XIV. COLONEL HURBON.

Another gallant soldier was Colonel Hurbon, a Spanish officer, who was employed as an engineer. He is said to have been the first man in the assaults on the fortress of Lahore during its siege by Maharaja Sher Singh, and Gardner states that Hurbon planned the earthworks at Sobraon. Cunningham, the historian of the Sikhs, who was himself an engineer, says that the lines showed no trace whatever of scientific skill or of unity of design. In his opinion Colonel Hurbon's influence and authority did not extend beyond a regiment or a brigade.

Colonel Hurbon is chiefly interesting as having been the only European officer who actually served with the Sikh army against the British.

XV. COLONEL STEINBACH.

Lieutenant-Colonel Henry Steinbach commanded an infantry regiment in the Sikh army, and wrote a little book about the Panjab. In the mutiny of the Sikh army in 1843 Colonel Steinbach narrowly escaped with his life. It is related that the men of his regiment adopted a most unpleasant method of showing their dislike and contempt for him.

He subsequently entered the service of Maharaja Gulab Singh, and commanded his army at the time of the second Sikh war.

XVI. CAPTAIN DE LA FONT.

Auguste de la Font was aide-de-camp to General Ventura, and in that capacity was in attendance on the General at Peshawar in 1839. When Ventura was prevented by the intrigues which followed the death of Ranjit Singh from proceeding to Kabul in command of the Muhammadan contingent of the Khalsa army, Captain de la Font acted as staff officer to Colonel Wade. In this capacity he rendered good service both in action at the taking of Fort Ali Masjid, and subsequently in aiding to keep the peace between the Khalsa contingent and Colonel Wade's somewhat unruly force.

At the siege of Lahore (described by Colonel Gardner) De la Font is said to have nearly gained access to the fortress by mining, when the operations were brought to a termination by Dhyan Singh.

XVII. CAPTAIN M'PHERSON.

This gentleman, described as "a respectable officer," after serving in Ranjit Singh's army, entered the service of the Nawab of Bhawalpur, who gave him command of a regiment of regular infantry.

Captain M'Pherson served with the Bhawalpur contingent in Sir Herbert Edwardes's campaign against Multan, and was killed at the head of his regiment at the battle of Sadusam on July 1, 1848. He was buried on the following morning with military honours.

XVIII. AND XIX. MESSRS CAMPBELL AND GARRON.

These gentlemen are mentioned by Masson the traveller as commanding regiments in the Sikh army. They are included in Gardner's list, but there is no further information concerning them.

Mr Campbell is very probably identical with the gallant officer of that name who raised Shah Shuja-ul-Mulk's Hindustani regiment, and was deserted by the Shah at Kandahar on the occasion of his defeat by Dost Muhammad. Mr Campbell's conduct was most gallant:

he was severely wounded, and was succoured by Dost Muhammad, whose service he entered. It is stated that his daughter is still living at Kabul.

Mr Garron may stand for Carron, a secret agent of the British Government, and a man of strange adventures.

Of the remaining officers but few particulars are to be gleaned.

Messrs Alvarine (23), Hommus (24), and Amise (25) died at Lahore at different periods. Hest (26), the Greek officer, was murdered in the streets of the same city. Captain De la Roche (27) was killed there by a fall from his horse.

Dubuignon (28), described as an estimable young man, was in the service of the Begum Sumroo. There he was picked up by General Ventura, who was visiting India for the good of his health. Ventura treated him with great kindness, and eventually married him to his own sister-in-law.

John Holmes, No. 29 on the list, and the last of whom any particulars were given, was a man of mixed parentage. He was a worthy old soldier, and passed for a Christian, at Peshawar, when Sir Herbert Edwardes was there, though he had more than one wife. John Holmes did good service with Edwardes and Van Cortlandt in the advance on Multan in 1848, and was eventually murdered by some of his own men. His family sent in a claim for compensation to the Indian Government, in which were specified, among other dependants, *two mothers*.

LIST OF CHARACTERS IN PANJAB HISTORY, FROM THE DEATH OF RANJIT SINGH TO THE BRITISH ANNEXATION.

SOVEREIGNS.

No.

1. Maharaja Ranjit Singh, died June 27, 1839.
2. " Kharrak Singh (son of No. 1), deposed, and subsequently poisoned, November 5, 1840.
3. " Nao Nihal Singh (son of No. 2), killed, Nov. 5, 1840.
4. Maharani Chand Kour (widow of No. 2 and Regent), murdered by order of No. 5, June 1842.
5. Maharaja Sher Singh (son of No. 1), murdered by No. 15, September 15, 1843.
6. Maharaja Dhulip Singh (son of No. 1), deposed, March 29, 1849.

PRINCES, MINISTERS, ETC.

7. Kashmira Singh (son of No. 1), killed by the Sikh army, July 1843.
8. Peshora Singh (son of No. 1), murdered, August 1844.
9. Partab Singh (son of No. 5), murdered by No. 15, Sept. 15, 1843.
10. Chet Singh (Minister to Kharrak Singh), murdered by No. 11, October 8, 1839.
11. Raja Dhyan Singh (Prime Minister), murdered by No. 15, September 15, 1843, } the Dogra brothers.
12. Raja Gulab Singh, afterwards Maharaja of Jammu and Kashmir, } the Dogra brothers.
13. Raja Suchet Singh, killed by the Sikh army, March 1843, } the Dogra brothers.
14. Hira Singh (son of No. 11), killed by the Sikh army, December 21, 1844.
15. Ajit Singh, Sindhanwalia, } brothers, killed by the Sikh army, September 1843.
16. Lehna Singh, Sindhanwalia, } brothers, killed by the Sikh army, September 1843.
17. Pandit Julla (Secretary to No. 14), killed by the Sikh army, December 21, 1844.
18. Jawahir Singh (uncle of No. 6), killed by the Sikh army, September 21, 1845.
19. Maharani Jindan (mother of No. 6), banished.

INDEX.

THE END.

PRINTED BY WILLIAM BLACKWOOD AND SONS.

Catalogue

of

Messrs Blackwood & Sons'

Publications

PHILOSOPHICAL CLASSICS FOR ENGLISH READERS.

EDITED BY WILLIAM KNIGHT, LL.D.,
Professor of Moral Philosophy in the University of St Andrews.

In crown 8vo Volumes, with Portraits, price 3s. 6d.

Contents of the Series.

DESCARTES, by Professor Mahaffy, Dublin.—BUTLER, by Rev. W. Lucas Collins, M.A.—BERKELEY, by Professor Campbell Fraser.—FICHTE, by Professor Adamson, Glasgow.—KANT, by Professor Wallace, Oxford.—HAMILTON, by Professor Veitch, Glasgow.—HEGEL, by the Master of Balliol.—LEIBNIZ, by J. Theodore Merz.—VICO by Professor Flint, Edinburgh.—HOBBES, by Professor Croom Robertson.—HUME, by the Editor.—SPINOZA, by the Very Rev. Principal Caird, Glasgow.—BACON: Part I. The Life, by Professor Nichol.—BACON: Part II. Philosophy, by the same Author.—LOCKE, by Professor Campbell Fraser.

FOREIGN CLASSICS FOR ENGLISH READERS.

EDITED BY MRS OLIPHANT.

CHEAP RE-ISSUE. In limp cloth, fcap. 8vo, price 1s. each.

Two Volumes will be issued Monthly in the following order:—

DANTE	The Editor.	*May.*
VOLTAIRE	General Sir E. B. Hamley, K.C.B.	*May.*
PASCAL	Principal Tulloch.	*June.*
PETRARCH	Henry Reeve, C.B.	*June.*
GOETHE	A. Hayward, Q.C.	*July.*
MOLIÈRE	The Editor and F. Tarver, M.A.	*July.*
MONTAIGNE	Rev. W. L. Collins.	*Aug.*
RABELAIS	Sir Walter Besant.	*Aug.*
CALDERON	E. J. Hasell.	*Sept.*
SAINT SIMON	Clifton W. Collins, M.A.	*Sept.*
CERVANTES	The Editor.	*Oct.*
CORNEILLE AND RACINE	Henry M. Trollope.	*Oct.*
MADAME DE SÉVIGNÉ	Miss Thackeray.	*Nov.*
LA FONTAINE, AND OTHER FRENCH FABULISTS	Rev. W. Lucas Collins, M.A.	*Nov.*
SCHILLER	James Sime, M.A.	*Dec.*
TASSO	E. J. Hasell.	*Dec.*
ROUSSEAU	Henry Grey Graham.	1899. *Jan.*
ALFRED DE MUSSET	C. F. Oliphant.	1899. *Jan.*

ANCIENT CLASSICS FOR ENGLISH READERS.

EDITED BY THE REV. W. LUCAS COLLINS, M.A.

CHEAP RE-ISSUE. In limp cloth, fcap. 8vo, price 1s. each.

Contents of the Series.

HOMER: ILIAD	The Editor.
HOMER: ODYSSEY	The Editor.
HERODOTUS	G. C. Swayne.
CÆSAR	Anthony Trollope.
VIRGIL	The Editor.
HORACE	Sir Theodore Martin.
ÆSCHYLUS	Bishop Copleston.
XENOPHON	Sir Alex. Grant.
CICERO	The Editor.
SOPHOCLES	C. W. Collins.
PLINY	Church and Brodribb.
EURIPIDES	W. B. Donne.
JUVENAL	E. Walford.
ARISTOPHANES	The Editor.
HESIOD AND THEOGNIS	J. Davies.
PLAUTUS AND TERENCE	The Editor.
TACITUS	W. B. Donne.
LUCIAN	The Editor.
PLATO	C. W. Collins.
GREEK ANTHOLOGY	Lord Neaves.
LIVY	The Editor.
OVID	Rev. A. Church.
CATULLUS, TIBULLUS, AND PROPERTIUS	J. Davies.
DEMOSTHENES	W. J. Brodribb.
ARISTOTLE	Sir Alex. Grant.
THUCYDIDES	The Editor.
LUCRETIUS	W. H. Mallock.
PINDAR	Rev. F. D. Morice.

CATALOGUE

OF

MESSRS BLACKWOOD & SONS'

PUBLICATIONS.

ALISON.

History of Europe. By Sir ARCHIBALD ALISON, Bart., D.C.L.

1. From the Commencement of the French Revolution to the Battle of Waterloo.
   LIBRARY EDITION, 14 vols., with Portraits. Demy 8vo, £10, 10s.
   ANOTHER EDITION, in 20 vols. crown 8vo, £6.
   PEOPLE'S EDITION, 13 vols. crown 8vo, £2, 11s.
2. Continuation to the Accession of Louis Napoleon.
   LIBRARY EDITION, 8 vols. 8vo, £6, 7s. 6d.
   PEOPLE'S EDITION, 8 vols. crown 8vo, 34s.

Epitome of Alison's History of Europe. Thirtieth Thousand, 7s. 6d.

Atlas to Alison's History of Europe. By A. Keith Johnston.
LIBRARY EDITION, demy 4to, £3, 3s.
PEOPLE'S EDITION, 31s. 6d.

Life of John Duke of Marlborough. With some Account of his Contemporaries, and of the War of the Succession. Third Edition. 2 vols. 8vo. Portraits and Maps, 30s.

Essays: Historical, Political, and Miscellaneous. 3 vols. demy 8vo, 45s.

ACROSS FRANCE IN A CARAVAN: BEING SOME ACCOUNT OF A JOURNEY FROM BORDEAUX TO GENOA IN THE "ESCARGOT," taken in the Winter 1889-90. By the Author of 'A Day of my Life at Eton.' With fifty Illustrations by John Wallace, after Sketches by the Author, and a Map. Cheap Edition, demy 8vo, 7s. 6d.

ACTA SANCTORUM HIBERNIÆ; Ex Codice Salmanticensi. Nunc primum integre edita opera CAROLI DE SMEDT et JOSEPHI DE BACKER, e Soc. Jesu, Hagiographorum Bollandianorum; Auctore et Sumptus Largiente JOANNE PATRICIO MARCHIONE BOTHAE. In One handsome 4to Volume, bound in half roxburghe, £2, 2s.; in paper cover, 31s. 6d.

ADOLPHUS. Some Memories of Paris. By F. ADOLPHUS. Crown 8vo, 6s.

AFLALO. A Sketch of the Natural History (Vertebrates) of the British Islands. By F. G. AFLALO, F.R.G.S., F.Z.S., Author of 'A Sketch of the Natural History of Australia,' &c. With numerous Illustrations by Lodge and Bennett. Crown 8vo, 6s. net.

AIKMAN.

Manures and the Principles of Manuring. By C. M. AIKMAN, D.Sc., F.R.S.E., &c., Professor of Chemistry, Glasgow Veterinary College; Examiner in Chemistry, University of Glasgow, &c. Crown 8vo, 6s. 6d.

Farmyard Manure: Its Nature, Composition, and Treatment. Crown 8vo, 1s. 6d.

ALLARDYCE.

The City of Sunshine. By ALEXANDER ALLARDYCE, Author of 'Earlscourt,' &c. New Edition. Crown 8vo, 6s.

Balmoral: A Romance of the Queen's Country. New Edition. Crown 8vo, 6s.

ANCIENT CLASSICS FOR ENGLISH READERS. Edited by Rev. W. LUCAS COLLINS, M.A. Price 1s. each. *For List of Vols. see p. 2.*

ANDERSON. Daniel in the Critics' Den. A Reply to Dean Farrar's 'Book of Daniel.' By ROBERT ANDERSON, LL.D., Barrister-at-Law, Assistant Commissioner of Police of the Metropolis; Author of 'The Coming Prince,' 'Human Destiny,' &c. Post 8vo, 4s. 6d.

AYTOUN.

Lays of the Scottish Cavaliers, and other Poems. By W. EDMONDSTOUNE AYTOUN, D.C.L., Professor of Rhetoric and Belles-Lettres in the University of Edinburgh. New Edition. Fcap. 8vo, 3s. 6d.
ANOTHER EDITION. Fcap. 8vo, 7s. 6d.
CHEAP EDITION. 1s. Cloth, 1s. 3d.

An Illustrated Edition of the Lays of the Scottish Cavaliers. From designs by Sir NOEL PATON. Cheaper Edition. Small 4to, 10s. 6d.

Bothwell: a Poem. Third Edition. Fcap., 7s. 6d.

Poems and Ballads of Goethe. Translated by Professor AYTOUN and Sir THEODORE MARTIN, K.C.B. Third Edition. Fcap., 6s.

The Ballads of Scotland. Edited by Professor AYTOUN. Fourth Edition. 2 vols. fcap. 8vo, 12s.

Memoir of William E. Aytoun, D.C.L. By Sir THEODORE MARTIN, K.C.B. With Portrait. Post 8vo, 12s.

BADEN-POWELL. The Saving of Ireland. Conditions and Remedies: Industrial, Financial, and Political. By Sir GEORGE BADEN-POWELL, K.C.M.G., M.P. Demy 8vo, 7s. 6d.

BEDFORD & COLLINS. Annals of the Free Foresters, from 1856 to the Present Day. By W. K. R. BEDFORD, W. E. W. COLLINS, and other Contributors. With 55 Portraits and 59 other Illustrations. Demy 8vo, 21s. *net.*

BELLAIRS. Gossips with Girls and Maidens, Betrothed and Free. By LADY BELLAIRS. New Edition. Crown 8vo, 3s. 6d. Cloth, extra gilt edges, 5s.

BELLESHEIM. History of the Catholic Church of Scotland. From the Introduction of Christianity to the Present Day. By ALPHONS BELLESHEIM, D.D., Canon of Aix-la-Chapelle. Translated, with Notes and Additions, by D. OSWALD HUNTER BLAIR, O.S.B., Monk of Fort Augustus. Cheap Edition. Complete in 4 vols. demy 8vo, with Maps. Price 21s. net.

BENTINCK. Racing Life of Lord George Cavendish Bentinck, M.P., and other Reminiscences. By JOHN KENT, Private Trainer to the Goodwood Stable. Edited by the Hon. FRANCIS LAWLEY. With Twenty-three full-page Plates, and Facsimile Letter. Third Edition. Demy 8vo, 25s.

BEVERIDGE.

Culross and Tulliallan; or, Perthshire on Forth. Its History and Antiquities. With Elucidations of Scottish Life and Character from the Burgh and Kirk-Session Records of that District. By DAVID BEVERIDGE. 2 vols. 8vo, with Illustrations, 42s.

Between the Ochils and the Forth; or, From Stirling Bridge to Aberdour. Crown 8vo, 6s.

BICKERDYKE. A Banished Beauty. By JOHN BICKERDYKE, Author of 'Days in Thule, with Rod, Gun, and Camera,' 'The Book of the All-Round Angler,' 'Curiosities of Ale and Beer,' &c. With Illustrations. Cheap Edition. Crown 8vo, 2s.

BIRCH.

Examples of Stables, Hunting-Boxes, Kennels, Racing Establishments, &c. By JOHN BIRCH, Architect, Author of 'Country Architecture,' &c. With 30 Plates. Royal 8vo, 7s.

Examples of Labourers' Cottages, &c. With Plans for Improving the Dwellings of the Poor in Large Towns. With 34 Plates. Royal 8vo, 7s.

Picturesque Lodges. A Series of Designs for Gate Lodges, Park Entrances, Keepers', Gardeners', Bailiffs', Grooms', Upper and Under Servants' Lodges, and other Rural Residences. With 16 Plates. 4to, 12s. 6d.

BLACK. Heligoland and the Islands of the North Sea. By WILLIAM GEORGE BLACK. Crown 8vo, 4s.

BLACKIE.

The Wisdom of Goethe. By JOHN STUART BLACKIE, Emeritus Professor of Greek in the University of Edinburgh. Fcap. 8vo. Cloth, extra gilt, 6s.

John Stuart Blackie: A Biography. By ANNA M. STODDART. With 3 Plates. Third Edition. 2 vols. demy 8vo, 21s.
POPULAR EDITION. With Portrait. Crown 8vo, 6s.

BLACKMORE.

The Maid of Sker. By R. D. BLACKMORE, Author of 'Lorna Doone,' &c. New Edition. Crown 8vo, 6s. Cheaper Edition. Crown 8vo, 3s. 6d.

Dariel: A Romance of Surrey. With 14 Illustrations by Chris. Hammond. Crown 8vo. 6s.

BLACKWOOD.

Annals of a Publishing House. William Blackwood and his Sons; Their Magazine and Friends. By Mrs OLIPHANT. With Four Portraits. Third Edition. Demy 8vo. Vols. I. and II. £2, 2s.

Blackwood's Magazine, from Commencement in 1817 to December 1897. Nos. 1 to 986, forming 161 Volumes.

Index to Blackwood's Magazine. Vols. 1 to 50. 8vo, 15s.

Tales from Blackwood. First Series. Price One Shilling each, in Paper Cover. Sold separately at all Railway Bookstalls.
They may also be had bound in 12 vols., cloth, 18s. Half calf, richly gilt, 30s. Or the 12 vols. in 6, roxburghe, 21s. Half red morocco, 28s.

Tales from Blackwood. Second Series. Complete in Twenty-four Shilling Parts. Handsomely bound in 12 vols., cloth, 30s. In leather back, roxburghe style, 37s. 6d. Half calf, gilt, 52s. 6d. Half morocco, 55s.

Tales from Blackwood. Third Series. Complete in Twelve Shilling Parts. Handsomely bound in 6 vols., cloth, 15s.; and in 12 vols., cloth, 18s. The 6 vols. in roxburghe, 21s. Half calf, 25s. Half morocco, 28s.

Travel, Adventure, and Sport. From 'Blackwood's Magazine. Uniform with 'Tales from Blackwood.' In Twelve Parts, each price 1s. Handsomely bound in 6 vols., cloth, 15s. And in half calf, 25s.

BLACKWOOD.

New Educational Series. *See separate Catalogue.*

New Uniform Series of Novels (Copyright).

Crown 8vo, cloth. Price 3s. 6d. each. Now ready:—

THE MAID OF SKER. By R. D. Blackmore.
WENDERHOLME. By P. G. Hamerton.
THE STORY OF MARGRÉDEL. By D. Storrar Meldrum.
MISS MARJORIBANKS. By Mrs Oliphant.
THE PERPETUAL CURATE, and THE RECTOR. By the Same.
SALEM CHAPEL, and THE DOCTOR'S FAMILY. By the Same.
A SENSITIVE PLANT. By E. D. Gerard.
LADY LEE'S WIDOWHOOD. By General Sir E. B. Hamley.
KATIE STEWART, and other Stories. By Mrs Oliphant.
VALENTINE AND HIS BROTHER. By the Same.
SONS AND DAUGHTERS. By the Same.
MARMORNE. By P. G. Hamerton.
REATA. By E. D. Gerard.
BEGGAR MY NEIGHBOUR. By the Same.
THE WATERS OF HERCULES. By the Same.
FAIR TO SEE. By L. W. M. Lockhart.
MINE IS THINE. By the Same.
DOUBLES AND QUITS. By the Same.
ALTIORA PETO. By Laurence Oliphant
PICCADILLY. By the Same. With Illustrations.
LADY BABY. By D. Gerard.
THE BLACKSMITH OF VOE. By Paul Cushing.
THE DILEMMA. By the Author of 'The Battle of Dorking.'
MY TRIVIAL LIFE AND MISFORTUNE. By A Plain Woman.
POOR NELLIE. By the Same.

Standard Novels. Uniform in size and binding. Each complete in one Volume.

FLORIN SERIES, Illustrated Boards. Bound in Cloth, 2s. 6d.

TOM CRINGLE'S LOG. By Michael Scott.
THE CRUISE OF THE MIDGE. By the Same.
CYRIL THORNTON. By Captain Hamilton.
ANNALS OF THE PARISH. By John Galt.
THE PROVOST, &c. By the Same.
SIR ANDREW WYLIE. By the Same.
THE ENTAIL. By the Same.
MISS MOLLY. By Beatrice May Butt.
REGINALD DALTON. By J. G. Lockhart.
PEN OWEN. By Dean Hook.
ADAM BLAIR. By J. G. Lockhart.
LADY LEE'S WIDOWHOOD. By General Sir E. B. Hamley.
SALEM CHAPEL. By Mrs Oliphant.
THE PERPETUAL CURATE. By the Same.
MISS MARJORIBANKS. By the Same.
JOHN: A Love Story. By the Same.

SHILLING SERIES, Illustrated Cover. Bound in Cloth, 1s. 6d.

THE RECTOR, and THE DOCTOR'S FAMILY. By Mrs Oliphant.
THE LIFE OF MANSIE WAUCH. By D. M. Moir.
PENINSULAR SCENES AND SKETCHES. By F. Hardman.
SIR FRIZZLE PUMPKIN, NIGHTS AT MESS, &c.
THE SUBALTERN.
LIFE IN THE FAR WEST. By G. F. Ruxton.
VALERIUS: A Roman Story. By J. G. Lockhart.

BON GAULTIER'S BOOK OF BALLADS. Fifteenth Edition. With Illustrations by Doyle, Leech, and Crowquill. Fcap. 8vo, 5s.

BOWHILL. Questions and Answers in the Theory and Practice of Military Topography. By Major J. H. BOWHILL. Crown 8vo, 4s. 6d. net. Portfolio containing 34 working plans and diagrams, 3s. 6d. net.

BRADDON. Thirty Years of Shikar. By Sir EDWARD BRADDON, K.C.M.G. With Illustrations by G. D. Giles, and Map of Oudh Forest Tracts and Nepal Terai. Demy 8vo, 18s.

BROUGHAM. Memoirs of the Life and Times of Henry Lord Brougham. Written by HIMSELF. 3 vols. 8vo, £2, 8s. The Volumes are sold separately, price 16s. each.

BROWN. The Forester: A Practical Treatise on the Planting and Tending of Forest-trees and the General Management of Woodlands. By JAMES BROWN, LL.D. Sixth Edition, Enlarged. Edited by JOHN NISBET, D.Œc., Author of 'British Forest Trees,' &c. In 2 vols. royal 8vo, with 350 Illustrations, 42s. net.

BROWN. A Manual of Botany, Anatomical and Physiological. For the Use of Students. By ROBERT BROWN, M.A., Ph.D. Crown 8vo, with numerous Illustrations, 12s. 6d.

BRUCE.

In Clover and Heather. Poems by WALLACE BRUCE. New and Enlarged Edition. Crown 8vo, 3s. 6d.

A limited number of Copies of the First Edition, on large hand-made paper, 12s. 6d.

Here's a Hand. Addresses and Poems. Crown 8vo, 5s. Large Paper Edition, limited to 100 copies, price 21s.

BUCHAN. Introductory Text-Book of Meteorology. By ALEXANDER BUCHAN, LL.D., F.R.S.E., Secretary of the Scottish Meteorological Society, &c. New Edition. Crown 8vo, with Coloured Charts and Engravings. [*In preparation.*

BURBIDGE.

Domestic Floriculture, Window Gardening, and Floral Decorations. Being Practical Directions for the Propagation, Culture, and Arrangement of Plants and Flowers as Domestic Ornaments. By F. W. BURBIDGE. Second Edition. Crown 8vo, with numerous Illustrations, 7s. 6d.

Cultivated Plants: Their Propagation and Improvement. Including Natural and Artificial Hybridisation, Raising from Seed, Cuttings and Layers, Grafting and Budding, as applied to the Families and Genera in Cultivation. Crown 8vo, with nnmerous Illnstrations, 12s. 6d.

BURGESS. The Viking Path: A Tale of the White Christ. By J. J. HALDANE BURGESS, Anthor of 'Rasmie's Büddie,' 'Shetland Sketches,' &c. Crown 8vo, 6s.

BURKE. The Flowering of the Almond Tree, and other Poems. By CHRISTIAN BURKE. Pott 4to, 5s.

BURROWS.

Commentaries on the History of England, from the Earliest Times to 1865. By MONTAGU BURROWS, Chichele Professor of Modern History in the University of Oxford; Captain R.N.; F.S.A., &c.; "Officier de l'Instruction Publique," France. Crown 8vo. 7s. 6d.

The History of the Foreign Policy of Great Britain. New Edition, revised. Crown 8vo, 6s.

BURTON.

The History of Scotland: From Agricola's Invasion to the Extinction of the last Jacobite Insurrection. By JOHN HILL BURTON, D.C.L., Historiographer-Royal for Scotland. Cheaper Edition. In 8 vols. Crown 8vo, 3s. 6d. each.

History of the British Empire during the Reign of Queen Anne. In 3 vols. 8vo. 36s.

The Scot Abroad. Third Edition. Crown 8vo, 10s. 6d.

The Book-Hunter. New Edition. With Portrait. Crown 8vo, 7s. 6d.

BUTCHER. Armenosa of Egypt. A Romance of the Arab Conqnest. By the Very Rev. Dean BUTCHER, D.D., F.S.A., Chaplain at Cairo. Crown 8vo, 6s.

BUTE. The Altus of St Columba. With a Prose Paraphrase and Notes. In paper cover, 2s. 6d.

BUTE, MACPHAIL, AND LONSDALE. The Arms of the Royal and Parliamentary Burghs of Scotland. By JOHN, MARQUESS OF BUTE, K.T., J. R. N. MACPHAIL, and H. W. LONSDALE. With 131 Engravings on wood, and 11 other Illustrations. Crown 4to, £2, 2s. net.

BUTLER. The Ancient Church and Parish of Abernethy, Perthshire. An Historical Study. By Rev. D. BUTLER, M.A., Minister of the Parish. With 13 Collotype Plates and a Map. Crown 4to, 25s. net.

BUTT.

Theatricals: An Interlude. By BEATRICE MAY BUTT. Crown 8vo, 6s.

Miss Molly. Cheap Edition, 2s.

Eugenie. Crown 8vo, 6s. 6d.

BUTT.
Elizabeth, and other Sketches. Crown 8vo, 6s.
Delicia. New Edition. Crown 8vo, 2s. 6d.

CAIRD. Sermons. By JOHN CAIRD, D.D., Principal of the University of Glasgow. Seventeenth Thousand. Fcap. 8vo, 5s.

CALDWELL. Schopenhauer's System in its Philosophical Significance (the Shaw Fellowship Lectures, 1893). By WILLIAM CALDWELL, M.A., D.Sc., Professor of Moral and Social Philosophy, Northwestern University, U.S.A.; formerly Assistant to the Professor of Logic and Metaphysics, Edin., and Examiner in Philosophy in the University of St Andrews. Demy 8vo, 10s. 6d. net.

CALLWELL. The Effect of Maritime Command on Land Campaigns since Waterloo. By Major C. E. CALLWELL, R.A. With Plans. Post 8vo, 6s. net.

CANTON. A Lost Epic, and other Poems. By WILLIAM CANTON. Crown 8vo, 5s.

CARSTAIRS.
Human Nature in Rural India. By R. CARSTAIRS. Crown 8vo, 6s.
British Work in India. Crown 8vo, 6s.

CAUVIN. A Treasury of the English and German Languages. Compiled from the best Authors and Lexicographers in both Languages. By JOSEPH CAUVIN, LL.D. and Ph.D., of the University of Göttingen, &c. Crown 8vo, 7s. 6d.

CHARTERIS. Canonicity; or, Early Testimonies to the Existence and Use of the Books of the New Testament. Based on Kirchhoffer's 'Quellensammlung.' Edited by A. H. CHARTERIS, D.D., Professor of Biblical Criticism in the University of Edinburgh. 8vo, 18s.

CHENNELLS. Recollections of an Egyptian Princess. By her English Governess (Miss E. CHENNELLS). Being a Record of Five Years' Residence at the Court of Ismael Pasha, Khédive. Second Edition. With Three Portraits. Post 8vo, 7s. 6d.

CHESNEY. The Dilemma. By General Sir GEORGE CHESNEY, K.C.B., M.P., Author of 'The Battle of Dorking,' &c. New Edition. Crown 8vo, 3s. 6d.

CHRISTISON. Early Fortifications in Scotland: Motes, Camps, and Forts. Being the Rhind Lectures in Archæology for 1894. By DAVID CHRISTISON, M.D., F.R.C.P.E., Secretary of the Society of Antiquaries of Scotland. With 379 Plans and Illustrations and 3 Maps. Fcap 4to, 21s. net.

CHRISTISON. Life of Sir Robert Christison, Bart., M.D., D.C.L. Oxon., Professor of Medical Jurisprudence in the University of Edinburgh. Edited by his SONS. In 2 vols. 8vo. Vol. I.—Autobiography. 16s. Vol. II.—Memoirs. 16s.

CHURCH. Chapters in an Adventurous Life. Sir Richard Church in Italy and Greece. By E. M. CHURCH. With Photogravure Portrait. Demy 8vo, 10s. 6d.

CHURCH SERVICE SOCIETY.
A Book of Common Order: being Forms of Worship issued by the Church Service Society. Seventh Edition, carefully revised. In 1 vol. crown 8vo, cloth, 3s. 6d.; French morocco, 5s. Also in 2 vols. crown 8vo, cloth, 4s.; French morocco, 6s. 6d.
Daily Offices for Morning and Evening Prayer throughout the Week. Crown 8vo, 3s. 6d.

CHURCH SERVICE SOCIETY.
Order of Divine Service for Children. Issued by the Church Service Society. With Scottish Hymnal. Cloth, 3d.

CLOUSTON. Popular Tales and Fictions: their Migrations and Transformations. By W. A. CLOUSTON, Editor of 'Arabian Poetry for English Readers,' &c. 2 vols. post 8vo, roxburghe binding, 25s.

COCHRAN. A Handy Text-Book of Military Law. Compiled chiefly to assist Officers preparing for Examination; also for all Officers of the Regular and Auxiliary Forces. Comprising also a Synopsis of part of the Army Act. By Major F. COCHRAN, Hampshire Regiment Garrison Instructor, North British District. Crown 8vo, 7s. 6d.

COLQUHOUN. The Moor and the Loch. Containing Minute Instructions in all Highland Sports, with Wanderings over Crag and Corrie, Flood and Fell. By JOHN COLQUHOUN. Cheap Edition. With Illustrations. Demy 8vo, 10s. 6d.

COLVILE. Round the Black Man's Garden. By Lady Z. COLVILE, F.R.G.S. With 2 Maps and 50 Illustrations from Drawings by the Author and from Photographs. Demy 8vo, 16s.

CONDER. The Bible and the East. By Lieut.-Col. C. R. CONDER, R.E., LL.D., D.C.L., M.R.A.S., Author of 'Tent Work in Palestine,' &c. With Illustrations and a Map. Crown 8vo, 5s.

The Hittites and their Language. With Illustrations and Map. Post 8vo, 7s. 6d.

CONSTITUTION AND LAW OF THE CHURCH OF SCOTLAND. With an Introductory Note by the late Principal Tulloch. New Edition, Revised and Enlarged. Crown 8vo, 3s. 6d.

COTTERILL. Suggested Reforms in Public Schools. By C. C. COTTERILL, M.A. Crown 8vo, 3s. 6d.

COUNTY HISTORIES OF SCOTLAND. In demy 8vo volumes of about 350 pp. each. With Maps. Price 7s. 6d. net.

Fife and Kinross. By ÆNEAS J. G. MACKAY, LL.D., Sheriff of these Counties.

Dumfries and Galloway. By Sir HERBERT MAXWELL, Bart., M.P

Moray and Nairn. By CHARLES RAMPINI, LL.D., Sheriff-Substitute of these Counties.

Inverness. By J. CAMERON LEES, D.D. [*Others in preparation.*

CRAWFORD. Saracinesca. By F. MARION CRAWFORD, Author of 'Mr Isaacs,' &c., &c. Cheap Edition. Crown 8vo, 3s. 6d.

CRAWFORD.

The Doctrine of Holy Scripture respecting the Atonement. By the late THOMAS J. CRAWFORD, D.D., Professor of Divinity in the University of Edinburgh. Fifth Edition. 8vo, 12s.

The Fatherhood of God, Considered in its General and Special Aspects. Third Edition, Revised and Enlarged. 8vo, 9s.

The Preaching of the Cross, and other Sermons. 8vo, 7s. 6d.

The Mysteries of Christianity. Crown 8vo, 7s. 6d.

CROSS. Impressions of Dante, and of the New World; with a Few Words on Bimetallism. By J. W. CROSS, Editor of 'George Eliot's Life, as related in her Letters and Journals.' Post 8vo, 6s.

CUMBERLAND. Sport on the Pamirs and Turkistan Steppes. By Major C. S. CUMBERLAND. With Map and Frontispiece. Demy 8vo, 10s. 6d.

CURSE OF INTELLECT. Third Edition. Fcap. 8vo, 2s. 6d. net.

CUSHING. The Blacksmith of Voe. By PAUL CUSHING, Author of 'The Bull i' th' Thorn,' 'Cut with his own Diamond.' Cheap Edition. Crown 8vo, 3s. 6d.

DARBISHIRE. Physical Maps for the use of History Students. By BERNHARD V. DARBISHIRE, M.A., Trinity College, Oxford. Two Series:—Ancient History (9 maps); Modern History (12 maps). [*In the press.*

DAVIES. Norfolk Broads and Rivers; or, The Waterways, Lagoons, and Decoys of East Anglia. By G. CHRISTOPHER DAVIES. Illustrated with Seven full-page Plates. New and Cheaper Edition. Crown 8vo, 6s.

DE LA WARR. An Eastern Cruise in the 'Edeline.' By the Countess DE LA WARR. In Illustrated Cover. 2s.

DESCARTES. The Method, Meditations, and Principles of Philosophy of Descartes. Translated from the Original French and Latin. With a New Introductory Essay, Historical and Critical, on the Cartesian Philosophy. By Professor VEITCH, LL.D., Glasgow University. Eleventh Edition. 6s. 6d.

DOGS, OUR DOMESTICATED: Their Treatment in reference to Food, Diseases, Habits, Punishment, Accomplishments. By 'MAGENTA.' Crown 8vo, 2s. 6d.

DOUGLAS.

The Ethics of John Stuart Mill. By CHARLES DOUGLAS, M.A., D.Sc., Lecturer in Moral Philosophy, and Assistant to the Professor of Moral Philosophy in the University of Edinburgh. Post 8vo, 6s. net.

John Stuart Mill: A Study of his Philosophy. Crown 8vo, 4s. 6d. net.

DOUGLAS. Chinese Stories. By ROBERT K. DOUGLAS. With numerons Illustrations by Parkinson, Forestier, and others. New and Cheaper Edition. Small demy 8vo, 5s.

DOUGLAS. Iras: A Mystery. By THEO. DOUGLAS, Author of 'A Bride Elect.' Cheaper Edition, in Paper Cover specially designed by Womrath. Crown 8vo, 1s. 6d.

DU CANE. The Odyssey of Homer, Books I.-XII. Translated into English Verse. By Sir CHARLES DU CANE, K.C.M.G. 8vo, 10s. 6d.

DUDGEON. History of the Edinburgh or Queen's Regiment Light Infantry Militia, now 3rd Battalion The Royal Scots; with an Acconnt of the Origin and Progress of the Militia, and a Brief Sketch of the Old Royal Scots. By Major R. C. DUDGEON, Adjntant 3rd Battalion the Royal Scots. Post 8vo, with Illnstrations, 10s. 6d.

DUNSMORE. Manual of the Law of Scotland as to the Relations between Agricultural Tenants and the Landlords, Servants, Merchants, and Bowers. By W. DUNSMORE. 8vo, 7s. 6d.

DZIEWICKI. Entombed in Flesh. By M. H. DZIEWICKI. Crown 8vo, 3s. 6d.

ELIOT.

George Eliot's Life, Related in Her Letters and Journals. Arranged and Edited by her husband, J. W. CROSS. With Portrait and other Illnstrations. Third Edition. 3 vols. post 8vo, 42s.

George Eliot's Life. With Portrait and other Illustrations. New Edition, in one volume. Crown 8vo, 7s. 6d.

Works of George Eliot (Standard Edition). 21 volumes, crown 8vo. In buckram cloth, gilt top, 2s. 6d. per vol.; or in roxburghe binding, 3s. 6d. per vol.

ADAM BEDE. 2 vols.—THE MILL ON THE FLOSS. 2 vols.—FELIX HOLT, THE RADICAL. 2 vols.—ROMOLA. 2 vols.—SCENES OF CLERICAL LIFE. 2 vols.—MIDDLEMARCH. 3 vols.—DANIEL DERONDA. 3 vols.—SILAS MARNER. 1 vol.—JUBAL. 1 vol.—THE SPANISH GIPSY. 1 vol.—ESSAYS. 1 vol.—THEOPHRASTUS SUCH. 1 vol.

Life and Works of George Eliot (Cabinet Edition). 24 volumes, crown 8vo, price £6. Also to be had handsomely bound in half and full calf. The Volumes are sold separately, bonnd in cloth, price 5s. each.

ELIOT.

Novels by George Eliot. New Cheap Edition. Printed on fine laid paper, and uniformly bound.

Adam Bede. 3s. 6d.—The Mill on the Floss. 3s. 6d.—Scenes of Clerical Life. 3s.—Silas Marner: the Weaver of Raveloe. 2s. 6d.—Felix Holt, the Radical. 3s. 6d.—Romola. 3s. 6d.—Middlemarch. 7s. 6d.—Daniel Deronda. 7s. 6d.

Essays. New Edition. Crown 8vo, 5s.

Impressions of Theophrastus Such. New Edition. Crown 8vo, 5s.

The Spanish Gypsy. New Edition. Crown 8vo, 5s.

The Legend of Jubal, and other Poems, Old and New. New Edition. Crown 8vo, 5s.

Scenes of Clerical Life. Popular Edition. Royal 8vo, in paper cover, price 6d.

Wise, Witty, and Tender Sayings, in Prose and Verse. Selected from the Works of GEORGE ELIOT. New Edition. Fcap. 8vo, 3s. 6d.

ELTON. The Augustan Ages. 'Periods of European Literature.' By OLIVER ELTON. In 1 vol. crown 8vo. [*In the press.*

ESSAYS ON SOCIAL SUBJECTS. Originally published in the 'Saturday Review.' New Edition. First and Second Series. 2 vols. crown 8vo, 6s. each.

FAITHS OF THE WORLD, The. A Concise History of the Great Religious Systems of the World. By various Authors. Crown 8vo, 5s.

FALKNER. The Lost Stradivarius. By J. MEADE FALKNER. Second Edition. Crown 8vo, 6s.

FENNELL AND O'CALLAGHAN. A Prince of Tyrone. By CHARLOTTE FENNELL and J. P. O'CALLAGHAN. Crown 8vo, 6s.

FERGUSON. Sir Samuel Ferguson in the Ireland of his Day. By LADY FERGUSON, Author of 'The Irish before the Conquest,' 'Life of William Reeves, D.D., Lord Bishop of Down, Connor, and Drumore,' &c., &c. With Two Portraits. 2 vols. post 8vo, 21s.

FERGUSSON. Scots Poems. By ROBERT FERGUSSON. With Photogravure Portrait. Pott 8vo, gilt top, bound in cloth, 1s. net.

FERRIER.

Philosophical Works of the late James F. Ferrier, B.A. Oxon., Professor of Moral Philosophy and Political Economy, St Andrews. New Edition. Edited by Sir ALEXANDER GRANT, Bart., D.C.L., and Professor LUSHINGTON. 3 vols. crown 8vo, 34s. 6d.

Institutes of Metaphysic. Third Edition. 10s. 6d.

Lectures on the Early Greek Philosophy. 4th Edition. 10s. 6d.

Philosophical Remains, including the Lectures on Early Greek Philosophy. New Edition. 2 vols. 24s.

FLINT.

Historical Philosophy in France and French Belgium and Switzerland. By ROBERT FLINT, Corresponding Member of the Institute of France, Hon. Member of the Royal Society of Palermo, Professor in the University of Edinburgh, &c. 8vo, 21s.

Agnosticism. Being the Croall Lecture for 1887-88. [*In the press.*

Theism. Being the Baird Lecture for 1876. Ninth Edition, Revised. Crown 8vo, 7s. 6d.

Anti-Theistic Theories. Being the Baird Lecture for 1877. Fifth Edition. Crown 8vo, 10s. 6d.

FOREIGN CLASSICS FOR ENGLISH READERS. Edited by Mrs OLIPHANT. Price 1s. *For List of Volumes, see page 2.*

FOSTER. The Fallen City, and other Poems. By WILL FOSTER. Crown 8vo, 6s.

FRANCILLON. Gods and Heroes; or, The Kingdom of Jupiter. By R. E. FRANCILLON. With 8 Illustrations. Crown 8vo, 5s.

FRANCIS. Among the Untrodden Ways. By M. E. FRANCIS (Mrs Francis Blundell), Author of 'In a North Country Village,' 'A Daughter of the Soil,' 'Frieze and Fustian,' &c. Crown 8vo, 3s. 6d.

FRASER.

Philosophy of Theism. Being the Gifford Lectures delivered before the University of Edinburgh in 1894-95. First Series. By ALEXANDER CAMPBELL FRASER, D.C.L. Oxford; Emeritus Professor of Logic and Metaphysics in the University of Edinburgh. Post 8vo, 7s. 6d. net.

Philosophy of Theism. Being the Gifford Lectures delivered before the University of Edinburgh in 1895-96. Second Series. Post 8vo, 7s. 6d. *net.*

FRASER. St Mary's of Old Montrose: A History of the Parish of Maryton. By the Rev. WILLIAM RUXTON FRASER, M.A., F.S.A. Scot., Emeritus Minister of Maryton; Author of 'History of the Parish and Burgh of Laurencekirk.' Crown 8vo, 3s. 6d.

FULLARTON.

Merlin: A Dramatic Poem. By RALPH MACLEOD FULLARTON. Crown 8vo, 5s.

Tanhäuser. Crown 8vo, 6s.

Lallan Sangs and German Lyrics. Crown 8vo, 5s.

GALT.

Novels by JOHN GALT. With General Introduction and Prefatory Notes by S. R. CROCKETT. The Text Revised and Edited by D. STORRAR MELDRUM, Author of 'The Story of Margrédel.' With Photogravure Illustrations from Drawings by John Wallace. Fcap. 8vo, 3s. net each vol.

ANNALS OF THE PARISH, and THE AYRSHIRE LEGATEES. 2 vols.—SIR ANDREW WYLIE. 2 vols.—THE ENTAIL; or, The Lairds of Grippy. 2 vols.—THE PROVOST, and THE LAST OF THE LAIRDS. 2 vols.

See also STANDARD NOVELS, *p.* 6.

GENERAL ASSEMBLY OF THE CHURCH OF SCOTLAND.

Scottish Hymnal, With Appendix Incorporated. Published for use in Churches by Authority of the General Assembly. 1. Large type, cloth, red edges, 2s. 6d.; French morocco, 4s. 2. Bourgeois type, limp cloth, 1s.; French morocco, 2s. 3. Nonpareil type, cloth, red edges, 6d.; French morocco, 1s. 4d. 4. Paper covers, 3d. 5. Sunday-School Edition, paper covers, 1d., cloth, 2d. No. 1, bound with the Psalms and Paraphrases, French morocco, 8s. No. 2, bound with the Psalms and Paraparases, cloth, 2s.; French morocco, 3s.

Prayers for Social and Family Worship. Prepared by a Special Committee of the General Assembly of the Church of Scotland. Entirely New Edition, Revised and Enlarged. Fcap. 8vo, red edges, 2s.

Prayers for Family Worship. A Selection of Four Weeks' Prayers. New Edition. Authorised by the General Assembly of the Church of Scotland. Fcap. 8vo, red edges, 1s. 6d.

One Hundred Prayers. Prepared by the Committee on Aids to Devotion. 16mo, cloth limp, 6d.

Morning and Evening Prayers for Affixing to Bibles. Prepared by the Committee on Aids to Devotion. 1d. for 6, or 1s. per 100.

GERARD.

Reata: What's in a Name. By E. D. GERARD. Cheap Edition. Crown 8vo, 3s. 6d.

Beggar my Neighbour. Cheap Edition. Crown 8vo, 3s. 6d.

The Waters of Hercules. Cheap Edition. Crown 8vo, 3s. 6d.

A Sensitive Plant. Crown 8vo, 3s. 6d.

GERARD.

A Foreigner. An Anglo-German Study. By E. GERARD. Crown 8vo, 6s.

The Land beyond the Forest. Facts, Figures, and Fancies from Transylvania. With Maps and Illustrations. 2 vols. post 8vo, 25s.

Bis: Some Tales Retold. Crown 8vo, 6s.

A Secret Mission. 2 vols. crown 8vo, 17s.

An Electric Shock, and other Stories. Crown 8vo, 6s.

GERARD.

A Forgotten Sin. By DOROTHEA GERARD. Crown 8vo, 6s.

A Spotless Reputation. Third Edition. Crown 8vo, 6s.

The Wrong Man. Second Edition. Crown 8vo, 6s.

Lady Baby. Cheap Edition. Crown 8vo, 3s. 6d.

Recha. Second Edition. Crown 8vo, 6s.

The Rich Miss Riddell. Second Edition. Crown 8vo, 6s.

GERARD. Stonyhurst Latin Grammar. By Rev. JOHN GERARD. Second Edition. Fcap. 8vo, 3s.

GORDON CUMMING.

At Home in Fiji. By C. F. GORDON CUMMING. Fourth Edition, post 8vo. With Illustrations and Map. 7s. 6d.

A Lady's Cruise in a French Man-of-War. New and Cheaper Edition. 8vo. With Illustrations and Map. 12s. 6d.

Fire-Fountains. The Kingdom of Hawaii: Its Volcanoes, and the History of its Missions. With Map and Illustrations. 2 vols. 8vo, 25s.

Wanderings in China. New and Cheaper Edition. 8vo, with Illustrations, 10s.

Granite Crags: The Yō-semité Region of California. Illustrated with 8 Engravings. New and Cheaper Edition. 8vo, 8s. 6d.

GRAHAM. Manual of the Elections (Scot.) (Corrupt and Illegal Practices) Act, 1890. With Analysis, Relative Act of Sederunt, Appendix containing the Corrupt Practices Acts of 1883 and 1885, and Copious Index. By J. EDWARD GRAHAM, Advocate. 8vo, 4s. 6d.

GRAND.

A Domestic Experiment. By SARAH GRAND, Author of 'The Heavenly Twins,' 'Ideala: A Study from Life.' Crown 8vo, 6s.

Singularly Deluded. Crown 8vo, 6s.

GRANT. Bush-Life in Queensland. By A. C. GRANT. New Edition. Crown 8vo, 6s.

GREGG. The Decian Persecution. Being the Hulsean Prize Essay for 1896. By JOHN A. F. GREGG, B.A., late Scholar of Christ's College, Cambridge. Crown 8vo, 6s.

GRIER.

In Furthest Ind. The Narrative of Mr EDWARD CARLYON of Ellswether, in the County of Northampton, and late of the Honourable East India Company's Service, Gentleman. Wrote by his own hand in the year of grace 1697. Edited, with a few Explanatory Notes, by SYDNEY C. GRIER. Post 8vo, 6s.

His Excellency's English Governess. Crown 8vo, 6s.

An Uncrowned King: A Romance of High Politics. Second Edition. Crown 8vo, 6s.

Peace with Honour. Crown 8vo, 6s.

A Crowned Queen: A Romance of a Minister of State. Crown 8vo, 6s.

GUTHRIE-SMITH. Crispus: A Drama. By H. GUTHRIE-SMITH. Fcap. 4to, 5s.

HAGGARD. Under Crescent and Star. By Lieut.-Col. ANDREW HAGGARD, D.S.O., Author of 'Dodo and I,' 'Tempest Torn,' &c. With a Portrait. Second Edition. Crown 8vo, 6s.

HALDANE. Subtropical Cultivations and Climates. A Handy Book for Planters, Colonists, and Settlers. By R. C. HALDANE. Post 8vo, 9s.

HAMERTON.

Wenderholme: A Story of Lancashire and Yorkshire Life. By P. G. HAMERTON, Author of 'A Painter's Camp.' New Edition. Crown 8vo, 3s. 6d.

Marmorne. New Edition. Crown 8vo, 3s. 6d.

HAMILTON.

Lectures on Metaphysics. By Sir WILLIAM HAMILTON, Bart., Professor of Logic and Metaphysics in the University of Edinburgh. Edited by the Rev. H. L. MANSEL, B.D., LL.D., Dean of St Paul's; and JOHN VEITCH, M.A., LL.D., Professor of Logic and Rhetoric, Glasgow. Seventh Edition. 2 vols. 8vo, 24s.

Lectures on Logic. Edited by the SAME. Third Edition, Revised. 2 vols., 24s.

Discussions on Philosophy and Literature, Education and University Reform. Third Edition. 8vo, 21s.

Memoir of Sir William Hamilton, Bart., Professor of Logic and Metaphysics in the University of Edinburgh. By Professor VEITCH, of the University of Glasgow. 8vo, with Portrait, 18s.

Sir William Hamilton: The Man and his Philosophy. Two Lectures delivered before the Edinburgh Philosophical Institution, January and February 1883. By Professor VEITCH. Crown 8vo, 2s.

HAMLEY.

The Operations of War Explained and Illustrated. By General Sir EDWARD BRUCE HAMLEY, K.C.B., K.C.M.G. Fifth Edition, Revised throughout. 4to, with numerous Illustrations, 30s.

National Defence; Articles and Speeches. Post 8vo, 6s.

Shakespeare's Funeral, and other Papers. Post 8vo, 7s. 6d.

Thomas Carlyle: An Essay. Second Edition. Crown 8vo, 2s. 6d.

On Outposts. Second Edition. 8vo, 2s.

Wellington's Career; A Military and Political Summary. Crown 8vo, 2s.

Lady Lee's Widowhood. New Edition. Crown 8vo, 3s. 6d. Cheaper Edition, 2s. 6d.

Our Poor Relations. A Philozoic Essay. With Illustrations, chiefly by Ernest Griset. Crown 8vo, cloth gilt, 3s. 6d.

The Life of General Sir Edward Bruce Hamley, K.C.B., K.C.M.G. By ALEXANDER INNES SHAND. With two Photogravure Portraits and other Illustrations. Cheaper Edition. With a Statement by Mr EDWARD HAMLEY. 2 vols. demy 8vo, 10s. 6d.

HANNAY. The Later Renaissance. By DAVID HANNAY. Being the second volume of 'Periods of European Literature.' Edited by Professor Saintsbury. Crown 8vo, 5s. net.

HARE. Down the Village Street: Scenes in a West Country Hamlet. By CHRISTOPHER HARE. Second Edition. Crown 8vo, 6s.

HARRADEN.

In Varying Moods: Short Stories. By BEATRICE HARRADEN, Author of 'Ships that Pass in the Night.' Twelfth Edition Crown 8vo, 3s. 6d.

Hilda Strafford, and The Remittance Man. Two Californian Stories. Tenth Edition. Crown 8vo, 3s. 6d.

Untold Tales of the Past. With 40 Illustrations by H. R Millar. Square crown 8vo, gilt top, 6s.

HARRIS.

From Batum to Baghdad, *viâ* Tiflis, Tabriz, and Persian Kurdistan. By WALTER B. HARRIS, F.R.G.S., Author of 'The Land of an African Sultan; Travels in Morocco,' &c. With numerous Illustrations and 2 Maps. Demy 8vo, 12s.

Tafilet. The Narrative of a Journey of Exploration to the Atlas Mountains and the Oases of the North-West Sahara. With Illustrations by Maurice Romberg from Sketches and Photographs by the Author, and Two Maps. Demy 8vo, 12s.

A Journey through the Yemen, and some General Remarks upon that Country. With 3 Maps and numerous Illustrations by Forestier and Wallace from Sketches and Photographs taken by the Author. Demy 8vo, 16s.

Danovitch, and other Stories. Crown 8vo, 6s.

HAY. The Works of the Right Rev. Dr George Hay, Bishop of Edinburgh. Edited under the Supervision of the Right Rev. Bishop STRAIN. With Memoir and Portrait of the Author. 5 vols. crown 8vo, bound in extra cloth, £1, 1s. The following Volumes may be had separately—viz.:

The Devout Christian Instructed in the Law of Christ from the Written Word. 2 vols., 8s.—The Pious Christian Instructed in the Nature and Practice of the Principal Exercises of Piety. 1 vol., 3s.

HEATLEY.

The Horse-Owner's Safeguard. A Handy Medical Guide for every Man who owns a Horse. By G. S. HEATLEY, M.R.C.V.S. Crown 8vo, 5s.

The Stock-Owner's Guide. A Handy Medical Treatise for every Man who owns an Ox or a Cow. Crown 8vo, 4s. 6d.

HEDDERWICK. Lays of Middle Age; and other Poems. By JAMES HEDDERWICK, LL.D., Author of 'Backward Glances.' Price 3s. 6d.

HEMANS.

The Poetical Works of Mrs Hemans. Copyright Edition. Royal 8vo, with Engravings, cloth, gilt edges, 7s. 6d.

Select Poems of Mrs Hemans. Fcap., cloth, gilt edges, 3s.

HENDERSON. The Young Estate Manager's Guide. By RICHARD HENDERSON, Member (by Examination) of the Royal Agricultural Society of England, the Highland and Agricultural Society of Scotland, and the Surveyors' Institution. With Plans and Diagrams. Crown 8vo, 5s.

HERKLESS. Cardinal Beaton: Priest and Politician. By JOHN HERKLESS, Professor of Church History, St Andrews. With a Portrait. Post 8vo, 7s. 6d.

HEWISON. The Isle of Bute in the Olden Time. With Illustrations, Maps, and Plans. By JAMES KING HEWISON, M.A., F.S.A. (Scot.), Minister of Rothesay. Vol. I., Celtic Saints and Heroes. Crown 4to, 15s. net. Vol. II., The Royal Stewards and the Brandanes. Crown 4to, 15s. net.

HIBBEN. Inductive Logic. By JOHN GRIER HIBBEN, Ph.D., Assistant Professor of Logic in Princeton University, U.S.A. Crown 8vo, 3s. 6d. net.

HILDEBRAND. The Early Relations between Britain and Scandinavia. Being the Rhind Lectures in Archæology for 1896. By Dr HANS HILDEBRAND, Royal Antiquary of Sweden. With Illustrations. In 1 vol. post 8vo. [*In the press.*

HOME PRAYERS. By Ministers of the Church of Scotland and Members of the Church Service Society. Second Edition. Fcap. 8vo, 3s.

HORNBY. Admiral of the Fleet Sir Geoffrey Phipps Hornby, G.C.B. A Biography. By Mrs FRED. EGERTON. With Three Portraits. Demy 8vo, 16s.

HUTCHINSON. Hints on the Game of Golf. By HORACE G. HUTCHINSON. Ninth Edition, Enlarged. Fcap. 8vo, cloth, 1s.

HYSLOP. The Elements of Ethics. By JAMES H. HYSLOP, Ph.D., Instructor in Ethics, Columbia College, New York, Author of 'The Elements of Logic.' Post 8vo, 7s. 6d. net.

IDDESLEIGH. Life, Letters, and Diaries of Sir Stafford Northcote, First Earl of Iddesleigh. By ANDREW LANG. With Three Portraits and a View of Pynes. Third Edition. 2 vols. post 8vo, 31s. 6d.

POPULAR EDITION. With Portrait and View of Pynes. Post 8vo, 7s. 6d.

INDEX GEOGRAPHICUS: Being a List, alphabetically arranged, of the Principal Places on the Globe, with the Countries and Subdivisions of the Countries in which they are situated, and their Latitudes and Longitudes. Imperial 8vo, pp. 676, 21s.

JEAN JAMBON. Our Trip to Blunderland; or, Grand Excursion to Blundertown and Back. By JEAN JAMBON. With Sixty Illustrations designed by CHARLES DOYLE, engraved by DALZIEL. Fourth Thousand. Cloth, gilt edges, 6s. 6d. Cheap Edition, cloth, 3s. 6d. Boards, 2s. 6d.

JEBB.

A Strange Career. The Life and Adventures of JOHN GLADWYN JEBB. By his Widow. With an Introduction by H. RIDER HAGGARD, and an Electrogravure Portrait of Mr Jebb. Third Edition. Demy 8vo, 10s. 6d.

CHEAP EDITION. With Illustrations by John Wallace. Crown 8vo, 3s. 6d.

Some Unconventional People. By Mrs GLADWYN JEBB, Author of 'Life and Adventures of J. G. Jebb.' With Illustrations. Crown 8vo, 3s. 6d.

JERNINGHAM.

Reminiscences of an Attaché. By HUBERT E. H. JERNINGHAM. Second Edition. Crown 8vo, 5s

Diane de Breteuille. A Love Story. Crown 8vo, 2s. 6d.

JOHNSTON.

The Chemistry of Common Life. By Professor J. F. W. JOHNSTON. New Edition, Revised. By ARTHUR HERBERT CHURCH, M.A. Oxon.; Author of 'Food: its Sources, Constituents, and Uses,' &c. With Maps and 102 Engravings. Crown 8vo, 7s. 6d.

Elements of Agricultural Chemistry. An entirely New Edition from the Edition by Sir CHARLES A. CAMERON, M.D., F.R.C.S.I., &c. Revised and brought down to date by C. M. AIKMAN, M.A., B.Sc., F.R.S.E., Professor of Chemistry, Glasgow Veterinary College. 17th Edition. Crown 8vo, 6s. 6d.

Catechism of Agricultural Chemistry. An entirely New Edition from the Edition by Sir CHARLES A. CAMERON. Revised and Enlarged by C. M. AIKMAN, M.A., &c. 95th Thousand. With numerous Illustrations. Crown 8vo, 1s.

JOHNSTON. Agricultural Holdings (Scotland) Acts, 1883 and 1889; and the Ground Game Act, 1880. With Notes, and Summary of Procedure, &c. By CHRISTOPHER N. JOHNSTON, M.A., Advocate. Demy 8vo, 5s.

JOKAI. Timar's Two Worlds. By MAURUS JOKAI. Authorised Translation by Mrs HEGAN KENNARD. Cheap Edition. Crown 8vo, 6s.

KEBBEL. The Old and the New: English Country Life. By T. E. KEBBEL, M.A., Author of 'The Agricultural Labourers,' 'Essays in History and Politics,' 'Life of Lord Beaconsfield.' Crown 8vo, 5s.

KERR. St Andrews in 1645-46. By D. R. KERR. Crown 8vo, 2s. 6d.

KINGLAKE.

History of the Invasion of the Crimea. By A. W. KINGLAKE. Cabinet Edition, Revised. With an Index to the Complete Work. Illustrated with Maps and Plans. Complete in 9 vols., crown 8vo, at 6s. each.

—— Abridged Edition for Military Students. Revised by Lieut.-Col. Sir GEORGE SYDENHAM CLARKE, K.C.M.G., R.E. In 1 vol. demy 8vo. [*In the press.*

History of the Invasion of the Crimea. Demy 8vo. Vol. VI. Winter Troubles. With a Map, 16s. Vols. VII. and VIII. From the Morrow of Inkerman to the Death of Lord Raglan With an Index to the Whole Work. With Maps and Plans. 28s.

KINGLAKE.

Eothen. A New Edition, uniform with the Cabinet Edition of the 'History of the Invasion of the Crimea.' 6s.

CHEAPER EDITION. With Portrait and Biographical Sketch of the Author. Crown 8vo, 3s. 6d. Popular Edition, in paper cover, 1s net.

KIRBY. In Haunts of Wild Game: A Hunter-Naturalist's Wanderings from Kahlamba to Libombo. By FREDERICK VAUGHAN KIRBY, F.Z.S. (Maqaqamba). With numerous Illustrations by Charles Whymper, and a Map. Large demy 8vo, 25s.

KNEIPP. My Water-Cure. As Tested through more than Thirty Years, and Described for the Healing of Diseases and the Preservation of Health. By SEBASTIAN KNEIPP, Parish Priest of Wörishofen (Bavaria). With a Portrait and other Illustrations. Authorised English Translation from the Thirtieth German Edition, by A. de F. Cheap Edition. With an Appendix, containing the Latest Developments of Pfarrer Kneipp's System, and a Preface by E. Gerard. Crown 8vo, 3s. 6d.

KNOLLYS. The Elements of Field-Artillery. Designed for the Use of Infantry and Cavalry Officers. By HENRY KNOLLYS, Colonel Royal Artillery; Author of 'From Sedan to Saarbrück,' Editor of 'Incidents in the Sepoy War,' &c. With Engravings. Crown 8vo, 7s. 6d.

LANG.

Life, Letters, and Diaries of Sir Stafford Northcote, First Earl of Iddesleigh. By ANDREW LANG. With Three Portraits and a View of Pynes. Third Edition. 2 vols. post 8vo, 31s. 6d.

POPULAR EDITION. With Portrait and View of Pynes. Post 8vo, 7s. 6d.

The Highlands of Scotland in 1750. From Manuscript 104 in the King's Library, British Museum. With an Introduction by ANDREW LANG. Crown 8vo, 5s. net.

LANG. The Expansion of the Christian Life. The Duff Lecture for 1897. By the Rev. J. MARSHALL LANG, D.D Crown 8vo, 5s.

LEES. A Handbook of the Sheriff and Justice of Peace Small Debt Courts. With Notes, References, and Forms. By J. M. LEES, Advocate, Sheriff of Stirling, Dumbarton, and Clackmannan. 8vo, 7s. 6d.

LINDSAY.

Recent Advances in Theistic Philosophy of Religion. By Rev. JAMES LINDSAY, M.A., B.D., B.Sc., F.R.S.E., F.G.S., Minister of the Parish of St Andrew's, Kilmarnock. Demy 8vo, 12s. 6d. net.

The Progressiveness of Modern Christian Thought. Crown 8vo, 6s.

Essays, Literary and Philosophical. Crown 8vo, 3s. 6d.

The Significance of the Old Testament for Modern Theology. Crown 8vo, 1s. net.

The Teaching Function of the Modern Pulpit. Crown 8vo, 1s. net.

LOCKHART.

Doubles and Quits. By LAURENCE W. M. LOCKHART. New Edition. Crown 8vo, 3s. 6d.

Fair to See. New Edition. Crown 8vo, 3s. 6d.

Mine is Thine. New Edition. Crown 8vo, 3s. 6d.

LOCKHART.

The Church of Scotland in the Thirteenth Century. The Life and Times of David de Bernham of St Andrews (Bishop), A.D. 1239 to 1253. With List of Churches dedicated by him, and Dates. By WILLIAM LOCKHART, A.M., D.D., F.S.A. Scot., Minister of Colinton Parish. 2d Edition. 8vo, 6s.

Dies Tristes: Sermons for Seasons of Sorrow. Crown 8vo, 6s.

LORIMER.

The Institutes of Law: A Treatise of the Principles of Jurisprudence as determined by Nature. By the late JAMES LORIMER, Professor of Public Law and of the Law of Nature and Nations in the University of Edinburgh. New Edition, Revised and much Enlarged. 8vo, 18s.

The Institutes of the Law of Nations. A Treatise of the Jural Relation of Separate Political Communities. In 2 vols. 8vo. Volume I., price 16s. Volume II., price 20s.

LUGARD. The Rise of our East African Empire: Early Efforts in Uganda and Nyasaland. By F. D. LUGARD, Captain Norfolk Regiment. With 130 Illustrations from Drawings and Photographs under the personal superintendence of the Author, and 14 specially prepared Maps. In 2 vols. large demy 8vo, 42s.

M'CHESNEY.

Miriam Cromwell, Royalist: A Romance of the Great Rebellion. By DORA GREENWELL M'CHESNEY. Crown 8vo, 6s.

Kathleen Clare: Her Book, 1637-41. With Frontispiece, and five full-page Illustrations by James A. Shearman. Crown 8vo, 6s.

M'COMBIE. Cattle and Cattle-Breeders. By WILLIAM M'COMBIE, Tillyfour. New Edition, Enlarged, with Memoir of the Author by JAMES MACDONALD, F.R.S.E., Secretary Highland and Agricultural Society of Scotland. Crown 8vo, 3s. 6d.

M'CRIE.

Works of the Rev. Thomas M'Crie, D.D. Uniform Edition. 4 vols. crown 8vo, 24s.

Life of John Knox. Crown 8vo, 6s. Another Edition, 3s. 6d.

Life of Andrew Melville. Crown 8vo, 6s.

History of the Progress and Suppression of the Reformation in Italy in the Sixteenth-Century. Crown 8vo, 4s.

History of the Progress and Suppression of the Reformation in Spain in the Sixteenth Century. Crown 8vo, 3s. 6d.

M'CRIE. The Public Worship of Presbyterian Scotland. Historically treated. With copious Notes, Appendices, and Index. The Fourteenth Series of the Cunningham Lectures. By the Rev. CHARLES G. M'CRIE, D.D. Demy 8vo, 10s. 6d.

MACDONALD. A Manual of the Criminal Law (Scotland) Procedure Act, 1887. By NORMAN DORAN MACDONALD. Revised by the LORD JUSTICE-CLERK. 8vo, 10s. 6d.

MACDOUGALL AND DODDS. A Manual of the Local Government (Scotland) Act, 1894. With Introduction, Explanatory Notes, and Copious Index. By J. PATTEN MACDOUGALL, Legal Secretary to the Lord Advocate, and J. M. DODDS. Tenth Thousand, Revised. Crown 8vo, 2s. 6d. net.

MACINTYRE. Hindu-Koh: Wanderings and Wild Sports on and beyond the Himalayas. By Major-General DONALD MACINTYRE, V.C., late Prince of Wales' Own Goorkhas, F.R.G.S. *Dedicated to H.R.H. The Prince of Wales.* New and Cheaper Edition, Revised, with numerous Illustrations. Post 8vo, 3s. 6d.

MACKAY.

Elements of Modern Geography. By the Rev. ALEXANDER MACKAY, LL.D., F.R.G.S. 55th Thousand, Revised to the present time. Crown 8vo, pp. 300, 3s.

The Intermediate Geography. Intended as an Intermediate Book between the Author's 'Outlines of Geography' and 'Elements of Geography.' Eighteenth Edition, Revised. Fcap. 8vo, pp. 238, 2s.

Outlines of Modern Geography. 191st Thousand, Revised to the present time. Fcap. 8vo, pp. 128, 1s.

Elements of Physiography. New Edition. Rewritten and Enlarged. With numerous Illustrations. Crown 8vo. [*In the press.*

MACKENZIE. Studies in Roman Law. With Comparative Views of the Laws of France, England, and Scotland. By Lord MACKENZIE, one of the Judges of the Court of Session in Scotland. Seventh Edition, Edited by JOHN KIRKPATRICK, M.A., LL.B., Advocate, Professor of History in the University of Edinburgh. In 1 vol., 8vo. [*In the press.*

MACPHERSON. Glimpses of Church and Social Life in the Highlands in Olden Times. By ALEXANDER MACPHERSON, F.S.A. Scot. With 6 Photogravure Portraits and other full-page Illustrations. Small 4to, 25s.

M'PHERSON. Golf and Golfers. Past and Present. By J. GORDON M'PHERSON, Ph.D., F.R.S.E. With an Introduction by the Right Hon. A. J. BALFOUR, and a Portrait of the Author. Fcap. 8vo, 1s. 6d.

MACRAE. A Handbook of Deer-Stalking. By ALEXANDER MACRAE, late Forester to Lord Henry Bentinck. With Introduction by Horatio Ross, Esq. Fcap. 8vo, with 2 Photographs from Life. 3s. 6d.

MAIN. Three Hundred English Sonnets. Chosen and Edited by DAVID M. MAIN. New Edition. Fcap. 8vo, 3s. 6d.

MAIR. A Digest of Laws and Decisions, Ecclesiastical and Civil, relating to the Constitution, Practice, and Affairs of the Church of Scotland. With Notes and Forms of Procedure. By the Rev. WILLIAM MAIR, D.D., Minister of the Parish of Earlston. New Edition, Revised. Crown 8vo, 9s. net.

MARCHMONT AND THE HUMES OF POLWARTH. By One of their Descendants. With numerous Portraits and other Illustrations. Crown 4to, 21s. net.

MARSHMAN. History of India. From the Earliest Period to the present time. By JOHN CLARK MARSHMAN, C.S.I. Third and Cheaper Edition. Post 8vo, with Map, 6s.

MARTIN.

The Æneid of Virgil. Books I.-VI. Translated by Sir THEODORE MARTIN, K.C.B. Post 8vo, 7s. 6d.

Goethe's Faust. Part I. Translated into English Verse. Second Edition, crown 8vo, 6s. Ninth Edition, fcap. 8vo, 3s. 6d.

Goethe's Faust. Part II. Translated into English Verse. Second Edition, Revised. Fcap. 8vo, 6s.

The Works of Horace. Translated into English Verse, with Life and Notes. 2 vols. New Edition. Crown 8vo, 21s.

Poems and Ballads of Heinrich Heine. Done into English Verse. Third Edition. Small crown 8vo, 5s.

The Song of the Bell, and other Translations from Schiller, Goethe, Uhland, and Others. Crown 8vo, 7s. 6d.

Madonna Pia: A Tragedy; and Three Other Dramas. Crown 8vo, 7s. 6d.

Catullus. With Life and Notes. Second Edition, Revised and Corrected. Post 8vo, 7s. 6d.

The 'Vita Nuova' of Dante. Translated, with an Introduction and Notes. Third Edition. Small crown 8vo, 5s.

Aladdin: A Dramatic Poem. By ADAM OEHLENSCHLAEGER. Fcap. 8vo, 5s.

Correggio: A Tragedy. By OEHLENSCHLAEGER. With Notes. Fcap. 8vo, 3s.

MARTIN. On some of Shakespeare's Female Characters. By HELENA FAUCIT, Lady MARTIN. Dedicated by permission to Her Most Gracious Majesty the Queen. Fifth Edition. With a Portrait by Lehmann. Demy 8vo, 7s. 6d.

MARWICK. Observations on the Law and Practice in regard to Municipal Elections and the Conduct of the Business of Town Councils and Commissioners of Police in Scotland. By Sir JAMES D. MARWICK, LL.D., Town-Clerk of Glasgow. Royal 8vo, 30s.

MATHESON.

Can the Old Faith Live with the New? or, The Problem of Evolution and Revelation. By the Rev. GEORGE MATHESON, D.D. Third Edition. Crown 8vo, 7s. 6d.

The Psalmist and the Scientist; or, Modern Value of the Religious Sentiment. Third Edition. Crown 8vo, 5s.

Spiritual Development of St Paul. Fourth Edition. Cr. 8vo, 5s.

The Distinctive Messages of the Old Religions. Second Edition. Crown 8vo, 5s.

Sacred Songs. New and Cheaper Edition. Crown 8vo, 2s. 6d.

MATHIESON. The Supremacy and Sufficiency of Jesus Christ our Lord, as set forth in the Epistle to the Hebrews. By J. E. MATHIESON, Superintendent of Mildmay Conference Hall, 1880 to 1890. Second Edition. Crown 8vo, 3s. 6d.

MAURICE. The Balance of Military Power in Europe. An Examination of the War Resources of Great Britain and the Continental States. By Colonel MAURICE, R.A., Professor of Military Art and History at the Royal Staff College. Crown 8vo, with a Map, 6s.

MAXWELL.

The Honourable Sir Charles Murray, K.C.B. A Memoir By Sir HERBERT MAXWELL, Bart., M.P., F.S.A., &c., Author of 'Passages in the Life of Sir Lucian Elphin.' With Five Portraits. Demy 8vo, 18s.

Life and Times of the Rt. Hon. William Henry Smith, M.P. With Portraits and numerous Illustrations by Herbert Railton, G. L. Seymour, and Others. 2 vols. demy 8vo, 25s.

POPULAR EDITION. With a Portrait and other Illustrations. Crown 8vo, 3s. 6d.

Scottish Land-Names: Their Origin and Meaning. Being the Rhind Lectures in Archæology for 1893. Post 8vo, 6s.

Meridiana: Noontide Essays. Post 8vo, 7s. 6d.

Post Meridiana: Afternoon Essays. Post 8vo, 6s.

A Duke of Britain. A Romance of the Fourth Century. Fourth Edition. Crown 8vo, 6s.

Dumfries and Galloway. Being one of the Volumes of the County Histories of Scotland. With Four Maps. Demy 8vo, 7s. 6d. net.

MELDRUM.

The Story of Margrédel: Being a Fireside History of a Fifeshire Family. By D. STORRAR MELDRUM. Cheap Edition. Crown 8vo, 3s. 6d.

Grey Mantle and Gold Fringe. Crown 8vo, 6s.

MELLONE. Studies in Philosophical Criticism and Construction. By SYDNEY HERBERT MELLONE, M.A. Lond., D.Sc. Edin. Post 8vo. 10s. 6d. net.

MERZ. A History of European Thought in the Nineteenth Century. By JOHN THEODORE MERZ. Vol. I., post 8vo, 10s. 6d. net.

MICHIE.

The Larch: Being a Practical Treatise on its Culture and General Management. By CHRISTOPHER Y. MICHIE, Forester, Cullen House. Crown 8vo, with Illustrations. New and Cheaper Edition, Enlarged, 5s.

The Practice of Forestry. Crown 8vo, with Illustrations. 6s.

MIDDLETON. The Story of Alastair Bhan Comyn; or, The Tragedy of Dunphail. A Tale of Tradition and Romance. By the Lady MIDDLETON. Square 8vo, 10s. Cheaper Edition, 5s.

MIDDLETON. Latin Verse Unseens. By G. MIDDLETON, M.A., Lecturer in Latin, Aberdeen University; late Scholar of Emmanuel College. Cambridge; Joint-Author of 'Student's Companion to Latin Authors.' Crown 8vo, 1s. 6d.

MILLER. The Dream of Mr H——, the Herbalist. By HUGH MILLER, F.R.S.E., late H.M. Geological Survey, Author of 'Landscape Geology.' With a Photogravure Frontispiece. Crown 8vo, 2s. 6d.

MILLS. Greek Verse Unseens. By T. R. MILLS, M.A., late Lecturer in Greek, Aberdeen University; formerly Scholar of Wadham College, Oxford; Joint-Author of 'Student's Companion to Latin Authors. Crown 8vo, 1s. 6d.

MINTO.

A Manual of English Prose Literature, Biographical and Critical: designed mainly to show Characteristics of Style. By W. MINTO, M.A., Hon. LL.D. of St Andrews; Professor of Logic in the University of Aberdeen. Third Edition, Revised. Crown 8vo, 7s. 6d.

Characteristics of English Poets, from Chaucer to Shirley. New Edition, Revised. Crown 8vo, 7s. 6d.

Plain Principles of Prose Composition. Crown 8vo, 1s. 6d.

The Literature of the Georgian Era. Edited, with a Biographical Introduction, by Professor KNIGHT, St Andrews. Post 8vo, 6s.

MOIR.

Life of Mansie Wauch, Tailor in Dalkeith. By D. M. MOIR. With CRUIKSHANK'S Illustrations. Cheaper Edition. Crown 8vo, 2s. 6d. Another Edition, without Illustrations, fcap. 8vo, 1s. 6d.

Domestic Verses. Centenary Edition. With a Portrait. Crown 8vo, 2s. 6d. net.

MOLE. For the Sake of a Slandered Woman. By MARION MOLE. Fcap. 8vo, 2s. 6d. net.

MOMERIE.

Defects of Modern Christianity, and other Sermons. By Rev. ALFRED WILLIAMS MOMERIE, M.A., D.Sc., LL.D. Fifth Edition. Crown 8vo, 5s.

The Basis of Religion. Being an Examination of Natural Religion. Third Edition. Crown 8vo, 2s. 6d.

The Origin of Evil, and other Sermons. Eighth Edition, Enlarged. Crown 8vo, 5s.

Personality. The Beginning and End of Metaphysics, and a Necessary Assumption in all Positive Philosophy. Fifth Ed., Revised. Cr. 8vo, 3s.

Agnosticism. Fourth Edition, Revised. Crown 8vo, 5s.

Preaching and Hearing; and other Sermons. Fourth Edition Enlarged. Crown 8vo, 5s.

Belief in God. Fourth Edition. Crown 8vo, 3s.

Inspiration; and other Sermons. Second Edition, Enlarged. Crown 8vo, 5s.

Church and Creed. Third Edition. Crown 8vo, 4s. 6d.

The Future of Religion, and other Essays. Second Edition. Crown 8vo, 3s. 6d.

The English Church and the Romish Schism. Second Edition. Crown 8vo, 2s. 6d.

MONCREIFF.

The Provost-Marshal. A Romance of the Middle Shires. By the Hon. FREDERICK MONCREIFF. Crown 8vo, 6s.

The X Jewel. A Romance of the Days of James VI. Cr. 8vo, 6s.

MONTAGUE. Military Topography. Illustrated by Practical Examples of a Practical Subject. By Major-General W. E. MONTAGUE, C.B., *P.S.C.*, late Garrison Instructor Intelligence Department, Author of 'Campaigning in South Africa.' With Forty-one Diagrams. Crown 8vo, 5s.

MONTALEMBERT. Memoir of Count de Montalembert. A Chapter of Recent French History. By Mrs OLIPHANT, Author of the 'Life of Edward Irving,' &c. 2 vols. crown 8vo, £1, 4s.

MORISON.

Doorside Ditties. By JEANIE MORISON. With a Frontispiece. Crown 8vo, 3s. 6d.

Æolus. A Romance in Lyrics. Crown 8vo, 3s.

MORISON.

There as Here. Crown 8vo, 3s.

*** *A limited impression on hand-made paper, bound in vellum, 7s. 6d.*

Selections from Poems. Crown 8vo, 4s. 6d.

Sordello. An Outline Analysis of Mr Browning's Poem. Crown 8vo, 3s.

Of "Fifine at the Fair," "Christmas Eve and Easter Day,' and other of Mr Browning's Poems. Crown 8vo, 3s.

The Purpose of the Ages. Crown 8vo, 9s.

Gordon: An Our-day Idyll. Crown 8vo, 3s.

Saint Isadora, and other Poems. Crown 8vo, 1s. 6d.

Snatches of Song. Paper, 1s. 6d.; cloth, 3s.

Pontius Pilate. Paper, 1s. 6d.; cloth, 3s.

Mill o' Forres. Crown 8vo, 1s.

Ane Booke of Ballades. Fcap. 4to, 1s.

MUNRO. The Lost Pibroch, and other Sheiling Stories. By NEIL MUNRO. Crown 8vo, 6s.

MUNRO.

Rambles and Studies in Bosnia-Herzegovina and Dalmatia. With an Account of the Proceedings of the Congress of Archæologists and Anthropologists held at Sarajevo in 1894. By ROBERT MUNRO, M.A., M.D., F.R.S.E., Author of 'The Lake-Dwellings of Europe,' &c. With numerons Illustrations. Demy 8vo, 12s. 6d. net.

Prehistoric Problems. With numerous Illustrations. Demy 8vo, 10s. net.

MUNRO. On Valuation of Property. By WILLIAM MUNRO, M.A., Her Majesty's Assessor of Railways and Canals for Scotland. Second Edition, Revised and Enlarged. 8vo, 3s. 6d.

MURDOCH. Manual of the Law of Insolvency and Bankruptcy: Comprehending a Summary of the Law of Insolvency, Notour Bankruptcy, Composition-Contracts, Trust-Deeds, Cessios, and Sequestrations; and the Winding-up of Joint-Stock Companies in Scotland; with Annotations on the various Insolvency and Bankruptcy Statutes; and with Forms of Procedure applicable to these Subjects. By JAMES MURDOCH, Member of the Faculty of Procurators in Glasgow. Fifth Edition, Revised and Enlarged. 8vo, 12s. net.

MYERS. A Manual of Classical Geography. By JOHN L. MYERS, M.A., Fellow of Magdalene College; Lecturer and Tutor, Christ Church, Oxford. In 1 vol. crown 8vo. [*In the press.*

MY TRIVIAL LIFE AND MISFORTUNE: A Gossip with no Plot in Particular. By A PLAIN WOMAN. Cheap Edition. Crown 8vo, 3s. 6d.

By the SAME AUTHOR.

POOR NELLIE. Cheap Edition. Crown 8vo, 3s. 6d.

NAPIER. The Construction of the Wonderful Canon of Logarithms. By JOHN NAPIER of Merchiston. Translated, with Notes, and a Catalogue of Napier's Works, by WILLIAM RAE MACDONALD. Small 4to, 15s. *A few large-paper copies on Whatman paper*, 30s.

NEAVES. Songs and Verses, Social and Scientific. By An Old Contributor to 'Maga.' By the Hon. Lord NEAVES. Fifth Edition. Fcap. 8vo, 4s.

NICHOLSON.

A Manual of Zoology, for the Use of Students. With a General Introdnction on the Principles of Zoology. By HENRY ALLEYNE NICHOLSON, M.D., D.Sc., F.L.S., F.G.S., Regius Professor of Natural History in the University of Aberdeen. Seventh Edition, Rewritten and Enlarged. Post 8vo, pp. 956, with 555 Engravings on Wood, 18s.

NICHOLSON.

Text-Book of Zoology, for Junior Students. Fifth Edition, Rewritten and Enlarged. Crown 8vo, with 358 Engravings on Wood, 10s. 6d.

Introductory Text-Book of Zoology. By PROFESSOR H. A. NICHOLSON and ALEXANDER BROWN, M.A., M.B., B.Sc., Lecturer on Zoology in the University of Aberdeen. New Edition, Revised and Enlarged. [*In the press.*

A Manual of Palæontology, for the Use of Students. With a General Introduction on the Principles of Palæontology. By Professor H. ALLEYNE NICHOLSON and RICHARD LYDEKKER, B.A. Third Edition, entirely Rewritten and greatly Enlarged. 2 vols. 8vo, £3, 3s.

The Ancient Life-History of the Earth. An Outline of the Principles and Leading Facts of Palæontological Science. Crown 8vo, with 276 Engravings, 10s. 6d.

On the "Tabulate Corals" of the Palæozoic Period, with Critical Descriptions of Illustrative Species. Illustrated with 15 Lithographed Plates and numerous Engravings. Super-royal 8vo, 21s.

Synopsis of the Classification of the Animal Kingdom. 8vo, with 106 Illustrations, 6s.

On the Structure and Affinities of the Genus Monticulipora and its Sub-Genera, with Critical Descriptions of Illustrative Species. Illustrated with numerous Engravings on Wood and Lithographed Plates. Super-royal 8vo, 18s.

NICHOLSON.

Thoth. A Romance. By JOSEPH SHIELD NICHOLSON, M.A., D.Sc., Professor of Commercial and Political Economy and Mercantile Law in the University of Edinburgh. Third Edition. Crown 8vo, 4s. 6d.

A Dreamer of Dreams. A Modern Romance. Second Edition. Crown 8vo, 6s.

OLIPHANT.

Masollam: A Problem of the Period. A Novel. By LAURENCE OLIPHANT. 3 vols. post 8vo, 25s. 6d.

Scientific Religion; or, Higher Possibilities of Life and Practice through the Operation of Natural Forces. Second Edition. 8vo, 16s.

Altiora Peto. Cheap Edition. Crown 8vo, boards, 2s. 6d.; cloth, 3s. 6d. Illustrated Edition. Crown 8vo, cloth, 6s.

Piccadilly. With Illustrations by Richard Doyle. New Edition, 3s. 6d. Cheap Edition, boards, 2s. 6d.

Traits and Travesties; Social and Political. Post 8vo, 10s. 6d.

Episodes in a Life of Adventure; or, Moss from a Rolling Stone. Cheaper Edition. Post 8vo, 3s. 6d.

Haifa: Life in Modern Palestine. Second Edition. 8vo, 7s. 6d.

The Land of Gilead. With Excursions in the Lebanon. With Illustrations and Maps. Demy 8vo, 21s.

Memoir of the Life of Laurence Oliphant, and of Alice Oliphant, his Wife. By Mrs M. O. W. OLIPHANT. Seventh Edition. 2 vols. post 8vo, with Portraits. 21s.

POPULAR EDITION. With a New Preface. Post 8vo, with Portraits. 7s. 6d.

OLIPHANT.

Annals of a Publishing House. William Blackwood and his Sons; Their Magazine and Friends. By Mrs OLIPHANT. With Four Portraits. Third Edition. Demy 8vo. Vols. I. and II. £2, 2s.

A Widow's Tale, and other Stories. With an Introductory Note by J. M. BARRIE. Crown 8vo, 6s.

Who was Lost and is Found. Second Edition. Crown 8vo, 6s.

Miss Marjoribanks. New Edition. Crown 8vo, 3s. 6d.

The Perpetual Curate, and The Rector. New Edition. Crown 8vo, 3s. 6d.

OLIPHANT.

Salem Chapel, and The Doctor's Family. New Edition. Crown 8vo, 3s. 6d

Chronicles of Carlingford. 3 vols. crown 8vo, in uniform binding, gilt top, 3s. 6d. each.

Katie Stewart, and other Stories. New Edition. Crown 8vo, cloth, 3s. 6d.

Katie Stewart. Illustrated boards, 2s. 6d.

Valentine and his Brother. New Edition. Crown 8vo, 3s. 6d

Sons and Daughters. Crown 8vo, 3s. 6d.

Two Stories of the Seen and the Unseen. The Open Door —Old Lady Mary. Paper covers, 1s.

OLIPHANT. Notes of a Pilgrimage to Jerusalem and the Holy Land. By F. R. OLIPHANT. Crown 8vo, 3s. 6d.

OSWALD. By Fell and Fjord; or, Scenes and Studies in Iceland. By E. J. OSWALD. Post 8vo, with Illustrations. 7s. 6d.

PAGE.

Introductory Text-Book of Geology. By DAVID PAGE, LL.D., Professor of Geology in the Durham University of Physical Science, Newcastle. With Engravings and Glossarial Index. New Edition. Revised by Professor LAPWORTH of Mason Science College, Birmingham. [*In preparation.*

Advanced Text-Book of Geology, Descriptive and Industrial. With Engravings, and Glossary of Scientific Terms. New Edition. Revised by Professor LAPWORTH. [*In preparation.*

Introductory Text-Book of Physical Geography. With Sketch-Maps and Illustrations. Edited by Professor LAPWORTH, LL.D., F.G.S., &c., Mason Science College, Birmingham. Thirteenth Edition, Revised and Enlarged. 2s. 6d.

Advanced Text-Book of Physical Geography. Third Edition. Revised and Enlarged by Professor LAPWORTH. With Engravings. 5s.

PATERSON. A Manual of Agricultural Botany. From the German of Dr A. B. FRANK, Professor in the Royal Agricultural College, Berlin. Translated by JOHN W. PATERSON, B.Sc., Ph.D., Free Life Member of the Highland and Agricultural Society of Scotland, and of the Royal Agricultural Society of England. With over 100 Illustrations. Crown 8vo, 3s. 6d.

PATON.

Spindrift. By Sir J. NOEL PATON. Fcap., cloth, 5s.

Poems by a Painter. Fcap., cloth, 5s.

PATON. Castlebraes. Drawn from "The Tinlie MSS." By JAMES PATON, B.A., Editor of 'John G. Paton: an Autobiography,' &c., &c. Crown 8vo, 6s.

PATRICK. The Apology of Origen in Reply to Celsus. A Chapter in the History of Apologetics. By the Rev. J. PATRICK, D.D. Post 8vo, 7s. 6d.

PAUL. History of the Royal Company of Archers, the Queen's Body-Guard for Scotland. By JAMES BALFOUR PAUL, Advocate of the Scottish Bar. Crown 4to, with Portraits and other Illustrations. £2, 2s.

PEARSE. Soldier and Traveller: Being the Memoirs of Alexander Gardner, Colonel of Artillery in the Service of Maharaja Ranjit Singh. Edited by Major HUGH PEARSE, 2nd Battalion the East Surrey Regiment. With an Introduction by the Right Hon. Sir RICHARD TEMPLE, Bart., G.C.S.I. With Two Portraits and Maps. In 1 vol. demy 8vo. [*In the press.*

PEILE. Lawn Tennis as a Game of Skill. By Lieut.-Col. S. C. F. PEILE, B.S.C. Revised Edition, with new Scoring Rules. Fcap. 8vo, cloth, 1s.

PETTIGREW. The Handy Book of Bees, and their Profitable Management. By A. PETTIGREW. Fifth Edition, Enlarged, with Engravings. Crown 8vo, 3s. 6d.

PFLEIDERER. Philosophy and Development of Religion. Being the Edinburgh Gifford Lectures for 1894. By OTTO PFLEIDERER, D.D., Professor of Theology at Berlin University. In 2 vols. post 8vo, 15s. net.

PHILLIPS. The Knight's Tale. By F. EMILY PHILLIPS, Author of 'The Education of Antonia.' Crown 8vo, 3s. 6d.

PHILOSOPHICAL CLASSICS FOR ENGLISH READERS. Edited by WILLIAM KNIGHT, LL.D., Professor of Moral Philosophy, University of St Andrews. In crown 8vo volumes, with Portraits, price 3s. 6d.

[*For List of Volumes, see page 2.*

POLLARD. A Study in Municipal Government: The Corporation of Berlin. By JAMES POLLARD, C.A., Chairman of the Edinburgh Public Health Committee, and Secretary of the Edinburgh Chamber of Commerce. Second Edition, Revised. Crown 8vo, 3s. 6d.

POLLOK. The Course of Time: A Poem. By ROBERT POLLOK, A.M. New Edition. With Portrait. Fcap. 8vo, gilt top, 2s. 6d.

PORT ROYAL LOGIC. Translated from the French; with Introduction, Notes, and Appendix. By THOMAS SPENCER BAYNES, LL.D., Professor in the University of St Andrews. Tenth Edition, 12mo, 4s.

POTTS AND DARNELL.

Aditus Faciliores: An Easy Latin Construing Book, with Complete Vocabulary By A. W. POTTS, M.A., LL.D., and the Rev. C. DARNELL, M.A., Head-Master of Cargilfield Preparatory School Edinburgh. Tenth Edition, fcap. 8vo, 3s. 6d.

Aditus Faciliores Graeci. An Easy Greek Construing Book, with Complete Vocabulary. Fifth Edition, Revised. Fcap. 8vo, 3s.

POTTS. School Sermons. By the late ALEXANDER WM. POTTS, LL.D., First Head-Master of Fettes College. With a Memoir and Portrait. Crown 8vo, 7s. 6d.

PRINGLE. The Live Stock of the Farm. By ROBERT O. PRINGLE. Third Edition. Revised and Edited by JAMES MACDONALD. Crown 8vo, 7s. 6d.

PUBLIC GENERAL STATUTES AFFECTING SCOTLAND from 1707 to 1847, with Chronological Table and Index. 3 vols. large 8vo, £3, 3s.

PUBLIC GENERAL STATUTES AFFECTING SCOTLAND, COLLECTION OF. Published Annually, with General Index.

RAMSAY. Scotland and Scotsmen in the Eighteenth Century. Edited from the MSS. of JOHN RAMSAY, Esq. of Ochtertyre, by ALEXANDER ALLARDYCE, Author of 'Memoir of Admiral Lord Keith, K.B.,' &c. 2 vols. 8vo, 31s. 6d.

RANJITSINHJI. The Jubilee Book of Cricket. By PRINCE RANJITSINHJI.

ÉDITION DE LUXE. Limited to 350 Copies, printed on hand-made paper, and handsomely bound in buckram. Crown 4to, with 22 Photogravures and 85 full-page Plates. Each copy signed by Prince Ranjitsinhji. Price £5, 5s. net.

FINE PAPER EDITION. Medium 8vo, with Photogravure Frontispiece and 106 full-page Plates on art paper. 25s. net.

POPULAR EDITION. With 107 full-page Illustrations. Sixth Edition. Large crown 8vo, 6s.

RANKIN.

A Handbook of the Church of Scotland. By JAMES RANKIN, D.D., Minister of Muthill; Author of 'Character Studies in the Old Testament, &c. An entirely New and much Enlarged Edition. Crown 8vo, with 2 Maps, 7s. 6d.

The First Saints. Post 8vo, 7s. 6d.

The Creed in Scotland. An Exposition of the Apostles' Creed. With Extracts from Archbishop Hamilton's Catechism of 1552, John Calvin's Catechism of 1556, and a Catena of Ancient Latin and other Hymns. Post 8vo, 7s. 6d.

The Worthy Communicant. A Guide to the Devout Observance of the Lord's Supper. Limp cloth, 1s. 3d.

The Young Churchman. Lessons on the Creed, the Commandments, the Means of Grace, and the Church. Limp cloth, 1s. 3d.

First Communion Lessons. 25th Edition. Paper Cover, 2d.

RANKINE. A Hero of the Dark Continent. Memoir of Rev. Wm. Affleck Scott, M.A., M.B., C.M., Church of Scotland Missionary at Blantyre, British Central Africa. By W. HENRY RANKINE, B.D., Minister at Titwood. With a Portrait and other Illustrations. Cheap Edition. Crown 8vo, 2s.

ROBERTSON.

The Poetry and the Religion of the Psalms. The Croall Lectures, 1893-94. By JAMES ROBERTSON, D.D., Professor of Oriental Languages in the University of Glasgow. In 1 vol. demy 8vo. [*In the press.*

The Early Religion of Israel. As set forth by Biblical Writers and Modern Critical Historians. Being the Baird Lecture for 1888-89. Fourth Edition. Crown 8vo, 10s. 6d.

ROBERTSON.

Orellana, and other Poems. By J. LOGIE ROBERTSON, M.A. Fcap. 8vo. Printed on hand-made paper. 6s.

A History of English Literature. For Secondary Schools. With an Introduction by Professor MASSON, Edinburgh University. Cr. 8vo, 3s.

English Verse for Junior Classes. In Two Parts. Part I.—Chaucer to Coleridge. Part II.—Nineteenth Century Poets. Crown 8vo, each 1s. 6d. net.

Outlines of English Literature for Young Scholars. With Illustrative Specimens. Crown 8vo, 1s. 6d.

ROBINSON. Wild Traits in Tame Animals. Being some Familiar Studies in Evolution. By LOUIS ROBINSON, M.D. With Illustrations by STEPHEN T. DADD. Demy 8vo, 10s. 6d. net.

RODGER. Aberdeen Doctors at Home and Abroad. The Story of a Medical School. By ELLA HILL BURTON RODGER. Demy 8vo, 10s. 6d.

ROSCOE. Rambles with a Fishing-Rod. By E. S. ROSCOE. Crown 8vo, 4s. 6d.

ROSS AND SOMERVILLE. Beggars on Horseback: A Riding Tour in North Wales. By MARTIN ROSS and E. Œ. SOMERVILLE. With Illustrations by E. Œ. SOMERVILLE. Crown 8vo, 3s. 6d.

RUTLAND.

Notes of an Irish Tour in 1846. By the DUKE OF RUTLAND, G.C.B. (Lord JOHN MANNERS). New Edition. Crown 8vo, 2s. 6d.

Correspondence between the Right Honble. William Pitt and Charles Duke of Rutland, Lord-Lieutenant of Ireland, 1781-1787. With Introductory Note by JOHN DUKE OF RUTLAND. 8vo, 7s. 6d.

RUTLAND.

Gems of German Poetry. Translated by the DUCHESS OF RUTLAND (Lady JOHN MANNERS). [*New Edition in preparation.*

Impressions of Bad-Homburg. Comprising a Short Account of the Women's Associations of Germany under the Red Cross. Crown 8vo, 1s. 6d.

Some Personal Recollections of the Later Years of the Earl of Beaconsfield, K.G. Sixth Edition. 6d.

Employment of Women in the Public Service. 6d.

Some of the Advantages of Easily Accessible Reading and Recreation Rooms and Free Libraries. With Remarks on Starting and Maintaining them. Second Edition. Crown 8vo, 1s.

A Sequel to Rich Men's Dwellings, and other Occasional Papers. Crown 8vo, 2s. 6d.

Encouraging Experiences of Reading and Recreation Rooms, Aims of Guilds, Nottingham Social Guide, Existing Institutions, &c., &c. Crown 8vo, 1s.

SAINTSBURY. The Flourishing of Romance and the Rise of Allegory (12th and 13th Centuries). By GEORGE SAINTSBURY, M.A., Professor of Rhetoric and English Literature in Edinburgh University. Being the first volume issued of "PERIODS OF EUROPEAN LITERATURE." Edited by Professor SAINTSBURY. Crown 8vo, 5s. net.

SCHEFFEL. The Trumpeter. A Romance of the Rhine. By JOSEPH VICTOR VON SCHEFFEL. Translated from the Two Hundredth German Edition by JESSIE BECK and LOUISA LORIMER. With an Introduction by Sir THEODORE MARTIN, K.C.B. Long 8vo, 3s. 6d.

SCHILLER. Wallenstein. A Dramatic Poem. By FRIEDRICH VON SCHILLER. Translated by C. G. N. LOCKHART. Fcap. 8vo, 7s. 6d

SCOTT. Tom Cringle's Log. By MICHAEL SCOTT. New Edition. With 19 Full-page Illustrations. Crown 8vo, 3s. 6d.

SCOUGAL. Prisons and their Inmates; or, Scenes from a Silent World. By FRANCIS SCOUGAL. Crown 8vo, boards, 2s.

SELKIRK. Poems. By J. B. SELKIRK, Author of 'Ethics and Æsthetics of Modern Poetry,' 'Bible Truths with Shakespearian Parallels,' &c. New and Enlarged Edition. Crown 8vo, printed on antique paper, 6s.

SELLAR'S Manual of the Acts relating to Education in Scotland. By J. EDWARD GRAHAM, B.A. Oxon., Advocate. Ninth Edition. Demy 8vo, 12s. 6d.

SETH.

Scottish Philosophy. A Comparison of the Scottish and German Answers to Hume. Balfour Philosophical Lectures, University of Edinburgh. By ANDREW SETH, LL.D., Professor of Logic and Metaphysics in Edinburgh University. Second Edition. Crown 8vo, 5s.

Hegelianism and Personality. Balfour Philosophical Lectures. Second Series. Second Edition. Crown 8vo, 5s.

Man's Place in the Cosmos, and other Essays. Post 8vo, 7s. 6d. net.

Two Lectures on Theism. Delivered on the occasion of the Sesquicentennial Celebration of Princeton University. Crown 8vo, 2s. 6d.

SETH. A Study of Ethical Principles. By JAMES SETH, M.A., Professor of Philosophy in Cornell University, U.S.A. Third Edition, Revised and Enlarged. Post 8vo, 7s. 6d.

SHADWELL. The Life of Colin Campbell, Lord Clyde. Illustrated by Extracts from his Diary and Correspondence. By Lieutenant-General SHADWELL C.B. With Portrait, Maps, and Plans. 2 vols. 8vo, 36s.

SHAND.

The Life of General Sir Edward Bruce Hamley, K.C.B., K.C.M.G. By ALEX. INNES SHAND, Author of 'Kilcarra,' 'Against Time,' &c. With two Photogravure Portraits and other Illustrations. Cheaper Edition, with a Statement by Mr Edward Hamley. 2 vols. demy 8vo, 10s. 6d.

Letters from the West of Ireland. Reprinted from the 'Times.' Crown 8vo, 5s.

SHARPE. Letters from and to Charles Kirkpatrick Sharpe. Edited by ALEXANDER ALLARDYCE, Author of 'Memoir of Admiral Lord Keith, K.B.,' &c. With a Memoir by the Rev. W. K. R. BEDFORD. In 2 vols. 8vo. Illustrated with Etchings and other Engravings. £2, 12s. 6d.

SIM. Margaret Sim's Cookery. With an Introduction by L. B. WALFORD, Author of 'Mr Smith: A Part of his Life,' &c. Crown 8vo, 5s.

SIMPSON. The Wild Rabbit in a New Aspect; or, Rabbit-Warrens that Pay. A book for Landowners, Sportsmen, Land Agents, Farmers, Gamekeepers, and Allotment Holders. A Record of Recent Experiments conducted on the Estate of the Right Hon. the Earl of Wharncliffe at Wortley Hall. By J. SIMPSON. Second Edition, Enlarged. Small crown 8vo, 5s.

SIMPSON. Side-Lights on Siberia. Some account of the Great Siberian Iron Road: The Prisons and Exile System. By J. Y. SIMPSON, M.A., B.Sc. With numerous Illustrations and a Map. Demy 8vo, 16s.

SINCLAIR. Audrey Craven. By MAY SINCLAIR. Second Edition. Crown 8vo, 6s.

SKELTON.

The Table-Talk of Shirley. By Sir JOHN SKELTON, K.C.B., LL.D., Author of 'The Essays of Shirley.' With a Frontispiece. Sixth Edition, Revised and Enlarged. Post 8vo, 7s. 6d.

SKELTON.

The Table-Talk of Shirley. Second Series. Summers and Winters at Balmawhapple. With Illustrations. Two Volumes. Second Edition. Post 8vo, 10s. net.

Maitland of Lethington; and the Scotland of Mary Stuart. A History. Limited Edition, with Portraits. Demy 8vo, 2 vols., 28s. net.

The Handbook of Public Health. A New Edition, Revised by JAMES PATTEN MACDOUGALL, Advocate, Legal Member of the Local Government Board for Scotland, Joint-Author of 'The Parish Council Guide for Scotland,' and ABIJAH MURRAY, Chief Clerk of the Local Government Board for Scotland. In Two Parts. Crown 8vo. Part I.—The Public Health (Scotland) Act, 1897, with Notes. Part II.—Circulars of the Local Government Board, &c. The Parts will be issued separately, and also complete in one Volume.

The Local Government (Scotland) Act in Relation to Public Health. A Handy Guide for County and District Councillors, Medical Officers, Sanitary Inspectors, and Members of Parochial Boards. Second Edition. With a new Preface on appointment of Sanitary Officers. Crown 8vo, 2s.

SKRINE. Columba: A Drama. By JOHN HUNTLEY SKRINE, Warden of Glenalmond; Author of 'A Memory of Edward Thring.' Fcap. 4to, 6s.

SMITH. Retrievers, and how to Break them. By Lieutenant-Colonel Sir HENRY SMITH, K.C.B. With an Introduction by Mr S. E. SHIRLEY, President of the Kennel Club. Dedicated by special permission to H.R.H. the Duke of York. In 1 vol. With Illustrations. Crown 8vo. [*In the press.*

SMITH.

Thorndale; or, The Conflict of Opinions. By WILLIAM SMITH, Author of 'A Discourse on Ethics,' &c. New Edition. Crown 8vo, 10s. 6d.

Gravenhurst; or, Thoughts on Good and Evil. Second Edition. With Memoir and Portrait of the Author. Crown 8vo, 8s.

The Story of William and Lucy Smith. Edited by GEORGE MERRIAM. Large post 8vo, 12s. 6d.

SMITH. Memoir of the Families of M'Combie and Thoms, originally M'Intosh and M'Thomas. Compiled from History and Tradition. By WILLIAM M'COMBIE SMITH. With Illustrations. 8vo, 7s. 6d.

SMITH. Greek Testament Lessons for Colleges, Schools, and Private Students, consisting chiefly of the Sermon on the Mount and the Parables of our Lord. With Notes and Essays. By the Rev. J. HUNTER SMITH, M.A., King Edward's School, Birmingham. Crown 8vo, 6s.

SMITH. The Secretary for Scotland. Being a Statement of the Powers and Duties of the new Scottish Office. With a Short Historical Introduction, and numerous references to important Administrative Documents. By W. C. SMITH, LL.B., Advocate. 8vo, 6s.

SNELL. The Fourteenth Century. "Periods of European Literature." By F. J. SNELL. In 1 vol. Crown 8vo. [*In the press.*

"SON OF THE MARSHES, A."

From Spring to Fall; or, When Life Stirs. By "A SON OF THE MARSHES." Cheap Uniform Edition. Crown 8vo, 3s. 6d.

Within an Hour of London Town: Among Wild Birds and their Haunts. Edited by J. A. OWEN. Cheap Uniform Edition. Cr. 8vo, 3s. 6d.

With the Woodlanders and by the Tide. Cheap Uniform Edition. Crown 8vo, 3s. 6d.

On Surrey Hills. Cheap Uniform Edition. Crown 8vo, 3s. 6d.

Annals of a Fishing Village. Cheap Uniform Edition. Crown 8vo, 3s. 6d.

SORLEY. The Ethics of Naturalism. Being the Shaw Fellowship Lectures, 1884. By W. R. SORLEY, M.A., Fellow of Trinity College, Cambridge, Professor of Moral Philosophy, University of Aberdeen. Crown 8vo, 6s.

SPIELMANN. Millais and his Works. By M. H. SPIELMANN. Author of 'History of Punch.' With 28 Full-page Illustrations. Large crown 8vo. Paper covers, 1s.; in cloth binding, 2s. 6d.

SPROTT. The Worship and Offices of the Church of Scotland. By GEORGE W. SPROTT, D.D., Minister of North Berwick. Crown 8vo, 6s.

STATISTICAL ACCOUNT OF SCOTLAND. Complete, with Index. 15 vols. 8vo, £16, 16s.

STEEVENS.

Egypt in 1898. By G. W. STEEVENS, Author of 'Naval Policy,' &c. With Illustrations. In 1 vol. crown 8vo. [*In the press.*

The Land of the Dollar. Crown 8vo, 6s.

With the Conquering Turk. With 4 Maps. Demy 8vo, 10s. 6d.

STEPHENS.

The Book of the Farm; detailing the Labours of the Farmer, Farm-Steward, Ploughman, Shepherd, Hedger, Farm-Labourer, Field-Worker, and Cattle-man. Illustrated with numerous Portraits of Animals and Engravings of Implements, and Plans of Farm Buildings. Fourth Edition. Revised, and in great part Re-written, by JAMES MACDONALD, F.R.S.E., Secretary Highland and Agricultural Society of Scotland. Complete in Six Divisional Volumes, bound in cloth, each 10s. 6d., or handsomely bound, in 3 volumes, with leather back and gilt top, £3, 3s.

*** Also being issued in 20 monthly Parts, price 2s. 6d. net each. [*Parts I.-XIII. ready.*

Catechism of Practical Agriculture. 22d Thousand. Revised by JAMES MACDONALD, F.R.S.E. With numerous Illustrations. Crown 8vo, 1s.

The Book of Farm Implements and Machines. By J. SLIGHT and R. SCOTT BURN, Engineers. Edited by HENRY STEPHENS. Large 8vo, £2, 2s.

STEVENSON. British Fungi. (Hymenomycetes.) By Rev. JOHN STEVENSON, Author of 'Mycologia Scotica,' Hon. Sec. Cryptogamic Society of Scotland. Vols. I. and II., post 8vo, with Illustrations, price 12s. 6d. net each.

STEWART. Advice to Purchasers of Horses. By JOHN STEWART, V.S. New Edition. 2s. 6d.

STODDART.

John Stuart Blackie: A Biography. By ANNA M. STODDART. With 3 Plates. Third Edition. 2 vols. demy 8vo, 21s.

POPULAR EDITION, with Portrait. Crown 8vo, 6s.

Sir Philip Sidney: Servant of God. Illustrated by MARGARET L. HUGGINS. With a New Portrait of Sir Philip Sidney. Small 4to, with a specially designed Cover. 5s.

STORMONTH.

Dictionary of the English Language, Pronouncing, Etymological, and Explanatory. By the Rev. JAMES STORMONTH. Revised by the Rev. P. H. PHELP. Library Edition. New and Cheaper Edition, with Supplement. Imperial 8vo, handsomely bound in half morocco, 18s. net.

Etymological and Pronouncing Dictionary of the English Language. Including a very Copious Selection of Scientific Terms. For use in Schools and Colleges, and as a Book of General Reference. The Pronunciation carefully revised by the Rev. P. H. PHELP, M.A. Cantab. Thirteenth Edition, with Supplement. Crown 8vo, pp. 800. 7s. 6d.

The School Dictionary. New Edition, Revised. [*In preparation.*

STORY. The Apostolic Ministry in the Scottish Church (The Baird Lecture for 1897). By ROBERT HERBERT STORY, D.D. (Edin.), F.S.A. Scot., Professor of Ecclesiastical History in the University of Glasgow; Principal Clerk of the General Assembly; and Chaplain to the Queen. Crown 8vo, 7s. 6d.

STORY.

Poems. By W. W. Story, Author of 'Roba di Roma,' &c. 2 vols., 7s. 6d.

Fiammetta. A Summer Idyl. Crown 8vo, 7s. 6d.

Conversations in a Studio. 2 vols. crown 8vo, 12s. 6d.

Excursions in Art and Letters. Crown 8vo, 7s. 6d.

A Poet's Portfolio: Later Readings. 18mo, 3s. 6d.

STRACHEY. Talk at a Country House. Fact and Fiction By Sir EDWARD STRACHEY, Bart. With a Portrait of the Author. Crown 8vo, 4s. 6d. net.

STURGIS. Little Comedies, Old and New. By JULIAN STURGIS. Crown 8vo, 7s. 6d.

TAYLOR. The Story of my Life. By the late Colonel MEADOWS TAYLOR, Author of 'The Confessions of a Thug,' &c., &c. Edited by his Daughter. New and Cheaper Edition, being the Fourth. Crown 8vo, 6s.

THEOBALD. A Text Book of Agricultural Zoology. By FRED. V. THEOBALD, M.A. (Cantab.), F.E.S., Foreign Member of the Association of Official Economic Entomologists, U.S.A., Zoologist to the S.E. Agricultural College, Wye, &c. With numerous Illustrations. In 1 vol. crown 8vo. [*In the press.*

THOMAS. The Woodland Life. By EDWARD THOMAS. With a Frontispiece. Square 8vo, 6s.

THOMSON.

The Diversions of a Prime Minister. By Basil Thomson. With a Map, numerous Illustrations by J. W. Cawston and others, and Reproductions of Rare Plates from Early Voyages of Sixteenth and Seventeenth Centuries. Small demy 8vo, 15s.

South Sea Yarns. With 10 Full-page Illustrations. Cheaper Edition. Crown 8vo, 3s. 6d.

THOMSON.

Handy Book of the Flower-Garden: Being Practical Directions for the Propagation, Culture, and Arrangement of Plants in Flower-Gardens all the year round. With Engraved Plans. By DAVID THOMSON, Gardener to his Grace the Duke of Buccleuch, K.T., at Drumlanrig. Fourth and Cheaper Edition. Crown 8vo, 5s.

The Handy Book of Fruit-Culture under Glass: Being a series of Elaborate Practical Treatises on the Cultivation and Forcing of Pines, Vines, Peaches, Figs, Melons, Strawberries, and Cucumbers. With Engravings of Hothouses, &c. Second Edition, Revised and Enlarged. Crown 8vo, 7s. 6d.

THOMSON. A Practical Treatise on the Cultivation of the Grape Vine. By WILLIAM THOMSON, Tweed Vineyards. Tenth Edition. 8vo, 5s.

THOMSON. Cookery for the Sick and Convalescent. With Directions for the Preparation of Poultices, Fomentations, &c. By BARBARA THOMSON. Fcap. 8vo, 1s. 6d.

THORBURN. Asiatic Neighbours. By S. S. THORBURN, Bengal Civil Service, Author of 'Bannú; or, Our Afghan Frontier,' 'David Leslie: A Story of the Afghan Frontier,' 'Musalmans and Money-Lenders in the Panjab.' With Two Maps. Demy 8vo, 10s. 6d. net.

THORNTON. Opposites. A Series of Essays on the Unpopular Sides of Popular Questions. By LEWIS THORNTON. 8vo, 12s. 6d.

TIELE. Elements of the Science of Religion. Part I.—Morphological. Being the Gifford Lectures delivered before the University of Edinburgh in 1896. By C. P. TIELE, Theol. D., Litt.D. (Bonon.), Hon. M.R.A.S., &c., Professor of the Science of Religion in the University of Leiden. In 2 vols. Vol. I. post 8vo, 7s. 6d. *net.*

TOKE. French Historical Unseens. For Army Classes. By N. E. TOKE, B.A. In 1 vol. crown 8vo. [*In the press.*

TRANSACTIONS OF THE HIGHLAND AND AGRICULTURAL SOCIETY OF SCOTLAND. Published annually, price 5s.

TRAVERS.

Mona Maclean, Medical Student. A Novel. By GRAHAM TRAVERS. Twelfth Edition. Crown 8vo, 6s.

Fellow Travellers. Fourth Edition. Crown 8vo, 6s.

TRYON. Life of Vice-Admiral Sir George Tryon, K.C.B. By Rear-Admiral C. C. PENROSE FITZGERALD. With Two Portraits and numerous Illustrations. Second Edition. Demy 8vo, 21s

TULLOCH.

Rational Theology and Christian Philosophy in England in the Seventeenth Century. By JOHN TULLOCH, D.D., Principal of St Mary's College in the University of St Andrews, and one of her Majesty's Chaplains in Ordinary in Scotland. Second Edition. 2 vols. 8vo, 16s.

Modern Theories in Philosophy and Religion. 8vo, 15s.

Luther, and other Leaders of the Reformation. Third Edition, Enlarged. Crown 8vo, 3s. 6d.

Memoir of Principal Tulloch, D.D., LL.D. By Mrs OLIPHANT, Author of 'Life of Edward Irving.' Third and Cheaper Edition. 8vo, with Portrait, 7s. 6d.

TWEEDIE. The Arabian Horse: His Country and People. By Major-General W. TWEEDIE, C.S.I., Bengal Staff Corps; for many years H.B.M.'s Consul-General, Baghdad, and Political Resident for the Government of India in Turkish Arabia. In one vol. royal 4to, with Seven Coloured Plates and other Illustrations, and a Map of the Country. Price £3, 3s. net.

TYLER. The Whence and the Whither of Man. A Brief History of his Origin and Development through Conformity to Environment. The Morse Lectures of 1895. By JOHN M. TYLER, Professor of Biology, Amherst College, U.S.A. Post 8vo, 6s. net.

VEITCH.

Memoir of John Veitch, LL.D., Professor of Logic and Rhetoric, University of Glasgow. By MARY R. L. BRYCE. With Portrait and 3 Photogravure Plates. Demy 8vo, 7s. 6d.

Border Essays. By JOHN VEITCH, LL.D., Professor of Logic and Rhetoric, University of Glasgow. Crown 8vo, 4s. 6d. *net.*

The History and Poetry of the Scottish Border: their Main Features and Relations. New and Enlarged Edition. 2 vols. demy 8vo, 16s.

Institutes of Logic. Post 8vo, 12s. 6d.

Merlin and other Poems. Fcap. 8vo, 4s. 6d.

Knowing and Being. Essays in Philosophy. First Series. Crown 8vo, 5s.

Dualism and Monism; and other Essays. Essays in Philosophy. Second Series. With an Introduction by R. M. Wenley. Crown 8vo, 4s. 6d. net.

VIRGIL. The Æneid of Virgil. Translated in English Blank Verse by G. K. RICKARDS, M.A., and Lord RAVENSWORTH. 2 vols. fcap. 8vo, 10s.

WACE. Christianity and Agnosticism. Reviews of some Recent Attacks on the Christian Faith. By HENRY WACE, D.D., late Principal of King's College, London; Preacher of Lincoln's Inn; Chaplain to the Queen. Second Edition. Post 8vo, 10s. 6d. net.

WADDELL. An Old Kirk Chronicle: Being a History of Auldhame, Tyninghame, and Whitekirk, in East Lothian. From Session Records, 1615 to 1850. By Rev. P. HATELY WADDELL, B.D., Minister of the United Parish. Small Paper Edition, 200 Copies. Price £1. Large Paper Edition, 50 Copies. Price £1, 10s.

WALDO. The Ban of the Gubbe. By CEDRIC DANE WALDO. Crown 8vo, 2s. 6d.

WALFORD. Four Biographies from 'Blackwood': Jane Taylor, Hannah More, Elizabeth Fry, Mary Somerville. By L. B. WALFORD. Crown 8vo, 5s.

WARREN'S (SAMUEL) WORKS:—

Diary of a Late Physician. Cloth, 2s. 6d.; boards, 2s

Ten Thousand A-Year. Cloth, 3s. 6d.; boards, 2s. 6d.

Now and Then. The Lily and the Bee. Intellectual and Moral Development of the Present Age. 4s. 6d.

Essays: Critical, Imaginative, and Juridical. 5s.

WENLEY.

Socrates and Christ: A Study in the Philosophy of Religion. By R. M. WENLEY, M.A., D.Sc., D.Phil., Professor of Philosophy in the University of Michigan, U.S.A. Crown 8vo, 6s.

Aspects of Pessimism. Crown 8vo, 6s.

WHITE.

The Eighteen Christian Centuries. By the Rev. JAMES WHITE. Seventh Edition. Post 8vo, with Index, 6s.

History of France, from the Earliest Times. Sixth Thousand. Post 8vo, with Index, 6s.

WHITE.

Archæological Sketches in Scotland—Kintyre and Knapdale. By Colonel T. P. WHITE, R.E., of the Ordnance Survey. With numerous Illustrations. 2 vols. folio, £4, 4s. Vol. I., Kintyre, sold separately, £2, 2s.

The Ordnance Survey of the United Kingdom. A Popular Account. Crown 8vo, 5s.

WILKES. Latin Historical Unseens. For Army Classes. By L. C. VAUGHAN WILKES, M.A. Crown 8vo, 2s.

WILLIAMSON. The Horticultural Handbook and Exhibitor's Guide. A Treatise on Cultivating, Exhibiting, and Judging Plants, Flowers, Fruits, and Vegetables. By W. WILLIAMSON, Gardener. Revised by MALCOLM DUNN, Gardener to his Grace the Duke of Buccleuch and Queensberry, Dalkeith Park. New and Cheaper Edition, enlarged. Crown 8vo, paper cover, 2s.; cloth, 2s. 6d.

WILLIAMSON. Poems of Nature and Life. By DAVID R. WILLIAMSON, Minister of Kirkmaiden. Fcap. 8vo, 3s.

WILLS. Behind an Eastern Veil. A Plain Tale of Events occurring in the Experience of a Lady who had a unique opportunity of observing the Inner Life of Ladies of the Upper Class in Persia. By C. J. WILLS, Author of 'In the Land of the Lion and Sun,' 'Persia as it is,' &c., &c. Cheaper Edition. Demy 8vo, 5s.

WILSON.

Works of Professor Wilson. Edited by his Son-in-Law, Professor FERRIER. 12 vols. crown 8vo, £2, 8s.

Christopher in his Sporting-Jacket. 2 vols., 8s.

Isle of Palms, City of the Plague, and other Poems. 4s.

Lights and Shadows of Scottish Life, and other Tales. 4s.

Essays, Critical and Imaginative. 4 vols., 16s.

The Noctes Ambrosianæ. 4 vols., 16s.

Homer and his Translators, and the Greek Drama. Crown 8vo, 4s.

WORSLEY.

Homer's Odyssey. Translated into English Verse in the Spenserian Stanza. By PHILIP STANHOPE WORSLEY, M.A. New and Cheaper Edition. Post 8vo, 7s. 6d. net.

Homer's Iliad. Translated by P. S. Worsley and Prof. Conington. 2 vols. crown 8vo, 21s.

YATE. England and Russia Face to Face in Asia. A Record of Travel with the Afghan Boundary Commission. By Captain A. C. YATE, Bombay Staff Corps. 8vo, with Maps and Illustrations, 21s.

YATE. Northern Afghanistan; or, Letters from the Afghan Boundary Commission. By Colonel C. E. YATE, C.S.I., C.M.G., Bombay Staff Corps, F.R.G.S. 8vo, with Maps, 18s.

YULE. Fortification: For the use of Officers in the Army, and Readers of Military History. By Colonel Sir HENRY YULE, Bengal Engineers. 8vo, with Numerous Illustrations, 10s.

5/98.

Lightning Source UK Ltd.
Milton Keynes UK
UKHW011557081121
393608UK00003B/712

9 789353 298937